Gender, Crime and Crim

This book examines the relationsh
explores both the gendered natur
nature of criminal victimisation. Covering ... . __
this new edition has been fully revised to reflect the wider changes,
development and influence of gendered thinking in these areas. It
brings together a range of key issues, including:

- Theories and concepts in feminist criminology,
- Gender and victimisation,
- Sexual and domestic violence,
- Male dominance in the criminal justice system,
- Gendered perspectives in law and criminal justice policy.

New to the third edition is increased coverage of gender and crime
in international perspective, particularly within the global south,
and emerging concepts of risk and security. This is essential reading
for advanced courses on gender and crime, women and crime, and
feminist criminology.

Kate Fitz-Gibbon is a Senior Lecturer in Criminology, researcher in
the Monash Gender and Family Violence program and an Honorary
Research Fellow at the School of Law and Social Justice at the University
of Liverpool. She is recognised as a leading researcher in family violence,
legal responses to lethal violence, and the effects of homicide law and
sentencing reform in Australian and international jurisdictions. In 2015
she received the prestigious Peter Mitchell Churchill Fellowship to examine
innovative and best practice legal responses to the prevention of intimate
homicide in the United Kingdom, Canada and the United States.

Sandra Walklate is Eleanor Rathbone Chair of Sociology at the
University of Liverpool and conjoint Chair of Criminology, Monash
University, Melbourne, Australia. She is Editor in Chief of the *British
Journal of Criminology* and in July 2014 was awarded the British
Society of Criminology's outstanding achievement award. She also
holds an adjunct professorial role at QUT in Brisbane. She has
been researching criminal victimisation since the early 1980s with a
particular focus on gendered violence(s) and the fear of crime.

"Gender is one of the most central and persistent organising principles of the criminal justice systems and policies around the globe. This book explains why offending, victimisation, policing, prisons, and the crime policies are inherently gendered. Fitz-Gibbon and Walklate weave their way through a complex map of gendered criminal justice practices, theories and policies. This map begins with a critical interrogation of the dominance of positivism on the emergence of criminology and victimology. This way of thinking was not only blinded by the lure of empiricism that failed to count much of importance (i.e. women as victims or offenders), but was also deeply embedded in a colonial imperialism of the global economy of knowledge. This book questions the efficacy of models of knowledge and policy transfer that only go from the global north to south, opening up the possibility of re-thinking victimology, as well as criminology from the experiences and theories of the global south. Wide ranging in scope – from a deconstruction of gendered concepts of risk and fear, the militaristic and masculinist nature of police work, law and the judiciary; and the challenges posed by feminism to the ongoing domination of men in the criminal justice workforce as well as masculinist viewpoints in criminology, victimology, and criminal justice practices. They conclude much has been achieved, but much more work needs to be done to redress these inequities. The book should be essential reading for a wide range of students, scholars, policy makers and criminal justice practitioners interested in crime, gender and criminal justice."

Kerry Carrington,
Professor and Head of School of Justice,
Faculty of Law, Queensland University of Technology, Australia

"This book provides a historically-informed, yet contemporary, analysis of gender in relation to key criminological and victimological theorists, issues and debates. The detailed and accessible approach taken by the authors makes this book an important resource for those interested in established and emerging themes concerning gender and criminal justice in an increasingly globalised domain."

Marian Duggan,
Lecturer in Criminology, School of Social Policy, Sociology and
Social Research, University of Kent, UK

Gender, Crime and Criminal Justice

Third Edition

**Kate Fitz-Gibbon and
Sandra Walklate**

Routledge
Taylor & Francis Group

LONDON AND NEW YORK

Third edition published 2018
by Routledge
2 Park Square, Milton Park, Abingdon, Oxon OX14 4RN

and by Routledge
711 Third Avenue, New York, NY 10017

Routledge is an imprint of the Taylor & Francis Group, an informa business

[First edition published by Willan 2001]
[Second edition published by Willan 2004]

British Library Cataloguing-in-Publication Data
A catalogue record for this book is available from the British Library

Library of Congress Cataloging-in-Publication Data
Names: Fitz-Gibbon, Kate (Lecturer in criminology), author. |
    Walklate, Sandra, author.
Title: Gender, crime and criminal justice / Kate Fitz-Gibbon and
    Sandra Walklate.
Description: 3rd Edition. | New York : Routledge, 2018. | Revised
    edition of Gender, crime, and criminal justice, 2004. | Includes
    bibliographical references and index.
Identifiers: LCCN 2017060231 | ISBN 9781138656369 (hardback) |
    ISBN 9781138656376 (pbk.) | ISBN 9781315621906 (ebook)
Subjects: LCSH: Crime—Sex differences. | Criminal behavior.
    | Victims of crimes. | Sex discrimination in criminal justice
    administration. | Feminist theory.
Classification: LCC HV6158 .W35 2018 | DDC 364.2/4—dc23
LC record available at https://lccn.loc.gov/2017060231

ISBN: 978-1-138-65636-9 (hbk)
ISBN: 978-1-138-65637-6 (pbk)
ISBN: 978-1-315-62190-6 (ebk)

Typeset in Sabon
by Apex CoVantage, LLC

Printed and bound in Great Britain by
TJ International Ltd, Padstow, Cornwall

Contents

Preface and acknowledgements

This book began its life in 1995 as *Gender and Crime: An Introduction* (published by Harvester Wheatsheaf) at a time when preoccupations with gender, particularly in the form of masculinity studies, were young in criminology (and victimology). In the intervening years the focus of that first book was given new life with Brian Willan of Willan Publishing in the form of the 2001 publication of *Gender, Crime and Criminal Justice*. The change of title itself indicates the extent to which concerns with gender had penetrated both areas of investigation in the intervening years. This book was published with the same title as a second edition in 2004 again by Willan Publishing. Since that time the world of publishing within social science generally and criminology in particular has changed. Pertinently, Willan Publishing has been absorbed by Routledge. At Routledge our thanks go to Tom Sutton (who has waited patiently for a further iteration of this book for some time) and Hannah Catterall, both of whom have offered sterling support to us, especially when changing circumstances demanded slippage in deadlines. Thank you, Tom and Hannah.

It is also important to point out that this version of *Gender, Crime and Criminal Justice* is more than just a third edition. There are major differences both in form and content in its pages reflecting the wider changes, development and influence of gendered thinking on both criminology and victimology. While the foundational conceptual chapters bear some similarity with earlier versions of this book (for obvious reasons), the rest has been reworked substantially. The other major difference is that this is now a co-authored book, bringing to its contents a global perspective that might have otherwise been missing. I am hugely grateful to my co-author Kate for both taking the risk of writing with me alongside her intellectual precision and imagination. The arrival of her twins Matilda and William in June 2017 added a joyful and memorable piquancy to writing with her about gender. It has truly been a rewarding experience. Thank you, Kate. In addition, I would like to acknowledge the ongoing and unstinting support of my partner and husband Ron Wardale, my colleagues at Liverpool University, namely Ross McGarry, Gabe Mythen, Barry Godfrey and Barry Goldson, and my newer, though no less important colleagues at Monash University, especially Jude McCulloch and JaneMaree Maher, all of whom provide intellectual stimulation along with so much more. Thanks to all of you.

…

To be invited to write the third edition of this book with Sandra has been an honour for which I am very grateful. It is always an intellectually stimulating, rewarding and joyful experience to work with Sandra but particularly so when writing in an area where her work has been so influential. My thanks go to Sandra for her patience and understanding as the arrival of William and Matilda necessitated special time away from the computer.

While working on a book covering this topic I have reflected on how lucky I am to work in a team at Monash University where a critical gendered perspective is always valued, and, with my colleagues, in particular JaneMaree Maher and Jude McCulloch. To my husband, Mick Young, whose support and encouragement while I typed away (between feeding and settling babies) is always so greatly appreciated.

Kate Fitz-Gibbon and Sandra Walklate
December 2017

About the authors

Kate Fitz-Gibbon is a Senior Lecturer in Criminology and researcher in the Monash Gender and Family Violence program in the School of Social Sciences at Monash University and an Honorary Research Fellow in the School of Law and Social Justice at the University of Liverpool. She is recognised as a leading researcher in family violence, legal responses to lethal violence, and the effects of homicide law and sentencing reform in Australian and international jurisdictions with her single-authored book, *Homicide Law Reform, Gender and the Provocation Defence: A Comparative Perspective* (Palgrave Macmillan) being cited in a judgment of the High Court of Australia (Lindsay v The Queen [2015] HCA 16). In 2015 she received the prestigious Peter Mitchell Churchill Fellowship to examine innovative and best practice legal responses to the prevention of intimate homicide in the United Kingdom, Canada and the United States. Her publications include an edited collection with Sandra Walklate, *Homicide, Gender and Responsibility: An International Perspective* (Routledge, 2016). She is a member of the Monash Family Violence Focus Research Program and is in receipt of funding from the Australian Research Council and Australia's National Research Organisation for Women's Safety, including a Discovery Grant (2017–20) on Securing Women's Safety: Preventing Intimate Partner Homicides.

Sandra Walklate is Eleanor Rathbone Chair of Sociology at the University of Liverpool, and conjoint Chair of Criminology, Monash University, Melbourne, Australia. She is Editor in Chief of the *British*

Journal of Criminology and in July 2014 was awarded the British Society of Criminology's outstanding achievement award. She also holds an adjunct professorial role at QUT in Brisbane. She has been researching criminal victimisation since the early 1980s with a particular focus on gendered violence(s) and the fear of crime. She has published widely on victimology (most recently the 2nd edition of *The Handbook of Victims and Victimology* with Routledge), and with colleagues at Liverpool University on terrorism and criminology and war. Her most recent publications include an edited collection with Kate Fitz-Gibbon, *Homicide, Gender and Responsibility: An International Perspective* (Routledge, 2016). She is the international partner of the Monash Family Violence Focus Research Program in receipt of an Australian Research Council Discovery Grant (2017–20) on Securing Women's Safety: Preventing Intimate Partner Homicides.

INTRODUCTION
WOMEN AND CRIME OR GENDER AND CRIME?

Introduction

In 1989 Braithwaite suggested that the first 'fact' any theory of crime should fit is that males disproportionately commit crime. In fact, thirty years earlier Wootton (1959: 32) commented: 'if men behaved like women, the courts would be idle and the prisons empty.' Indeed, the maleness of crime is discernible across the globe, irrespective of particular national jurisdictions or particular categories of crime. Yet, despite the increasing presence of a wide range of literature concerned to address this issue, the disciplines of both criminology and victimology still struggle to embrace the implications of recognising the inherent maleness of crime and to develop appropriately informed criminal justice responses to it. The purpose of this book is to map this struggle and to chart a path through it. As will become evident, any path through this struggle is contested.

Crucial to this contestation are two basic concepts: sex and gender. These concepts, and the relationship between them, may be understood in different ways and the purpose of this introduction is to outline how these terms have been understood and the approach adopted towards them throughout this book. To be clear, our purpose here is not to be preoccupied with the strengths and weaknesses of the different data sources about who commits crime, who the victims are, what kinds of crime are committed and how these might be patterned by sex and/or gender. Neither are we concerned to ask questions about whether or not men or women commit crime for the same or different reasons and under what circumstances. Many of these issues are already well documented in the existing literature. Moreover, any specific issues that arise from these questions will be dealt with as they become pertinent to the more substantives issues discussed in the chapters that follow. Our purpose in this Introduction is to consider the basic conceptual apparatus underpinning what informs the data-gathering process in relation to understandings of sex and gender. We will discuss each of these terms in turn.

What does the term 'sex' mean?

When criminology was in its infancy the term 'sex' was uncontested. It was used in a simple, straightforward fashion that reflected the binary thinking associated with the knowledge base of the nineteenth century. Children born with the outwardly obvious physical characteristics of being male or female were sexed in line with those characteristics. However, as scientific knowledge has moved on, particularly within the realm of genetics, it has become increasingly apparent that even biologically, human beings do not always or necessarily fall into either of these categories. Nor do they always wish to be confined by an either/or classification. Thus the more genetics has revealed about human beings the less clear a simple distinction between male and female, based solely on physical attributes, has become. However, having recognised this complexity, the chance that any one individual possesses the biological characteristics of both sexes in equal measure is statistically rare. In most instances a person possesses the biological characteristics of being predominantly male or predominantly female.

The growth in genetics has led some to question the value of using biology as a way of defining sex, arguing that even the terms used within this area of work are social constructions (Butler 1993). Such interventions notwithstanding, it is the case that most of the time people treat individuals designated as male differently from individuals designated as female. Indeed, Gartner and McCarthy (2014: 5) state:

> In many societies, sex determines where people live (e.g. patri- versus matri-local), their kinship, their inheritance, and the allocation of valued resources. Moreover, a variety of cultural values and social norms contribute to sex roles that demarcate behaviours deemed appropriate for males and females.

So, while the simplistic attribution of sex on the basis of physical characteristics alone is now not so clear cut, it remains the case globally that attributions of sex (being female or being male) still matter for people's routine daily lives, particularly in relation to their experiences of crime and criminal victimisation, as the chapters that follow illustrate. Following Barberet (2014: 3), we would concur that:

> [C]riminology's subjects of study (crime, victimisation, institutional responses) now make sex a very difficult variable to ignore,

because research confirms some very clear, nearly universal differences between men and women as offenders, victims and criminal justice professionals: marked differences in rates and patterns of offending and victimization and differential participation in the criminal justice workplace.

What does the term 'gender' mean?

For criminology and victimology, alongside a wide range of social science disciplines, the increasing appreciation of *gender* as distinct from sex clearly distinguishes current debates about crime and criminal victimisation than those dominant at the time in which Wootton (1959) was writing. As Chapters 1 and 2 (of this volume) demonstrate, the influence of different feminisms and developments in studies of masculinities has been central to reorienting those debates from a preoccupation with sex to one focused far more on gender. However, this reorientation in itself hides a number of issues with the term 'gender', since not all theorists and researchers, let alone policy makers, use this term in the same way. For some, following the thinking of Butler (1993) referred to earlier, 'gender' has simply been substituted for 'sex', or the two terms are used interchangeably as though they mean the same. As is suggested in our discussion of sexual violence in Chapter 4, this conflation is problematic for a number of reasons, not least of which because it denies the evidence that some crimes are sexual both in their motivation and expression. Such denial does not necessarily assist in either understanding or explaining offending, victimisation or system responses.

Conversely some commentators use the term 'gender' to refer to the socially constructed norms and expectations associated with masculinity and femininity which become embedded in an individual's gender identity. The danger here is that gender in this sense reflects similar binary and dichotomous thinking associated with earlier uses of the term 'sex'. This kind of understanding of gender assumes that it is immutable: determined and unchanging and, as with the earlier deterministic use of the term 'sex', this use of the term 'gender' fails to recognise that gender constructs can change over time and with socio-cultural contexts. While, as Renzetti (2013: 7) observes, 'The social world is, in short, fundamentally gendered', such gendering does not take the same shape and form everywhere, for everyone, throughout time. Thus gender too is not static. As the discussion in Chapter 2 demonstrates, much work within masculinity theory has endeavoured to tease out masculinities in much the same way as the work within feminism (Chapter 1) talks contemporarily of femininities. Indeed, while there are links to be understood among sex, gender, masculinities and femininities, these links are neither simple nor straightforward. They are messy, fuzzy, situated and layered. At the same time, such conceptual nuances notwithstanding, the strain towards binary thinking persists, as does the conflation of sex with gender. Thus the picture is messy even before the complexities of sexuality are added to the mix.

Criminology and victimology have for the most part side-stepped the complexities of the debates touched upon above ever since. While much feminist-informed work has remained dedicated to make women visible within these areas of concern in all their complexity, such efforts have been slow to produce change. Hence the title of the fourth edition of Belknap's book, *Invisible Woman: Gender, Crime and Justice* (2015). Here, following Renzetti (2013), we recognise that biology is not destiny and neither are the social prescriptions of gender. Biology and culture interact constantly with one another in processes in which human beings have agency, even if that agency is under certain conditions circumscribed. In understanding crime, victimisation and criminal justice the trick is working out the conditions under which individuals make choices, events 'just happen' to them, and when what transpires is a complex mixture of these processes. Sometime sex is the dominant variable. Sometimes gender is. Yet, as the reference to Barberet's (2014) recent work suggests, charting a path through this complexity remains contested territory.

'Women and crime' or 'gender and crime'?

Early feminist incursions into criminology did not focus so much on the maleness of crime (as implied by the reference to Braithwaite above) but were more concerned to talk about 'women and crime'.

This focus began with the seminal work of Smart (1976), and was continued by Leonard (1982), Heidensohn (1985), Morris (1987) and Naffine (1987). All these texts, while varied in content and theoretical approach, were concerned to challenge conventional criminological wisdoms concerning women and crime and, in so doing, pushed to make women more visible within those criminological wisdoms. Each of these writers shared a number of common concerns.

First, they wanted to move the criminological empirical agenda towards addressing a key and what appeared to be a constant feature of the data on crime: it is a male-dominated activity. Second, they wanted to move the criminological theoretical agenda towards appreciating the diverse possibilities of feminist theorising and its potential contribution to explaining that empirical data. Third, several of these texts reflected a concern to appreciate that women's relationship to the crime problem needed to be understood not only in terms of their offending behaviour, but also in relation to women's experiences as victims of crime. Fourth, this connects this body of work to that of Barberet (2014: 3), who states:

> Equity is still a main concern in most of the research within feminist criminology, and sex-disaggregated data are still a common demand of activists and state feminists working at both international and national levels.

Indeed, Barberet makes a sound observation here. It is particularly pertinent to be reminded of both the activist origins of feminism alongside the unevenness, globally, in data gathering in criminal justice practices. These are ongoing concerns for feminists working in this field. Fifth, all of these writers were of the view that male dominance within criminal activity might be better understood as a product of gender differences rather than as a product of sex differences. However, a dilemma remains in the light of these concerns: to centre 'women and crime' or 'gender and crime'? Each of these positions offers a different focus for criminology and victimology.

We acknowledge that there are a number of difficulties associated with focusing solely on the 'women and crime' question. Brown

(1986: 35) outlined some of them. She argued that the more the woman question was treated as a separate and separable issue within criminology, the more that mainstream (read 'malestream') criminology was left to its own devices, untouched by feminist criticism, and therefore presumed to be accurate when it talked about (male) crime. Put simply, it left criminology (and for the purposes here victimology) and its domain assumptions untouched and unquestioned. Thus questions relating to women could always potentially be seen as othered and marginal to the central concerns of the discipline. From this vantage point behaviour was always likely to be measured against some masculine norm; which may or may not provide an adequate framework for explaining crime for men or for women. Thus for Brown the 'women and crime' approach in its very label presumed two things. First, it presumed that it was possible to substitute the biological category of sex with the socio-cultural category of gender. In other words, women's criminality, for example, could be explained not by reference to biology but by reference to the ways in which women who fail to meet stereotypical expectations of femininity are stigmatised and thereby fall foul of the criminal justice system: its policies and practices. This approach presumes that it is possible to replace biologically rooted understandings (sex) with socially rooted ones (gender). Expressed in this way it is a position which hints at essentialism. This is problematic not only because essentialism presumes immutable differences, but perhaps more importantly, particularly in policy terms, it also hides the tendency within such work to assume that questions of gender only refer to women, thus ignoring men and their relationship with masculinity(ies).

The expression of masculinity in its various forms constitutes a key feature of understanding the criminal justice process and all its related activities in *gendered* terms. An exploration of masculinity, its expression in criminal behaviour, the impact it has on men who are victimised, and its central presence in key professional areas within the criminal justice system, permits the development of a way of thinking about the crime problem which neither universalises men's experiences nor neglects women's. It is this perspective on the crime problem that provides a more accurate framework for thinking about gender and crime rather than about women and crime or about sex differences and crime. Thus while it is without doubt that feminist-inspired empirical work and feminist theorising offers much to both criminology and victimology – and that includes feminist work which has concentrated on and still does concentrate on the 'women and crime' question – here we have chosen to put gender to the fore. Thus we echo, and build upon, the work of Wootton and Braithwaite in putting the maleness of crime in the centre.

Nevertheless, it is important to recognise that the ongoing powerful effects of the expectations associated with femininity illustrated in Cain's edited collection *Growing Up Good* (1989) remain. This is illustrated in the ongoing puzzled response to, for example, women who kill their children, or the female suicide bomber. Both of these examples challenge historically deeply rooted cultural presumptions concerning appropriate femininity. They are acts that carry more or less draconian consequences in terms of criminal justice responses (in relation to the first of these in particular) dependent upon the socio-cultural context in which they occur (see Razali *et al.*, 2017). Similarly, the powerful effects of the social expectations associated with masculinity may also be discerned in the ongoing puzzled response to men who present themselves as victims. Moreover, while this is changing (even for those men considered the most masculine, namely soldiers: see McGarry and Walklate 2011), it is still the case that, in terms of criminal justice responses, much remains to be done (see, *inter alia*, Javaid 2016). The complexities associated with uncovering and responding to male crime victimisation are explored in further detail in Chapter 2.

Thus, since the early feminist incursions into criminology, and later victimology, much has changed (or at least has had the potential to change) within each of these areas of investigation, and much has remained the same. In a recent assessment of Carol Smart's (1976) *Women, Crime and Criminology*, Collier (2017: 46) states that it 'raises important issues no less relevant today than when it was first published'. In this spirit, in the chapters that follow we endeavour to chart a course through these areas of investigation with a view to examining what has been done but also what is yet to be done. As the rest of this book unfolds it will become apparent that much of the work which remains to be done focuses attention not only on the complex relationship between sex, gender and sexuality but also on the question of how and under what conditions any of these variables either singly or in conjunction with each other become the salient variable(s) in making sense of crime, victimhood and perpetration as well as criminal justice policy and practice.

Organisation and overview of this book

Part I of this book focuses on theory. Within this part, Chapters 1 and 2 address the different feminist perspectives and the different theoretical developments on masculinity, and their respective impact on both criminology and victimology. These two chapters indicate the challenge posed to both criminology and victimology by feminist perspectives on crime, criminal victimisation and criminal justice, and the extent to which the questions posed by feminisms are intricately linked to the presence (or otherwise) of concerns with masculinities within each of these disciplinary domains. Taken together these chapters constitute the conceptual foundations upon which the chapters that follow are built.

Part II addresses questions of practice. In this context practice refers as much to the practices of the disciplinary areas under investigation as it does to the actual work of criminal justice practitioners and agencies. These chapters are particularly concerned to unpack in a little more detail the ways in which gendered conceptual assumptions inform both how and what is considered to be an appropriate way of thinking about the substantial concerns of criminology and victimology. Specifically, Chapter 3 unpacks the assumptions embedded in the way in which the concepts of fear, risk and security have been understood and how those assumptions have proceeded to be built into policy responses; for example, practices of risk assessment and/or the increasing concern with vulnerability. Chapter 4 advances these concerns one stage further by taking a closer look at the relationship between gender and sexual violence. In furthering our efforts to offer a nuanced understanding of gender, this chapter considers three different contexts in which sexual violence occurs: the interpersonal, the institutional and state-sponsored sexual violence. This facilitates a more detailed appreciation of the capacity of criminology and/or victimology to make sense of sexual violence in each of these domains.

Part III concerns itself more directly with policy. Chapter 5 asks the question as to whether or not criminal justice work is men's work. Criminal justice systems around the world have been traditionally male centric in theory and male dominated in operation. This chapter explores the extent to which questions relating to gender continue to pervade the work of criminal justice professionals. In so doing the chapter considers the extent to which a traditionally male-dominated criminal justice system, particularly in relation to policing, adequately responds to gendered crimes, such as domestic violence and sexual assault (also part of the subject of Chapter 4). Chapter 6 builds upon this exploration by examining the gendered dimensions and influences in law and criminal justice policy. Across a number of jurisdictions there have now been over two decades of policy work and advocacy that has had gender in mind. This chapter draws upon several examples of this work, including the Feminist Judgments Project, debates surrounding gender and the judiciary, and recent reforms introduced to improve women's experience of using self-defence in trials of homicide to consider the efficacy or otherwise of changing legal interventions.

The Conclusion reviews not only the foregoing content but also offers a view on the extent to which gender remains a salient variable in understanding the nature and extent of crime, criminal victimisation and system responses. The Conclusion also considers the importance of studies focused on intersectionality and those that draw upon the role of the state in endeavouring to answer questions surrounding gender, crime and criminal justice. Given the international orientation of the book as a whole, the case will be made that in considering the ongoing salience there is a need to listen carefully to voices not only from the global north but also those from the global south (*qua* Carrington 2015). The implications for victimology and criminology in appreciating crime and victimhood in this global perspective are considered and emphasised.

Conclusion

As is apparent from this Introduction, and as was intimated earlier, much has changed and much has remained the same in the presence and impact of the debates with which this book is concerned since its first publication in 1995. While there is indeed much more substantive material concerned with gender available to the reader, it remains questionable as to the extent to which such concerns have impacted upon the fundamental domain assumptions of both victimology and criminology in those intervening years. This is the subject matter of Chapter 1. However, in charting a path through this material this book makes no claim to be exhaustive in its coverage of this material. Nonetheless, it is anticipated that the reader will at least get a flavour of what has been achieved and what has yet to be done. It is not an even picture on either count but it is hoped that having read this book the reader will be equipped with the conceptual armoury and an understanding of some of the substantive data and issues that continue to make gender an important concept for criminological and victimological exploration.

Recommendations for further reading

While now over forty years old, time spent reading Carol Smart's (1976) *Women, Crime and Criminology* will not be wasted effort. Appreciating the kinds of questions posed by Smart and reflecting upon the extent to which these questions have or have not been addressed four decades on is a good exercise in which to engage. In similar fashion reading Monk and Sim's (2017) *Women, Crime and Criminology: A Celebration* affords a unique opportunity for considering further the achievements of Smart's contribution.

References

Barberet, R. (2014) *Women, Crime, and Criminal Justice*. London: Routledge.
Belknap, J. (2015) *The Invisible Woman: Gender, Crime and Justice* (4th edition). Stanford, CT: Cengage Learning.

Braithwaite, J. (1989) *Crime, Power and Reintegration*. London: Heinemann.

Brown, B. (1986) Women and crime: the dark figures of criminology. *Economy and Society* 15(3): 355–402.

Butler, J. (1993) *Bodies that Matter*. London: Routledge.

Cain, M. (ed.) (1989) *Growing Up Good*. London: Sage.

Carrington, K. (2015) *Feminism and Global Justice*. London: Routledge.

Collier, R. (2017) Redressing the balance? Masculinities, law and criminology – Rethinking the 'man question' forty years on. In H. Monk and J. Sim (eds) *Women, Crime and Criminology: A Celebration* (pp.23–56). London: EG Press.

Gartner, R. and McCarthy, B. (2014) Introduction. In R. Gartner and B. McCarthy (eds) *The Oxford Handbook of Gender, Sex, and Crime* (pp. 1–18). Oxford: Oxford University Press.

Heidensohn, F. (1985) *Women and Crime*. London: Macmillan.

Javaid, A. (2016) Feminism, masculinity and male rape: bringing male rape 'out of the closet'. *Journal of Gender Studies* 25(3): 283–293.

Leonard, E.B. (1982) *A Critique of Criminology Theory: Women, Crime and Society*. London: Longman.

McGarry, R. and Walklate, S. (2011) The soldier as victim: peering through the looking glass. *British Journal of Criminology* 46(6): 900–917.

Monk, H. and Sim, J. (eds) (2017) *Women, Crime and Criminology: A Celebration*. London: EG Press.

Morris, A. (1987) *Women, Crime and Criminal Justice*. Oxford: Blackwell.

Naffine, N. (1987) *Female Crime*. Sydney: Allen and Unwin.

Razali, S., Kirkman, M. and Fisher, J. (2017) Research on a socially, ethically, and legally complex phenomenon: women convicted of filicide in Malaysia. *International Journal for Crime, Justice and Social Democracy* 6(2): 34–45. DOI: 10.5204/ijcjsd.v6i2.337.

Renzetti, C. (2013) *Feminist Criminology*. London: Routledge.

Smart, C. (1976) *Women, Crime and Criminology*. London: Routledge and Kegan Paul.

Wootton, B. (1959) *Social Science and Social Pathology*. London: George Allen and Unwin.

Part I

THEORY

CRIMINOLOGY, VICTIMOLOGY AND FEMINISM

Introduction

Criminology and victimology are two areas of investigation characterised by their substantive topic of interest: crime in the case of the former, victims (of crime) in the case of the latter. As a consequence, each of these 'disciplines' is peopled by a wide range of other specialists (sociologists, psychologists, economists and so on), all of whom make claims about understanding and/or explaining crime and criminal victimisation. Thus criminology and victimology are highly contested, theoretically diverse and hotly debated areas of investigation. The interconnections among criminology, victimology and criminal justice policy afford an added piquancy to these debates. Such issues notwithstanding, criminology and victimology share much in common. These commonalities reflect what Gouldner (1973) once referred to as domain assumptions: assumptions embedded so deeply in their disciplinary view of the world that they frame how an area of investigation does its work. All (social) science disciplines operate with such assumptions.

Some of these assumptions have recently been called into question in relation to the influence and presence of what Connell (2007) has termed 'Northern theorising'. This theorising, she argues, reflects the deployment of concepts and assumptions developed in the Northern hemisphere and applied throughout the rest of the world as though these concepts and methods are pertinent everywhere. In criminology this kind of theorising reflects domain assumptions around Occidentalism (Cain 2000), a deep attachment to positivism (Young 2011; see also Walklate (2008) on victimology), and presumptions around geography (Aas 2012). All of these features of the discipline have been the subject of critical scrutiny for the ways in which they limit the discipline's imagination. So much so that latterly, Carrington *et al.* (2016) have called for the development of a 'Southern criminology' agenda whereby the voices of the South are interjected into the debates traditionally confined to Northern scholars (see also the interventions of de Sousa Santos 2014). Such critiques notwithstanding, the focus of this chapter is to explore the extent to which the domain assumptions of criminology and victimology in relation to gender frame how each of these areas of investigation thinks about crime, the criminal and the victim of crime.

In so doing, this chapter will offer an overview of the origins of each of these 'disciplines' as one way of providing some insight into what they each take for granted about gender. Put simply, it will consider the extent to which criminology and victimology persist in being 'gender-blind' and will examine the (various) feminist responses to this problem. As Dekeseredy (2016: 1) reminds us, 'One thing that all feminist responses have in common is prioritizing the concept of gender', though, as discussed in the Introduction to this book and developed in this chapter, they do not all agree on how this 'prioritizing' should be achieved, or indeed, once having prioritised it, how it might inform the investigative process and with what impact. A second feature shared by feminists is the desire to engage in rigorous empirical work. How this is done involves challenging, as Dekeseredy (2016; 2) also points out, 'the twin bastilles of positivism and abstracted empiricism'. This chapter interrogates the role and presence of positivism, abstracted empiricism, and how they can frame the capacity of criminology and/or victimology to consider gender. The first question then is: How, if at all, might criminology and victimology be thought of as gender-blind?

In some ways this may be considered an odd place to start. After all, feminism from the late nineteenth century up until the present has been actively challenging presumptions around men and women, with some commentators writing contemporarily about a fourth wave of feminism as doing so. Moreover, it is now routinely possible to read policy documents of all kinds apparently informed by gender and to listen to criminal justice professionals discuss issues relating to gender as part of the focus of their work. Yet at the same time it remains possible to pick up criminology books discussing mainstream issues around crime, its causes and impact, and to find no reference to gender in the index. So the question arises, as implied in the introductory chapter to this book: What does this contemporary talk about gender amount to? Furthermore, to what extent have criminology and victimology genuinely re-examined their respective domain assumptions about this concept? In order to examine this it will be useful to say a little more about what is meant by gender-blindness or what Belknap (2015) calls 'the invisible woman'.

Thinking about gender-blindness

Historically, criminology and victimology been blind to 'differences' of all kinds, like race, ethnicity and culture, alongside being imbued with the kind of Northern theorising criticised by Connell (2007). Yet while the capacity to 'see' race, ethnicity, sexuality and class is at least empirically increasingly evident (as discussed in Chapter 2), the question of gender arguably remains persistently problematic. This is in part a result of the knowledge base upon which each of these areas of investigation has been built. Thus, in order to get to the roots of gender-blindness, it is important to ask: How is it that criminologists and victimologists know things?

Asking this question brings to the surface a way of thinking which presumes that the world is a masculine world. Smith (1987: 74) expressed the problem in the following way:

> The knower turns out after all not to be 'abstract knower' perching on an Archimedian point but a member of a definite social category occupying definite positions in the society.

Once it is recognised that the knower is always male, and that the position of this (male) knower informs what counts as knowledge and whose knowledge counts, the deep-rooted nature of gender-blindness becomes apparent. To make the point more clearly and reiterate the examination of sex and gender set up in the Introduction, the human world does not consist of androgynous subjects. It comprises males and females who are differently attributed with masculine and feminine qualities. Moreover, as was intimated in the Introduction and further considered here, while sex and gender are thought of in far more flexible terms contemporarily than they were several decades ago, it remains the case that using the term 'human' as if it captured the (potentially) diverse ways of thinking about the world implied by Smith above is problematic. The fundamental privileging and elision of male knowledge with human knowledge constitutes gender-blindness and throws into sharp focus what underpins the knowledge-production process. It is at this deep level that criminology and victimology share in gender-blindness. This has been one of the focal concerns of feminism, since it poses questions about whose knowledge, and what kind of knowledge, is privileged. These questions are central to understanding the domain assumptions of relevance here.

Gendering criminology

Criminology, like other social science disciplines, is depicted as a 'modern' discipline. Its nature and focus flowed from the historical period known in the Northern hemisphere as the Enlightenment. The Enlightenment encouraged the belief in reason as opposed to religious belief as the basis on which to make decisions. This belief in the power of reason, specifically the reasoning capacities of men, centred the reasoned power of science and the scientific enterprise. Criminology and latterly victimology carry the hallmarks of these historical shifts and are found in these areas of investigation in the ongoing presence/dominance of positivism. While the precise nature of positivism as a way of knowing is open to debate, Taylor *et al.* in *The New Criminology* (1973) deduced that criminology's commitment to this way of framing empirical knowledge equipped the discipline with three characteristics: the quantification of behaviour; a belief in objectivity; and a deterministic view of human behaviour (see also Roshier 1989). Taken together, these characteristics reflect a commitment to search for a universal explanation of crime, importantly a search that has travelled the globe, that would lend itself to appropriate policy intervention. This search, delineated by Young (2011) as a 'nomothetic impulse', has blighted much criminological endeavour. The roots of gender-blindness are buried here, since this nomothetic impulse conveys much about what there is to be known, by whom and about whom. In order to excavate this further it is of value to appreciate the prevailing scientific context in which those considered to be the Founding Fathers of criminology, later victimology, formulated their ideas.

Eagle Russett (1989: 63) states:

> Women and savages, together with idiots, criminals and patho-
> logical monstrosities, were a constant source of anxiety to male
> intellectuals in the late nineteenth century.

According to Eagle Russett, this anxiety could be discerned in the four principles underpinning nineteenth-century 'sexual science' within which it is possible to trace the birth of early criminology. The principles of this science were, according to Eagle Russett, the law of biogenetics, the notion of the greater variability of the male of the species, the drive within the species to conserve energy, and the physiological division of labour. Of these four principles, the most influential was the law of biogenetics. This law stated: 'ontology recapitulates phylogeny.' In other words, every individual organism revisits the development of its species within its own developmental history. This principle of recapitulation was one of the unifying and organising principles of what was then referred to as criminal anthropology. It is here that the origins of the discipline are to be found, particularly in the seminal work of Ceasare Lombroso. Influenced by the Darwinian thinking associated with this emergent biogenetics, Lombroso drew from these ideas to inform his concept of atavism. Assuming that the process of recapitulation usually produced biologically normal individuals, Lombroso envisaged the criminal as a throwback, an atavistic degeneration, to an earlier biological ancestry. Indeed, more contemporaneously the tendency for criminals to mark themselves with tattoos, for example, led Lombroso to argue that this was evidence of their closer relationship with 'savages', a form of human deemed to be located at an earlier point of the human species development on the Darwinian evolutionary scale. The concept of atavism explained the abnormality, understood as criminality, in an individual. Not confined to explaining male criminality, Lombroso's concept was also applied to females and children. Consequently the idea of the 'atavistic criminal' served a double helping of inadequacy to the female criminal.

To explicate this point more fully, in general terms Victorian science viewed women as a 'developmental anomaly' (Eagle Russett

1989: 74). The biogenetic laws presumed that the ultimate stage of evolutionary development was that reached by the white, Caucasian male. This resulted in certain presumptions about women; primarily that they suffered from arrested development. This rendered the criminal woman particularly problematic. Lombroso and Ferraro reached this conclusion in *The Female Offender* (1895). The female criminal was seen as a 'monster': she constituted both a throwback to an earlier species type and was arrested in her development as a member of her species. It is worth remembering that, influenced by the principles of positivism as a way of generating knowledge, Lombroso and Ferraro were searching for a universal explanation of crime. This search constituted the female criminal as problematic because of her presumed (inherent) species conservatism rather than her deviance per se. Thus, Brown (1990: 50) asserts:

> [T]he important thing about Lombroso and Ferrero's book is not biological determinism but the siting of women's conformity as the object of criminological analysis.

Yet this siting of women's conformity as the object of analysis was lost in much of the related work that followed, with some notable exceptions (see, *inter alia*, Wootton 1959; Heidensohn 1985; Cain 1989). However, of note here is that the principles of biogenetics deployed by Lombroso and Ferraro placed males and females (children and savages) on different points of the evolutionary scale. The greater development of the male (reflected in the greater variability in the male of any species) was likely to produce a greater variation in atavistic degeneration. Whereas the greater conservatism (less variability), alongside the arrested development of the female of the species, resulted in her degeneracy (in this case criminal behaviour) being all the more problematic when it occurred. Thus, the principle of the biogenetic law afforded Lombroso and Ferraro theoretical consistency for their explanation of the male and female criminal.

This search for a unifying explanation of criminal behaviour did not start and finish with the work of Lombroso and Ferraro specifically and the criminal anthropologists, or biological positivists as they are more conventionally referred to more broadly. It is a recurrent feature of criminological theorising. For example, the idea that female criminals are driven by their differently constructed nervous system (Thomas 1923) or their hormones (Dalton 1991) stands as testimony to the influence of this way of thinking. Biologism, as these approaches are sometimes referred to – in other words, explaining behaviour in terms of intrinsic biological make-up – was not confined solely to explaining the female criminal. Neither should it be forgotten that that which Hall-Williams (1982) labels the 'chemistry of crime' infiltrates a range of criminological work, from twin studies through to chromosome studies through to more contemporary neural imaging of the criminal brain. Many of these studies have focused either implicitly or explicitly on men, particularly on violent men. Of course, such a concern is entirely consonant with the deep-rooted view of male offenders derived from a presumption of the greater variability of the male of the species. Importantly when taken together this work denudes the offender of a sense of agency. Nonetheless, what is particularly significant about the influence of these nineteenth-century scientists, and their biologically rooted explanations of the differences between males and females, is the way in which these ideas permeated later work. This influence is particularly displayed in research which presumes that the differences between males and females are 'natural', biological and/or given, all of which are forms of gender-blindness.

As suggested above, the criminal anthropologists (biological positivists) laid a particular foundation for the ensuing development of criminological explanations. In drawing upon the ideas associated with nineteenth-century science, both in their commitment to positivism and to the biologically derived presumptions concerning the nature of sex differences, they provided a deep-rooted framework for thinking about and explaining crime. Moreover, the influence of nineteenth-century concepts of the evolutionary process and the way in which these were applied to explanations of sex differences has, arguably, made a significant contribution to cultural concepts of these same differences. In other words, they have framed the ways in which thinking about males and females, masculinity and femininity, have been constructed. While overt biological concerns were not necessarily present in all subsequent criminological explanations, few of these explanations lacked the desire to search for a universal explanation of criminal behaviour. Later criminological work, for example, moved away from the purely physical and/or biological as causal factors of crime towards explanations that focused on mental and/or personality factors, emotional stability, child-rearing practices and/or deprivation of an 'adequate' upbringing. While none of this work was explicitly gendered, implicitly it often presumed that the differences between the sexes were both natural and universal. Sexual differences in these studies, if not seen as biologically given, were sometimes seen to be the product of sex role stereotyping during upbringing. Hence biological difference is presumed to produce social difference. This latter view of the process of the production of sex differences influenced the more sociologically inspired subcultural studies of delinquency and deviance of the 1950s and 1960s.

While females are not completely absent from the studies of the 1950s and 1960s (hence the oft-quoted statement from Cohen (1955) that 'boys collect stamps, and girls collect boys'), these are studies which repeatedly focus on the greater criminal activity of the male and the (unacknowledged) greater conformity of the female. In commenting on some of this work, Naffine (1987: 31) points out that as a result, 'Femaleness emerges as an anomaly'. This clearly echoes the tenets of nineteenth-century sexual science identified by Eagle Russett (1989) and, of course, embedded in much of this subcultural work is the structural functionalist sociology of Talcott Parsons. Functionalism presumes that sex differences are biologically given, and these biological givens dictate subsequent exposure to differential socialisation. For example, given that it is natural for women to bear children, socialisation prepares them for this role; hence the presumed preoccupation for girls in forming a stable relationship with a boy, and the preoccupation for boys in actively creating their public identities as men to be reckoned with. These ideas on sexual difference made it very difficult for the subcultural theorists to attend to the female deviant in any other way than when she was deviant from her expected, biologically given, sex role. Thus this work became preoccupied with female status offences associated with the expression of 'deviant' sexuality, promiscuity and/or prostitution.

It is without doubt that the threat posed by girls exploring their sexuality outside prescribed social rules and expectations was, and is, considered to be a very real one. The social control exerted over and by young working-class girls in their use and experience of the label 'slag' stands as a very real indicator of this (Lees 1989). Similarly, more contemporary preoccupations with the dangers of sexting and other examples of technologically facilitated violence may also be considered 'dangerous' because of the challenges posed to the exploration of sexuality outside of prescribed rules (see, *inter alia*, Crofts *et al.* 2015). Subcultural theorists, however, did not view the impact of such status offences in quite the same terms. These offences were taken as illustrations of the kind of criminal behaviour girls engaged in rather than such behaviour being seen as the product of the differential mechanisms of control to which girls were subjected. The perpetual failure to see female crime in anything other than 'sexual' terms is reflected in the control theory of Hirschi (1969); the liberation thesis of Adler (1975); and, ironically, in the work of labelling theorists themselves. They all denude the female offender of any sense of agency other than that which matched stereotypical/cultural sex role expectations.

To summarise: Naffine (1987) argues that for the most part female crime has traditionally been associated with legitimate endeavours to find a mate or to sustain a relationship with a male. More succinctly, female crime was viewed solely as a means through which women sought male companionship. Women were not seen to be aggressive or violent because that was (and still is, as will be highlighted in later chapters) inconsistent with the feminine ideal. So, while there have been a variety of approaches to explaining crime since the days of Lombroso, all of which have dealt differently, and more or less visibly, with the question of female criminality (for discussions of this work see e.g. Naffine 1987; Heidensohn 1985; Smart 1976), none of this work is void of the deeply embedded assumption that crime is men's work, not women's (Jefferson 1993). This presumption pervades criminology as a discipline both in terms of who counts as a criminologist and what counts as criminological work (see e.g. the observations made by Scraton 1990, and latterly by Cook 2016). However, it is a presumption that takes its toll on the discipline in ways much deeper than who currently counts as 'one of the boys'. Re-enter the nomothetic impulse (Young 2011). This impulse, driven by positivism, results in even contemporary work, like that of life-course criminology, leaving gender largely unexamined as a variable. This work takes as a given that men are much more likely to commit crime than women and moves forward on the basis of this presumption without asking why (see Chapter 2 for a discussion of how this impacts upon the visibility of male victimisation). In reviewing life-course criminology MacMillan and McCarthy (2014: 357) consequently conclude that:

> Unfortunately, many recent studies that use a life course orientation to examine offending (or desistance) do not examine the extent to which gender conditions the patterns documented even though they make use of data on both men and women.

Arguably this more than illustrates the drive for universal explanations embedded in the acceptance of positivism and its presumptions about who can know things, what there is to be known, about what.

This summary of criminology has implicitly and explicitly drawn upon the kinds of questions raised by second-wave feminism. In the context of criminology this feminist work has been concerned to render the female criminal visible and has posed a serious challenge to the discipline. Thus it is possible to suggest that while criminology may have thought a great deal about sex differences, it has roundly failed to think in more nuanced ways about gender. Nineteenth-century scientific work concerned with sex differences has played a crucial part in contributing to this failure, as has the ongoing dominance of positivism and its associated search for universal explanations. The question remains as to the extent to which victimology has been subjected to the same influences.

Gendering victimology

Victimology as a distinct area of study emerged later than criminology. Its origins are usually located in the work of Von

Hentig and Mendelsohn, among others, in the late 1940s. As lawyers-cum-criminologists, both of these writers were concerned to understand the relationship between the victim and offender, and both endeavoured to construct 'victim typologies' as one way of achieving such an understanding. Each gave a very different focus to their typologies. Von Hentig was concerned with categories of victim proneness; Mendelsohn with victim culpability. While neither of these writers intended to suggest that there was a 'born victim', they were nevertheless searching for ways of differentiating the potential victim from the non-victim which could be used to make sense of all victimising situations. This approach is clearly consonant with the work of the early criminologists.

Victim typologies remained a key feature of early victimological work. Later versions of this kind of work were much more sophisticated than those of Von Hentig and Mendelsohn but they nevertheless shared the early criminological worldview that if criminals could be identified and typologised in some way then so could victims. In this way it may be seen that victimology, unsurprisingly, also shared those fundamental tenets of early criminology: determinism, differentiation and pathology. This way of thinking about the victim reflected an underpinning view that there is a normal person measured against whom the victim somehow falls short.

Taking this as their starting point, the typologies of both Mendelsohn and Von Hentig, and much work that followed on from them, presumed that the white, heterosexual male was the measuring stick informing who could and could not be a victim (see Walklate 2003). The influence of nineteenth-century science is more than apparent here. As we will explore throughout this book, the questions of what and who is considered to be reasonable and/or rational (see Chapter 6), and/or more prone or not to victimisation (see Chapter 2), are gendered ones. In particular when Mendelsohn's concept of victim culpability became translated into a concept of victim precipitation, the impact of what may be considered reasonable or rational behaviour for a victim was keenly felt. An understanding of this concept is particularly relevant in appreciating victimology and its developments, and we will consider it here in a little more detail.

The concept of victim precipitation was originally formulated by Wolfgang (1957) in his work on homicide and further developed in the later work by Amir (1971) on rape. Essentially this concept draws attention to the criminal act as involving two (or more) individuals and is concerned to understand the relative contribution of each party to the commission of that act. Derived as it is from a more legalistic understanding of the notion of culpability, its use has been seen to be particularly controversial when applied to understanding culpability and responsibility in rape and sexual assault cases. Amir's (1971) study of rape provoked a particularly strong reaction for a number of reasons. Not only were there empirical difficulties with his findings (for a detailed discussion of these difficulties see Morris 1987); the connotations of victim-blaming were very difficult to shed from the concept of victim precipitation, however carefully formulated. As a concept, victim precipitation clearly encouraged a consideration of the contribution of a victim's behaviour towards the crime committed against them. The focus on the victim's contribution to what occurred, as opposed to the contribution of the perpetrator, marks what Karmen (1990) has called the move from 'crime prevention' towards 'victimisation prevention'. In the context of burglary, it may be seen to be unfair, though perhaps reasonable, to expect people to lock their doors in order to help prevent a burglary taking place. And while this may seem straightforward, this perspective is problematic when applied to interpersonal crimes. In the context of rape or sexual assault, for example, the notion that somehow the victim could have engaged in more reasonable behaviour to prevent the incident misunderstands the fundamental nature of such an incident. It also serves to muddy allocations of responsibility and culpability in understanding such acts. Put simply for now, the concept of victim precipitation presumes equality between participants where none may exist. This raises all kinds of questions as to what constitutes reasonable behaviour in situations where the individuals concerned do not possess, at a minimum, the same physical power with which to negotiate the situation. More generally this concept cannot therefore be applied to situations which are a product of power relations or in particular gendered power relationships. As a concept, it cannot 'see' gender.

Although victimology, as originally formulated, was concerned with the relationship between the victim and the offender, the focus on the behaviour of the victim and the policy possibilities generated from this has been very influential. This is particularly illustrated in the translation of Von Hentig's concept of victim proneness into the concept of lifestyle. This is largely associated with the work of Hindelang *et al.* (1978), who sought to develop a framework which could help one to understand the regular patterning of criminal victimisation rather than how a particular incident occurred. Again, influenced by functionalism, their propositions largely directed attention to such factors as how much time an individual spent outside their home, what activities they were engaged in, how they moved about, and so on. This way of thinking about the role of the victim in contributing to their victimisation fed significantly into the crime survey business of the nineteenth century and has also contributed towards a reorientation of the crime prevention industry from crime prevention to victimisation prevention alluded to by Karmen (1990). Indeed, the concept of lifestyle, as something that is measurable and comprising separate and separable incidents, is so deeply embedded in the now widespread use and deployment of the criminal victimisation survey that it has almost achieved the status of a domain assumption in its own right. Yet, as will be discussed in later chapters with reference to the realities of intimate partner violence, this concept is unable to capture the everyday, routine lives of those for whom life is regularly punctuated by violence: it is 'just part of life' (Genn 1988: 92–93).

Taken together, the concepts of victim precipitation and lifestyle formed the core of much early victimological thinking. This core constitutes what Miers (1989: 3) termed positivistic victimology, defined as:

> The identification of factors which contribute to a non-random pattern of victimisation, a focus on interpersonal crimes of violence, and a concern to identify victims who may have contributed to their own victimisation.

The parallels here with criminology are clear: the emphasis on measurement and identification, added to differentiation, determinism and pathology, result in the same nomothetic impulse (Young 2011). This impulse takes its toll in different ways within victimology than within criminology, though that toll may be found primarily within the ever-sophisticated deployment of the criminal victimisation survey. As implied above, the capacity of such surveys to capture the routine nature of the impact of crime upon people's everyday lives is suspect, but is particularly suspect when it comes to measuring violence (see e.g. Walby *et al.* 2017). Deeply rooted in this method are problematic questions about who to count, what to count, when to count, and what to do having counted, especially in relation to violence against women (Walklate 2014) fundamentally asking: Whose knowledge counts?

In one sense the process of understanding and identifying the influence of what counts as science and consequently what counts as scientific knowledge underpins the gendering of the victim in a very similar way to that which occurred in gendering the criminal. These processes do not surface in expressions relating directly to evolution-ism within victimology, but they do surface as having been influenced by the cultural legacy emanating from those ideas. For example, according to Von Hentig's typology of victim proneness it is women (children, the elderly, people from ethnic minorities) who feature as being particularly victim prone. Indeed, this typology lends itself very easily to contemporary policy preoccupations with vulnerability (dis-cussed in Chapter 3). The concept of victim precipitation presumes some legal notion of reasonable (or ordinary) behaviour which, when examined carefully, frequently means reasonable, white, male, entre-preneurial behaviour (Naffine, 1990; see also Chapter 6 for a critique of the ordinary man of criminal law). In the work of Hindelang *et al.* (1978), their propositions are derived from a highly functionalist view of the world. A world in which the concept of lifestyle presumes that individuals adapt to their structural location; and that they do this differently and passively according to the characteristics they possess: age, race, sex and so on. Such adaptations then become reflected in an individual's routine public life; that is, their daily street activities. This implicitly accepts the sex role model and thereby accepts a very male view of what counts as a high-risk place: the street.

These examples reflect a deeply embedded male view of the problem of victimisation. At a conceptual level this problem arises in defining the scope of the discipline, and at an empirical level in defining that which needs to be measured. These assumptions gender the discipline: women are victims, men are not. However, it is not only victimology that has contributed to the gendering of the victim in this way. It has to be said that much feminist work, while developing outside of victimology both conceptually and empirically, has also contributed to this process. That feminist work, focusing as it did on the nature and extent of male violence, especially sexual violence towards women, has created the impression that only women (and female children) are victimised by such violence, as explored in greater depth in Chapter 2.

This is not to downplay the political importance of all that was achieved by feminist academics and activists in drawing attention to campaigning against rape and 'domestic' violence; nor is it intended to underestimate the importance of the feminist focus on the concept of the female 'survivor' rather than 'victim'. Here, we recognise that labels have been important. As such, it must be said that neither should this be read as a denial of the overwhelming evidence that women and children suffer most at the hands of men, and particularly men they know (see Chapter 4). This is a consistent fact across time, cultures and geographical space. However, despite these caveats, this work, taken alongside mainstream victimological work, constructs a worldview constituting the potential victim as being, in many instances, a powerless female.

This review has thus far offered a vision of a criminology that presumes the criminal to be male and a vision of victimological work which implicitly presumes that victims of crime are least likely to be male and, as such, least likely to hold power or control. Of course, when these presumptions are examined a little more carefully it is also important to point out that the variables of class, faith, sexuality and ethnicity impact upon these considerations in different and important ways. This does not change the nature of these core presumptions, however. Feminists have argued that the presumptions of maleness within both of these disciplines and their associated inability to see gender have their origin in the influence of positivism. The origins of this gendered view of science and the scientific process will be considered next.

Male science, male knowledge

The belief that science could transform and control nature has its origins in the seventeenth century. Bacon, for example, believed that the 'man of science' could 'make nature a "slave" to man's needs and desires' (Sydie 1989: 205). For Bacon, nature was to be controlled and nature was female. This association of women with nature, or being closer to nature as in the nineteenth-century work on sex differences discussed above does, pervades philosophical thinking about scientific knowledge. As Kellner Fox states:

> Having divided the world into two parts the knower (mind) and the knowable (nature) scientific ideology goes on to prescribe a very specific relation between the two. It prescribes the interactions which can consummate this union, that is which can lead to knowledge. Not only are mind and nature assigned gender, but in characterising scientific and objective thought as masculine, the very activity by which the knower can acquire knowledge is also genderised.
>
> (Quoted in Sydie, 1989: 205)

This gendered science view assigns women not only as a dangerous 'Other' (the nature to be controlled) but also assigns to women a particular status as knowers in relation to men (*qua* Smith 1987). Recognising that the construction of knowledge is a product of a definite social relationship of this kind involves recognising that the rules underpinning such knowledge construction render some forms of knowledge legitimate and acceptable while other forms are not. Thus the 'scientifically validated' ideas of the nineteenth century render some knowledge forms legitimate and others not. This leads to two questions: What kind of knowledge counts as scientific knowledge, and how does this production of knowledge count as a gendered process?

It is usual to associate 'scientific' knowledge with knowledge seen to be dispassionate, disinterested, impartial and abstract. These values are considered to be transcendental: uncontaminated by time, space and values. These are also the characteristics associated with knowledge that is considered to be rational. In the context of nineteenth-century science, this equates to a gendered outcome in that male knowledge was equated with rational knowledge with women's knowledge (almost a contradiction in terms) being consigned to 'emotional work'. Thus the presumption underpinning such dichotomous thinking, as Sydie (1989) has illustrated, is of 'natural woman' and 'cultured man'. Early criminology, and later victimology, reflected these views of males and females and the process of knowledge production: the male of the species is the norm, the searcher for knowledge, and the female of the species is closer to nature, abnormal and the provider of nurture. Once these domain assumptions are acknowledged, all kinds of questions surface: Who can be a knower? What kinds of things can be known? And what is meant by objectivity? (Harding 1987). There are different feminist responses to each of these questions and each will be considered in turn in the discussion that follows.

Liberal feminism

Liberal feminism is a useful place to start in examining feminist responses to questions about science, since some of the ideas informing this position are associated with writers whose work coexisted with the emergent nineteenth-century science discussed above. This arguably begins with the work of Mary Wollstonecraft, followed by Harriet Taylor and John Stuart Mill. Interestingly, given our discussion here, Wollstonecraft valued rationality. In response to Rousseau, she wanted Rousseau's Sophie to have the same educational opportunities as his Emile. It was irrational, she argued, to deny women's autonomy and capacity for rational thought. Reason and equality are two key features of the liberal feminist tradition. Consequently, much liberal feminist political work has been associated with the pursuit of equal rights. Indeed, Heidensohn (2013: 253) points out that 'In the sphere of criminal justice studies, liberal feminism has had a power-ful impact on analyses of equity and discrimination.'

Liberal feminism is also associated with a particular methodo-logical position labelled feminist empiricism (Harding 1987). This approach presumes that it is 'bad' science which produces sexist bias in empirical work. In other words, the rules of science and sci-entific enquiry are in themselves sound; what is amiss is how they are applied. To alleviate this problem feminist empiricists would argue for the presence of more women researchers and would take as a given the need to include women in any empirical data-gathering processes. In many ways the appeal of feminist empiri-cism is obvious: it leaves the conventional standards of what counts as 'good' research untouched, and thereby remains committed to the traditional principles and processes of science and scientific knowledge. Adherence to these principles, however, constitutes a fundamental dilemma for the liberal feminist. These principles take as given the yardstick by which we judge any knowledge pro-duced as a male one. In other words, this position, while promot-ing equal treatment in research and the empirical examination of theories with respect to men and women, leaves intact the assump-tion that male values are equivalent to human values; i.e. they apply to everyone. This assumption has led some critics to argue that liberal feminism reflects a 'normative dualism' (Jaggar 1983) which implicitly accepts the nineteenth-century view that women are closer to nature. It valorises rational (male) knowledge, and devalues other (female) ways of knowing.

While this may be considered a fundamental flaw in liberal femi-nism, it does not mean that either as a methodological or a political strategy this viewpoint is without strengths. Indeed, there is still much to be gained from pursuing the equal opportunity stance associated with this position for women and other disadvantaged groups (see further Renzetti 2017). Conceptually speaking, however, the liberal feminist position conflates questions associated with sex differences with questions posed by gender. This is not the case with radical feminism.

Radical feminism

In contrast to liberal feminism, radical feminism focuses more clearly on the issue of men's oppression of women and is more squarely situated within the burgeoning campaigning voices of second-wave feminism. Crucial to radical feminist analyses are questions of sexuality and sexual violence. This is seen as the locus of male power (MacKinnon 1989; Radford 2013). Radical feminist analysis has had much to say about reproduction, mothering and women's experiences of male (often sexual) violence. This emphasis on understanding the expression of female sexuality through the lens of patriarchal social relationships is central to all of them. As Tong (1989) pointed out, the radical feminist only needs to ask such questions as: Who rapes whom? Who batters whom? For whom does pornography exist? For whom does prostitution exist? For the ultimate answer to the question, For whom does female sexuality exist? Men.

Radical feminism, while centring the importance of male power over other forms of domination, is however exposed to the problems of essentialism and reductionism. It suggests that there are immutable differences between males and females and with male and female behaviour explained by reference to these differences. The impact of this is far-reaching, since it has the effect of leaving women, and women's experiences, undifferentiated. Thus the category 'woman' is left unconsidered and untouched. Yet at the same time it is a position which strives to allow women to speak for themselves: to have a different voice.

This viewpoint also conveys similar messages about men and men's experiences – they too are undifferentiated and some of the questions that arise as a result of this are explored in greater detail in Chapter 2. More specifically, as Carrington (2017: 202) observes, radical feminism constructed 'fictive subjectivities whose statuses before criminal justice and the law were quite diverse' (see also Carrington 2015). Despite these problems the strength of radical feminism over liberal feminism lies in the fact that it does not conflate the issue of male power and domination with other social processes or conditions. It also proposes strategies for action and resistance (Radford 2013) and as such bears comparison with socialist feminism, especially in relation to the methodological imperatives which flow from it.

Socialist feminism

Socialist feminism is an outgrowth of Marxist feminist dissatisfaction with the gender-blind concept of class. Marxist analysis subsumed women's oppression as being less important than the oppression experienced as a result of social class and in so doing failed to recognise the domestic (and unpaid) nature of much of women's work. Socialist feminism identifies a concern not to reduce gender inequality to patriarchal social relations, as in radical feminism, but to conceptualise the particular conditions under which women were both oppressed by capitalism and dominated by men. Thus socialist feminism focuses its attention on the interplay between capitalism and patriarchy. While there is much debate within socialist feminism concerning which of these systems – capitalism or patriarchy – has primacy, in empirical terms this position frequently translates into a concern with the ways in which the structural variables of gender, age, class and race have a compounding effect on one another within capitalist/patriarchal social systems. The connecting thread with radical feminism, in methodological terms, is the notion of a 'standpoint'.

The idea of a standpoint is derived from Hegelian philosophy. Hegel argued that it was through struggle that the proletariat gained knowledge. Struggle provided the proletariat with access not only to their own knowledge and experience of being oppressed, but also to the knowledge and understanding about the process of oppression and who the oppressors are. Thus the knowledge of the proletariat could be considered more complete knowledge, since it was derived from both sides of the system of oppression. Feminist standpoint theorists, for the purposes of this overview deemed to encompass both radical and socialist feminists, have used this idea to understand and elevate the nature of women's knowledge and experiences.

To be clear, the dualistic thinking associated with nineteenth-century liberalism places women on the nature side of the nature/culture dualism. Standpoint theorists argue that women, placed as they are on one side of this dualism, therefore have access to knowledge and experience derived from both being placed closer to nature and at the same time as participants in social and cultural processes. So in some senses women are both a part of, and simultaneously outside of, the social order: they straddle the nature/culture divide. Women's routine lives consist of the ability to constantly negotiate this dualism. Thus, rather like the struggle experienced by the proletariat, women's struggle equips them with more complete knowledge and experience of the social order; that is, more objective knowledge. Feminists who adhere to this standpoint view on the nature of knowledge are not only clearly stating that knowledge is context-bound, thus tempering scientific claims to universality; they are also accepting its highly contentious and political nature.

Nonetheless, this socialist position also has some shortcomings. This is most noticeable in its tendency to replace one universalising knowledge base with another (albeit rooted in women's experiences). At the same time it runs the risk of eliminating or downgrading difference. This is a problem which applies equally to uniform and unifying views of women's experiences as well as to those of men. Postmodern feminism certainly could not be accused of this.

Postmodern feminism

Two themes underpin postmodern feminism. These are deconstructionism and the celebration of 'Otherness'. The exploration of 'otherness' stems from the work of Simone de Beauvoir. For her, to be the 'other' represented the condition of oppression. For postmodern feminists, this condition comprises much more. Otherness represents openness, plurality, diversity and difference. This emphasis on the positive side of 'Otherness', the features of otherness which have been excluded or marginalised by phallocentric thinking, promotes a critical stance towards everything; that is, a need to deconstruct the ideas, language, and the structures on which otherness is based. This emphasis on the celebration of difference and deconstruction renders meaningless the search for a universal truth or a unified concept of the self. Such searches are symptomatic of a phallocentric drive for an ordered, unified universe which feminist postmodernism intrinsically denies. For example, the category 'woman', used as it is to denote all women, is highly problematic, since it denies the diversity and difference present in women's experiences: be it white, black, lesbian, regional, culturally and linguistically diverse.

This emphasis on diversity, difference and the desire to deconstruct the language structures of the modern world has led many critics to argue that postmodernism simply produces chaos and, by implication, is particularly problematic for those who lay claim to the universalising forces of science and scientific knowledge. For the postmodernist, such claims are a fiction. For them, there can never be a feminist science, only the many stories that women tell. Thus at a methodological level, and in terms of setting an agenda for empirical research in particular, such a perspective is highly sceptical of the claims of a criminology (or a victimology) tied to the (modernist) project of progress and policy formation as reflected in a commitment to positivism.

Third- and fourth-wave feminism

In some ways postmodern feminism has become transformed into what many commentators refer to as 'third-wave feminism'. Budgeon (2015: 4), for example, suggests that:

> Third wave feminism signals a break with previous feminist theory by fundamentally challenging the dualisms associated with Western thought.

This challenge is readily discerned in the short overview of postmodern feminism indicated above. Moreover, Budgeon (2015) goes on to observe that third-wave feminism, in challenging this dualism, centres the diversity of women's experiences and in so doing both heightens the problem of rendering such experiences uniform and also makes problematic what centring such experiences may amount to. For the purposes of criminology and victimology, this position certainly places severe pressure on any claims to speak on behalf of women, or indeed men, as criminal, victim or criminal justice professional.

More recently some commentators have observed the presence of a 'fourth-wave' feminism. Munro (2013), for example, suggests that the increasing presence of the Internet and its capacity for imaginative use has provided women with the space for a 'call-out culture':

> This culture is indicative of the continuing influence of the third wave, with its focus on micropolitics and challenging sexism and misogyny insofar as they appear in everyday rhetoric, advertising, film, television and literature, the media, and so on.
>
> (Munro 2013: 23)

Indeed, the Internet has certainly provided a space for women to connect globally in ways not previously imagined. Moreover, it provides an opportunity and ease for engaging differently in advocacy, campaign and research work (in this latter respect see Carrington and Larkin 2016). However, it is a moot point as to whether these opportunities constitute a different knowledge base or just a different set of opportunities to engage in the same/similar challenges that earlier feminist work has done. In any event there is a great deal of scope for criminology and victimology to make sense of what is happening in this space for whom and to whom, and how this is informed by gender (see, for example, the edited collection on gender, technology and domestic violence by Segrave and Vitis 2017).

In summary, all of these different feminist perspectives attempt to deal with the knowledge-production process in different ways. Liberal feminism calls for the implementation of 'correct' and unbiased procedures, radical and social feminism, for the elevation of women's knowledge as more complete knowledge, and postmodern feminism as sceptical of any claims for producing generalised knowledge of any kind. It is a moot point whether or not third-/fourth-wave feminism adds anything more to this. Of all these positions, liberal feminism is the least threatening to conventional concepts of science and knowledge, since it accepts many of the foundations of that approach as valid. Radical, socialist and postmodern feminisms, however, pose a much greater threat to these traditional notions of what counts as rational knowledge. Regardless, all of these perspectives have the potential for, and have already impacted upon, criminology and/ or victimology in different ways. The nature of that impact and its contribution to broader understandings of the gendering of crime is, however, open to debate.

Feminism and criminology: a contradiction in terms?

In some respects it is possible to argue that liberal feminism has had the longest historical impact upon criminology. First, there have always been women researchers looking at the problems associated with crime and criminal justice. There may not have been very many of them at times (or in some cases currently), and the work they produced may not have been particularly radical, but they were nevertheless present and they were examining the sex differentials associated with crime, especially delinquency (see e.g. Wootton 1959; Glueck and Glueck 1950; Cowie *et al.* 1968). In other words, there is a historical her-story of women researching within criminology and a her-story of work addressing female offending behaviour. Second, much of that liberally inspired work took discrimination as its common focus. For example, the work of Pollak (1950), concerned as it was with understanding the influence that chivalry might play in the under-documenting of women's criminality, is, at the same time, a study of discriminatory practice. This kind of practice has been explored in ever more detailed and specific circumstances; in magistrates' courts (Eaton 1986), in prison (Carlen 1983; Dobash *et al.* 1986), and in women's experiences as victims of crime (Chambers and Millar 1983; Edwards 1989). That these factors simply represent sexist practices, however, is not easy to assert. Some studies suggest that women are treated more leniently by the courts; others suggest a harsher outcome. Such contradictory conclusions point to the complex way in which factors such as age, class, race, marital status and previous criminal record interact with one other.

What is clear is that this work has yielded a wealth of information concerning the complex way in which factors interact to produce different outcomes for different female offenders and victims of crime. Indeed, it is the sheer weight of that evidence which points to the need to understand women's experiences of the criminal justice system by reference to factors outside the operation of the criminal justice system itself. The work of Carlen (1988) is especially important in this respect. As her work illustrates, women who find themselves in prison are those whose criminalisation has been over-determined by the threefold effect of racism, sexism and classism, none of which are reducible to the other and all of which, for Carlen, highlight the need to connect the debate around women and crime to the broader issue of social justice. Importantly this work, if it connects with a feminist perspective at all, is socialist in orientation and certainly flags up the more recent development of studies on intersectionality (see Potter 2014 and the Conclusion to this book). The process of moving to debates outside of criminology in order to understand women's (and men's) experiences of the criminal justice system is one feature of what Cain has called 'transgressive criminology'.

Transgressive criminology is concerned to identify the similarities between women's and girl's experiences both as offenders and as non-offenders. For Cain (1990) this transgressive criminology disrupts the nature of the discipline and is constituted by reflexivity, deconstruction and reconstruction. Reflexivity demands that the concerns of women and girls are not downgraded but recognised as a legitimate way of making sense of social reality. For example, working-class girls may have a very realistic assessment of their life chances and the relationship that this has with perceptions of their sexuality. If so, researchers need to recognise this and to be able to deconstruct its internal logic: to get beyond its mere appearance towards an understanding of the ways and the sites in which such logic is deployed. The third element of Cain's approach is political, recognising that many women 'know' about the painful disjunction between how they feel and how they live. It is within this gap that the promise of political possibility and social change is constituted. Indeed, this concept of a transgressive criminology is one that has been taken up both conceptually (see e.g. O'Neill and Seal 2012) and methodologically (see e.g. O'Neill 2016). Methodologically, the items on the 'criminological' agenda for Cain are, therefore, women-only studies, studies which explore the totality of their lives as women rather than about crime per se, and studies of men. This criminology must take on board the question of 'what in the social construction of maleness is so profoundly criminogenic: why do males so disproportionately turn out to be criminals?' (Cain 1990: 12). Ways of beginning to construct an answer to this question are considered in Chapter 2.

Feminism and victimology: a contradiction in terms?

The marginalisation of feminism by victimology has been commented upon on more than one occasion. Victimology has, for the most part, been seen as a 'weapon of ideological oppression' (Rock 1986). Some aspects of this uneasy relationship between victimology and radical feminism in particular are epitomised in their respective use of the terms 'victim' and 'survivor'. Genealogically, the term 'victim' connotes the sacrificiant who was often female. Moreover, the word itself, when gendered as in French, is denoted as female. Feminists recognising the power of such linguistic use regard the term 'victim' as emphasising passivity and powerlessness, in contrast to the active resistance to oppression in which women routinely engage to sustain their survival. Of course, while these terms are often presented as oppositional to one another, experientially speaking they frequently are not. It is possible to think in terms of an active or passive victim, as it is to identify an active or passive survivor. Indeed, an argument may be mounted which presents these concepts as capturing different elements of the same process and moreover are rooted in women's own experiences of their lives (Kirkwood 1993). However, the challenge posed by feminism to victimology lies much deeper than a conceptual debate such as this one (though this is not to say that such a debate is not meaningful).

Victimology has been no exception to the 'regime of rationality' of the 'abstract knower' (*qua* Smith 1987). As discussed above, victimology, like other social science endeavours, has been characterised as positivistic, so the feminist challenge to victimology goes beyond a critique of the discipline as a weapon of ideological oppression. It strikes at the very heart of the discipline's understanding of what it is to be scientific, and concomitantly how the central concerns of this discipline may be defined and understood. So, the question remains, in a rather similar way to the notion of a transgressive criminology: Could there be a feminist-informed victimology? The work of Davies (2012, 2017) and Walklate (2003) suggests that there are clear possibilities for this approach but for that to happen it is necessary for victimology, as with criminology, to loosen the shackles of positivism.

Criminology and victimology, as the earlier discussion in this chapter illustrates, are both tied to the (modernist) project of effecting social change through the policy process. Both of these disciplines presume that this can be achieved through a central adherence to the scientific enterprise; that is, through a search for a unitary, causal explanation of crime and/or criminal victimisation. Crime and criminal victimisation are central to their existence, so by implication the concept of crime cannot be deconstructed. As Alison Young (1992: 76) stated: 'Woman is always criminal, always deviant, always censured. This condition is utterly normal.' Thus Smart (1990) suggested that criminology needs feminism more than feminism needs criminology. However, the resistance to loosening the shackles of positivism runs deep. For many writers not unsympathetic to postmodern criticisms of universal claims to Truth, the required disentangling from the modernist (progressive) projects of criminology and victimology is far too threatening. Yet it is also without doubt that the feminist challenge to these disciplines has changed their nature and substantive content quite profoundly since the 1950s. It may be then that there is just more work to be done.

Conclusion: feminist criminology/feminist victimology; projects in construction?

Of all the feminist perspectives discussed here, liberal feminism has had the most discernible impact upon criminology and victimology to date. The reasons for this are found not only in the kind of work this perspective has generated, but also in its implicit acceptance of the conventional rules of science and the knowledge-production process. Such liberal feminist work reflects a tendency, however, to narrow feminist concerns to the 'women and crime' question as though this represented an area demanding specialised explanation (see also the Introduction to this book). Radical- and socialist-inspired feminism has led to the construction of agendas for criminology and, in the context of victimisation studies, for victimology, draws upon theoretical concepts and concerns outside of the criminological and victimological domains. This has led feminist researchers of different theoretical and political persuasions to focus on the interconnections between gender and the crime experience. In other words, this work directs criminology (and victimology) to take seriously how an understanding of men and masculinities, among other variables, can contribute to an understanding of the phenomenon called crime.

So, from the 'woman question' of liberal feminism we are returned to the 'man question' of radical and socialist feminism, and the challenge these positions present for these respective disciplines and their underlying construction of what counts as knowledge. Thus one may be tempted to agree with those feminist writers who in their different ways deny the tenability of a 'feminist criminology' or a 'feminist victimology'. Nonetheless, feminist work has, and still does, pose important questions for criminology and victimology, as the ensuing chapters in this book more than illustrate. Indeed, the questions posed for criminology and victimology around Northern theorising, geography and voice, and the emergent 'Southern' criminology, owe some debt to the feminist heritage mapped here. Carrington (2015: 12) elucidates this position in arguing for the extension of the criminological gaze by actively engaging with those historically excluded by 'the Anglophone and monocultural metropolitan biases' and to 'widen its research agendas to include the distinctively different gendered patterns of crime and violence that occur across the globe' (ibid.: 2). The following chapters will endeavour to illustrate the ways in which such globalised feminist perspectives can cast different lights on the shape and form of crime and victimisation. The question is, as Tony Jefferson (1993) so aptly expressed it twenty-five years ago, 'Is criminology [or victimology] man enough to take it?'

Recommendations for further reading

Joanne Belknap's (2015) *The Invisible Woman: Gender, Crime and Justice* offers a very detailed empirically informed analysis of the ways in which gender manifests itself in the criminal justice system and, while rooted primarily in data from the United States, the patterns documented by Belknap may be found in a wide range of other jurisdictions. Kerry Carrington's (2015) *Feminism and Global Justice* adds a much-needed global dimension to the debates documented in this chapter, and Pam Davies' (2012) *Gender, Crime and Victimisation* offers a more nuanced understanding as seen through the lens of victimology. Finally, Clare Renzetti's (2013) *Feminist Criminology* provides a clear, accessible and more detailed account of the contribution of the different feminisms to criminology discussed here.

References

Aas, K. (2012) 'The Earth is but one but the world is not': Criminological theory and its geopolitical divisions. *Theoretical Criminology* 16(1): 5–20.

Adler, I. (1975) *Sisters in Crime*. New York: McGraw-Hill.

Amir, M. (1971) *Patterns of Forcible Rape*. Chicago, IL: University of Chicago Press.

Belknap, J. (2015) *The Invisible Woman: Gender, Crime and Justice* (4th edition). Stanford, CT: Cengage Learning

Brown, B. (1990) Reassessing the critique of biologism. In L. Gelsthorpe and A. Morris (eds) *Feminist Perspectives in Criminology*. Buckingham: Open University Press, pp. 41–56.

Budgeon, S. (2015) *Third-wave Feminism and the Politics of Gender in Late Modernity*. Basingstoke: Palgrave-Macmillan.

Cain, M. (1989) Feminists transgress criminology. In M. Cain (ed.) *Growing Up Good*. London: Sage, pp. 1–18.

Cain, M. (1990) Towards transgression: new directions in feminist criminology. *International Journal of the Sociology of Law* 18: 1–18.

Cain, M. (2000) Orientalism, occidentalism and the sociology of crime. *British Journal of Criminology* 40(2): 239–260.

Carlen, P. (1983) *Women's Imprisonment*. London: Routledge and Kegan Paul.

Carlen, P. (1988) *Women, Crime and Poverty*. Milton Keynes: Open University Press.

Carrington, K. (2015) *Feminism and Global Justice*. London: Routledge.

Carrington, K. (2017) Radical feminism. In A. Brisman, E. Carrabine and N. South (eds) *The Routledge Companion to Criminological Theory and Concepts*. London: Routledge, pp. 201–204.

Carrington, K. and Larkin, A. (2016) The politics of doing imaginative criminological research. In M. Hviid-Jacobsen and S. Walklate (eds) *Liquid Criminology*. London: Routledge, pp. 188–204.

Carrington, K., Hogg, R. and Sozzo, M. (2016) Southern criminology. *British Journal of Criminology* 56(1): 1–20.

Chambers, G. and Millar, A. (1983) *Investigating Sexual Assault*. Edinburgh: Scottish Office.

Cohen, A.K. (1955) *Delinquent Boys*. New York: Free Press.

Connell, R. (2007) The Northern theory of globalization. *Sociological Theory* 25(4): 368–385.

Cook, K.J. (2016) Has criminology awakened from its 'androcentric slumber'? *Feminist Criminology* 11(4): 334–353.

Cowie, J., Cowie, V. and Salter, E. (1968) *Delinquency in Girls*. London: Heinemann.

Crofts, T., Lee, M., McGovern, A. and Milivojevic, S. (2015) *Sexting and Young People*. Basingstoke: Palgrave-Macmillan.

Dalton, K. (1991) *Once a Month*. London: Fontana.

Davies, P. (2012) *Gender, Crime and Victimisation*. London: Sage.

Davies, P. (2017) The gender agenda. In S. Walklate (ed.) *Handbook of Victims and Victimology* (2nd edition). London: Routledge, pp. 107–123.

Dekeseredy, W. (2016) Understanding woman abuse in intimate heterosexual relationships: the enduring relevance of feminist ways of knowing. *Journal of Family Violence* online first. DOI 10.1007/s10896-016-9861-8.

de Sousa Santos, B. (2014) *Epistemologies of the South: Justice against Epistemicide*. Boulder, CO: Paradigm Publishers.

Dobash, R.P., Dobash, R.E. and Gutteridge, S. (1986) *The Imprisonment of Women*. Oxford: Blackwell.

Eagle Russett, C. (1989) *Sexual Science: The Victorian Construction of Motherhood*. Cambridge, MA: Harvard University Press.

Eaton, M. (1986) *Justice for Women? Family, Court and Social Control*. Milton Keynes: Open University Press.

Edwards, S. (1989) *Policing 'Domestic' Violence*. London: Sage.

Genn, H. (1988) Multiple victimisation. In M. Maguire and J. Pointing (eds) *Victims of Crime: A New Deal?* Buckingham: Open University Press, pp. 90–100.

Glueck, S. and Glueck, E. (1950) *Unravelling Juvenile Delinquency*. Cambridge, MA: Harvard University Press.

Gouldner, A.W. (1973) *For Sociology: Renewal and Critique in Sociology Today*. Harmondsworth: Penguin.

Hall-Williams, J.E. (1982) *Criminology and Criminal Justice*. London: Butterworths.

Harding, S. (ed.) (1987) *Feminism and Methodology*. Milton Keynes: Open University Press.

Heidensohn, F. (1985) *Women and Crime*. London: Macmillan.

Heidensohn, F. (2013) Liberal feminism. In E. McLaughlin and J. Muncie (eds) *The Sage Dictionary of Criminology* (3rd edition). London: Sage, pp. 253–254.

Hindelang, M.J., Gottfredson, M.R. and Garofalo, J. (1978). *A Theory of Personal Violence*. Cambridge, MA: Ballinger.

Hirschi, T. (1969) *Causes of Delinquency*. Berkeley: University of California Press.

Jaggar, A.M. (1983) *Feminist Politics and Human Nature*. Totowa, NJ: Rowman and Allanfield.

Jefferson, T. (1993) Theorising Masculine Subjectivity. Plenary address, Masculinities and Crime Conference, University of Brunel, September.

Karmen, A. (1990) *Crime Victims: An Introduction to Victimology*. Pacific Grove, CA: Brooks Cole.

Kirkwood, C. (1993) *Leaving Abusive Partners*. London: Sage.

Lees, S. (1989) Learning to love. In M. Cain (ed.) *Growing Up Good*. London: Sage, pp. 19–37.

Lombroso, C. and Ferraro, W. (1895) *The Female Offender*. London: T. Fisher Unwin.

MacKinnon, C. (1989) *Feminism Unmodified*. Cambridge, MA: Harvard University Press.

MacMillan, R. and McCarthy, B. (2014) Gender and offending in a lifecourse context. In R. Gartner and B. McCarthy (eds) *The Oxford Handbook of Gender, Sex, and Crime*. Oxford: Oxford University Press, pp. 343–361.

Miers, D. (1989) Positivist victimology: a critique. *International Review of Victimology* 1(1): 3–22.

Morris, A. (1987) *Women, Crime and Criminal Justice*. Oxford: Blackwell.

Munro, E. (2013) Feminism: a fourth wave? *Political Insight*, September, pp. 22–25.

Naffine, N. (1987) *Female Crime*. Sydney: Allen and Unwin.

Naffine, N. (1990) *Law and the Sexes*. London: Allen and Unwin.

O'Neill, M. (2016) Studying the marginalized with mixed methods. In M. Hviid-Jacobsen and S. Walklate (eds) *Liquid Criminology*. London: Routledge, pp. 81–99.

O'Neill, M. and Seal, L. (2012) *Transgressive Imaginations*. Basingstoke: Palgrave-Macmillan.

Pollak, O. (1950) *The Criminality of Women*. New York: A.S. Barnes/Perpetua.

Potter, H. (2014) *Criminology and Intersectionality*. London: Routledge.

Radford, J. (2013) Radical feminism. In E. McLaughlin and J. Muncie (eds) *The Sage Dictionary of Criminology* (3rd edition). London: Sage, pp. 361–363.

Renzetti, C. (2017) Feminist criminologies. In A. Brisman, E. Carrabine and N. South (eds) *The Routledge Companion to Criminological Theory and Concepts*. London: Routledge, pp. 172–176.

Rock, P. (1986) *Helping Victims of Crime*. Oxford: Clarendon Press.

Roshier, B. (1989) *Controlling Crime*. Milton Keynes: Open University Press.

Scraton, P. (1990) Scientific knowledge or masculine discourses? Challenging patriarchy in criminology. In L. Gelsthorpe and A. Morris (eds) *Feminist Perspectives in Criminology*. Buckingham: Open University Press, pp. 10–25.

Segrave, M. and Vitis, L. (eds) (2017) *Gender, Technology and Violence*. London: Routledge.

Smart, C. (1976) *Women, Crime and Criminology*. London: Routledge and Kegan Paul.

Smart, C. (1990) Feminist approaches to criminology: or post-modern woman meets atavistic man. In L. Gelsthorpe and A. Morris (eds) *Feminist Perspectives in Criminology*. Buckingham: Open University Press, pp. 70–84.

Smith, D. (1987) *The Everyday World as Problematic: A Feminist Sociology*. Milton Keynes: Open University Press.

Sydie, R. (1989) *Natural Women, Cultured Men*. Milton Keynes: Open University Press.

Taylor, I., Walton, P. and Young, J. (1973) *The New Criminology*. London: Routledge and Kegan Paul.

Thomas, W.I. (1923) *The Unadjusted Girl*. Boston, MA: Little Brown.

Tong, R. (1989) *Feminist Thought: A Comprehensive Introduction*. London: Unwin Hyman.

Walby, S., Towers, J., Balderston, S., Corradi, C., Francis, B., Heiskanen, M., Helweg-Larsen, K., Mergaert, L., Olive, P., Palmer, E., Stöckl, H. and Strid, S. (2017) *The Concept and Measurement of Violence against Women and Men*. Bristol: Policy Press.

Walklate, S. (2003) Can there be a feminist victimology? In P. Davies and P. Francis (eds) *Understanding Victimisation*. London: Macmillan, pp.28–45.

Walklate, S. (2008) Local contexts and globalised knowledge: what can international criminal victimisation surveys tell us about women's diverse lives? In M. Cain and A. Howe (eds) *Women, Crime and Social Harm*. Oxford: Hart Publishing, pp. 201–214.

Walklate, S. (2014) Sexual violence against women? Still a controversial issue for victimology? *International Review of Victimology* 20(1): 71–84.

Wolfgang, M.E. (1957) *Patterns in Criminal Homicide*. Philadelphia, PA: University of Pennsylvania Press.

Wootton, B. (1959) *Social Science and Social Pathology*. London: George, Allen and Unwin.

Young, A. (1992) Feminism and the body of criminology. In D.P. Farrington and S. Walklate (eds) *Offenders and Victims: Theory and Policy*. Selected papers from The British Criminology Conference 1991. British Society of Criminology, ISTD, pp. 62–82.

Young, J. (2011) *The Criminological Imagination*. Cambridge: Polity Press.

CRIMINOLOGY, VICTIMOLOGY AND MASCULINISM

Chapter **2**

Introduction

A 21-year-old man assaults a 36-year-old man with a single punch to the head in the early hours of a morning while both are out at a nightclub in Nottingham. The victim died in hospital within a day from trauma caused by the punch (Therrien 2017). Elsewhere, a 'gang' of five men engage in a series of robberies – at least one armed – of security cash transit vans (Lion 2016). Finally, after a 'boozy evening' out together a husband kills his wife, a mother of three, in a jealous rage following an argument in which he accused her of flirting with another man earlier in the evening (Culley 2017). These cases are unconnected. They occurred at different times and in different English (UK) locations. And while they also involve different people the composition of each is interesting – they involve predominately men: men as perpetrators, men as victims, men as individuals and men as a collective. Against this backdrop, we are reminded of a quote from Grosz (1987: 5, cited by Liddle 1994: 65), who said:

> What is it about men, not as working class, not as migrant, not as underprivileged individual, but as men that induces them to commit crime? Here it is no longer women who are judged by the norms of masculinity and found to be 'the problem'. Now it is men and not humanity who are openly acknowledged as the objects and subjects of investigation.

Foregrounding men as 'the problem' in relation to the question of crime became an increasingly important part of the criminological equation during the 1990s. As the previous chapter has illustrated, criminology and victimology, as academic disciplines, have operated with particular gendered assumptions in relation to women. The purpose of this chapter is to engage in a similar exploratory process in relation to men both as perpetrators and as victims. However, first it will be useful to consider some of the different ways in which it is possible to think about men and their relationship with constructions of masculinity.

Thinking about masculinity

The body of research on masculinity has expanded markedly since the early 1980s. However, although an increasing number of both academic and media commentators have endeavoured to draw attention to the relationship between maleness and crime, there remains a limited body of research, with the exception of that discussed later in this chapter, which has applied these developments systematically to either criminology or victimology. This lack of application does not mean that the issue of masculinity has been absent from criminological discourse; rather, the opposite is perhaps more accurate: in one form or another, the presence of men and masculinity is clearly evident, even if in a hidden form. How that presence has influenced criminology and victimology has varied over time and disciplinary lines; from the way in which the subject matter of these disciplines has been defined to the way in which empirical findings have been explained. As such, this chapter begins with the broad question of how we may begin to understand the relationship between men and the question of masculinity in more general terms.

Four decades ago, in 1977, Andrew Tolson wrote *The Limits of Masculinity*. Tolson's book explored the different types of gender identities, emphasising the possibility of a plurality of gender identities. He sought to recognise that masculinity was not simply a one-dimensional phenomenon that could be understood in terms of opposition to femininity. Neither, Tolson argued, was it possible to talk about a universal form of masculinity. Its expression varied across cultures and between generations. These twin themes of the multidimensionality and specificity of masculinity heralded the emergence of a key debate for those concerned to understand men and their expressions of themselves as men. Tolson's observations about the nature of masculinity and its expression alert us to one of the central features of this debate: Is there one transcendent form of masculinity or are there many diverse masculinities? Tolson's work is also important in that it implies that it is as important to develop an understanding of masculinity in terms of gender relations as it is to explore what masculinity means for individual men.

The way in which these issues are addressed, however, varies depending upon the kind of theoretical framework in which we choose to understand the concept of masculinity itself. Some of the theoretical considerations encountered in Chapter 1 re-emerge here. This is particularly the case with respect to evaluating the relevance and value of different feminist perspectives on this issue; though, as we will see, the current debate on masculinity owes a significant debt to that feminist work. First, following Tolson (1977), it will be useful to consider the question of how it may be possible to develop a framework in which to understand both masculinity and femininity.

Morgan (1992) offers one way of organising understandings of masculinity and femininity. His framework locates this question within the broader context of gender relations. He suggests that there are two key concepts through which gender relations may be differently defined and understood. These are the concepts of power and difference. Analytically, these ideas may be related to each other in any one of four ways. First, Morgan (1992) poses that the relationship between power and difference may be denied; in other words, the existence of gender as a significant feature of the organisation of our social lives may be ignored. Second, and in somewhat stark contrast to the first of Morgan's understandings, the importance of power relationships may be stressed at the expense of understanding difference. In the context of radical feminism, for example, this relationship centres importance of concepts such as patriarchy, oppression, exploitation and domination. In this relationship the question of difference is sacrificed in favour of the question of power; that is, masculinity and femininity are seen to derive from socially constructed power relationships.

The third approach suggested by Morgan poses the converse relationship between difference and power. This option emphasises difference and minimises power. Here the exploration of the differences, not only between masculinity and femininity but also within them, is celebrated and given primacy. Such a celebration of difference can take a number of forms. For example, it could be rooted in the individual difference approach associated with biology (more on biological explanations for crime and criminality later). Latterly, however, an emphasis on difference has been more directly associated with, and derived from, postmodernism. The expression of femininity and masculinity is understood from this vantage point as the product of individual negotiation and expression.

Finally, Morgan's (1992) fourth approach poses that it is possible to develop an understanding of the relationship between power and difference which defines them both as interdependent. This framework endeavours to identify ways in which social systems give primacy to some versions of masculinity and femininity over others. Such primacy values some versions more highly than others and thus renders them more powerful than others. This process, of course, has significant consequences for the versions of masculinity and/or femininity deemed 'the other'; that is, less valued and thereby less powerful. As we will explore below, this kind of analysis is also characteristic of the work of Connell (1987).

Morgan's schema provides a useful starting point from which to develop an understanding of the ways in which concepts of masculinity have influenced criminology (and by extension the sub-discipline of victimology). Each of these different ways of thinking about the relationship between power and difference may be found in criminological work. Given the primacy placed on gender in this text, it would be highly contradictory to explore Morgan's first way of thinking about gender relations, since this option denies the importance of gender as a variable. Suffice it to say that much criminological work has done just this, especially historically. Although, as Chapter 1 endeavoured to illustrate, such a denial was in part a product of an uncritical acceptance of deeply embedded assumptions about the nature of the scientific enterprise and what could count as knowledge. Given that the central purpose of this text is to consider the relevance of gender to conversations on crime and criminal justice, we will spend some time considering the implications of the other three options in Morgan's schema; each of which have, arguably, made their presence felt in criminology and victimology in different ways and at different times.

In order to do this we will first focus on the influence on criminology of sex role theory borrowed from social psychology as an

illustration of option three; categorical theory as characterised by
Connell (1987) as an illustration of option two; and the notion of
'doing gender' borrowed from the work of Messerschmidt (1993,
1997) as an illustration of option four. In each case we will consider
some illustrative substantive criminological material to highlight the
value of the options under discussion.

Sex role theory

The concept of 'role' is central to social psychology and some versions of sociology. As a concept it is used as a way of organising
people's behaviour into a meaningful whole. It acts as a mechanism
for understanding the ways in which social expectations, actions
and behaviour reflect stereotypical assumptions about behavioural
expectations; that is, what it is that should be done, by whom and
under what circumstances. In the context of understanding gender
relations, this leads to the identification of distinctive male roles
and female roles. Such roles are presumed to outline the appropriate behavioural sets and associated expectations for men (males)
and women (females). Sex role theory takes as a given the biological origins of defining the differences between males and females.
These biological origins constitute the canvas on which specific
behavioural sets, called sex roles, are painted through the process of
socialisation. As a theory, then, it is rooted in biological assumptions
concerning what count as the defining characteristics of being male
and female.

In the criminological context, the work of both Sutherland (1947)
and Parsons (1937) embraced sex role theory and wielded a particular influence over criminology's grasp of the maleness of the crime
problem. We will briefly examine the ideas of each of these key scholars in turn, followed by a closer examination of the seminal work of
Cohen (1955) and Connell (1987).

Sutherland

Sutherland started from the position that criminal behaviour was
learned behaviour like any other. He argued that people learned

criminal behaviour when exposed to an 'excess of definitions' favouring deviant as opposed to conventional (or rule-abiding) behaviour. This view of criminal behaviour focused not only on the importance of the socialisation process in learning crime but also on understanding the importance of the value attached to the behaviour learned. In other words, it is not just a matter of with whom you associate but also the kinds of meanings those associations provide for an individual with respect to engaging in criminal behaviour. Thus an individual may know how to act criminally, but may not do so in the absence of the values, motives and attitudes which support such behaviour. The more an individual is exposed to such support, the more likely it is that that individual will share in that behaviour. For Sutherland, then, criminal behaviour was learned behaviour like any other behavioural response rather than being the product of some innate atavistic or degenerative drive.

Within this general framework Sutherland pointed to distinctive sex patterns, arguing that boys are more likely to become delinquent than girls are. This, he suggested, occurs for two reasons. First, because boys are less strictly controlled by the socialisation process in general than girls are. Second, because in that process boys are taught to be tough, aggressive, active, risk-seekers; all characteristics which Sutherland considered to be prerequisites for involvement in the criminal world. These two factors taken together, he argued, mean that boys are more frequently exposed to the kinds of learning situations in which criminality becomes a possibility. This happens despite the fact that in other respects both boys and girls may be growing up together in the same economically deprived neighbourhoods. Thus Sutherland was of the view that there is something more to be understood about boys' involvement in the criminal world than can be explained by reference to socio-economic factors alone.

This general theory of criminal behaviour was labelled by Sutherland as the theory of 'differential association'. When it is applied to an understanding of criminal behaviour in general it may be seen to offer a framework substantially different in some respects to that proposed by the biological positivists. However, when applied specifically to understanding the differences between male and female involvement in delinquent behaviour, there are a number of issues that this theory treats as unproblematic.

First, as a theory, it is rooted in the presumption of sex role theory and thereby a notion of biological difference. Being rooted in this way, this position consequently accepts implicitly a view that biological difference constitutes part of the explanation for any observed behavioural differences, despite the importance that sex role theory attributes to the socialisation process. It must be remembered that in sex role theory the socialisation process only provides the mechanism through which specific learning takes place; in other words, the fact that girls get pregnant and not boys (i.e. biological difference constitutes the basis for explaining both their different experience of the socialisation process and their subsequent different rate of criminality).

Parsons

The work of functionalist sociologist Talcott Parsons added a further dimension to thinking about the relationship between sex differences, the socialisation process and the maleness of criminal behaviour. Parsons placed the family at the centre of the social learning associated with sex roles. In the family children learn that the expressive role – the role associated with nurturing, caring and keeping the family together – is what women do. The instrumental role, on the other hand, that concerned with achievement, goal attainment and breadwinning, is what men do. In the work of Parsons, these roles are the basis for the stability of society from one generation to the next. Moreover, society in general and the family in particular are presumed to operate at their most effective when the family is constructed along these lines. This presumption is made on the basis that because women have the reproductive capacity to bear children they are thus deemed to be best suited for the expressive role, a role which is consequently denied to men and which young men experience as being denied to them.

The process of learning these sex roles poses different problems for boys than for girls. Exposed to feminine care, girls have little difficulty in finding appropriate role models to emulate. Boys, on the other hand, do not have a readily and routinely available male model to follow. Exposed to the female model as young children, they quickly learn that the feminine role model is not one for which they will be accepted as men. Parsons argues, therefore, that boys engage in what he calls 'compensatory compulsory masculinity'. In other words, boys actively reject any behaviour seen to be feminine, such as tenderness, gentleness and the expression of emotion. In the place of these feminine qualities boys pursue those whom they observe to be masculine: being powerful, tough and rough. The pursuit of these masculine characteristics is engaged in vigorously in order to avoid any doubt being cast on the boys' sense of themselves as men or of them being recognised by others as men. Using this approach, Parson contends that this pursuit of masculinity, and its approved forms of expression, results in boys engaging in antisocial behaviour much more often than girls. It is this greater likelihood to engage in anti-social behaviour that is subsequently related to their greater chance of engaging in delinquency. This view of the relationship between sex differences and the socialisation process is implicit in some of the formative work on delinquency within criminology.

Cohen

The work of Cohen (1955) draws together the work of Sutherland and Parsons and was very influential in the development of delin-quency studies during the 1950s and 1960s. As stated in Chapter 1, Cohen did attempt to address the observed sex differences associated with delinquent behaviour by drawing upon the work of Parsons in particular. Following Parsons, Cohen accepted that the process of socialisation in the home was neither a smooth nor an easy process for boys. He accepted the view that the lack of a readily available masculine role model in the home alongside the ready availability of a feminine role associated with nurturing raised anxious questions for boys. Given that the nurturing role in the domestic context is so readily identified as 'being good', boys are left unsure as to how to be good yet not be seen to be feminine. The resultant anxiety generated by this for boys is, according to Cohen, resolved in the street gang. Here the assertion of power through physical prowess rather than negotiation, the taking of risks rather than keeping safe, the thrill and excitement of breaking the rules rather than accepting them; all provide not only the avenues and the motivation for delinquent behaviour but also for an expression of themselves as young men. Cohen, however, did not focus his analysis of delinquency in this way. Cohen presumed that delinquency was primarily a working-class phenomenon; so his explanation of delinquent behaviour ultimately downgrades what he has to say about masculinity in favour of upgrading an emphasis on class and, more specifically, class conflict. For Cohen, the delinquent subculture is to be seen as a consequence of a working-class collective response to the shared experience of being judged by middle-class values and the frustration that results.

This does not mean that Cohen did not recognise other possible motivations for delinquent behaviour – he did. For example, he viewed female delinquency primarily in terms of the expression of deviant sexuality; and he viewed middle-class delinquent behaviour primarily in terms of 'drag racing' or 'joy-riding' (in the 1950s' American sense of the term). This latter type of delinquent behaviour was also seen by Cohen as a masculine protest against female authority. Yet, despite the intriguing nature of some of the observations Cohen makes about gender in relation to delinquency, his concern with social class left these observations relatively underdeveloped but with a very influential effect on a whole generation of delinquency studies.

Cohen's observations are not without their problems. Cohen, like Sutherland, presumed that the biological basis of sex role theory is a non-problematic starting point for understanding routes into crime. This alerts us to the way in which the difficulties associated with sex roles became embedded within this kind of criminological thinking. While sex role theory does have its attractions as a starting point for understanding gender relations in general, as well as the gendered expression of criminal behaviour in particular, its biological orientation is problematic.

Connell

Expanding upon the work of sex role theorists, Connell (1987) has pointed out that there are a number of reasons why sex role theory provides a useful starting point for explanations concerned with gender and gender difference. She offers three reasons why this may be the case. In the first instance, Connell argues that sex role theory moves beyond biology as a way of explaining sex differences in behaviour. As an approach, she proposes that sex role theory replace biology with learned social expectations. Second, sex role theory provides a mechanism whereby an understanding of the impact of social structure may be inserted into an understanding of individual personality. The process of socialisation is obviously crucial in this, and this facilitates a way of thinking about the contribution played by different kinds of institutions in mediating the effects of structure on individuals. Third, given the emphasis on the socialisation process, sex role theory offers a politics of change. If men and women are what they are because of the oppressive experience and impact of the socialisation process, then if this process can be changed, so too can men and women. This suggests a fluidity and flexibility that is not present from the biological vantage point.

There is, however, a central difficulty embedded within these favourable assessments of sex role theory; that is, the difficulty highlighted by the fundamental resilience of the biological category of sex. Connell (1987: 50–51) explains:

> The very terms 'female role' and 'male role', hitching a biological term to a dramaturgical one, suggests what is going on. [.] With sex roles, the underlying biological dichotomy seems to have persuaded many theorists that there is no power relationship here at all. The 'female role' and the 'male role' are tacitly treated as equal.

Moreover, there is something further hidden here. Sex role theory, given its emphasis on social expectations, has more often than not been concerned to identify that which *should* be the case in social relationships as opposed to that which is actually the case. In other words, it concerns itself with what is considered to be normative as opposed to that which actually occurs empirically. If we take the impact of this alongside the resilience of the biological category of sex, it has the resultant effect of disabling role theory's grasp of gender relations. In other words, sex role theory cannot see gender in terms of negotiated power relationships. It can at best only see gender as given through fundamentally biologically determined individual adaptations to social expectations.

This emphasis on what is normative, as distinct from what actually occurs in practice, has the impact of drawing attention away from social reality in terms of power relationships, and simultaneously draws attention away from the critical question of whose interests may best be served by such concerns. In other words, emphasis on the normative aspects of social behaviour, what people should do, serves the interests of particular groups in society: the socially powerful. This is of particular importance in relation to understanding the influence of academic and policy agendas informed by sex role theory. One consequence of this is that while attention is focused on the normative dimensions to gender relations, other aspects remain under-explored. Thus disentangling the tension between the normative and the actually experienced is particularly important in order to develop a more accurate picture of the nature and impact of gender relations. Such a disentangling reveals some interesting insights into the question of masculinity. How may this be achieved?

In the context of understanding masculinity, Brittain (1989) has drawn a similar distinction to that being made here in identifying what he calls 'masculinism' as distinct from 'masculinity'. According to Brittain, masculinism comprises the ideological roots of masculinity and attributes masculinity with essential transcendent qualities. These qualities point to a number of assumptions frequently made about gender relations. For example, that there is a fundamental difference between men and women, that heterosexuality is normal, that men's nature determines their behaviour. In other words, masculinism naturalises male domination; it is deemed natural. Sex role theory, in its inability to transcend the temptations of the biological perspective, buys into such masculinism. It reflects a fundamental belief that differences between the sexes as displayed in behaviour are natural in their origins. In this way sex role theory lends further support to the interests of male domination. Consequently, in its failure to question such ideological roots, sex role theory does a further disservice to actually experienced femininity and masculinity insofar as it can capture neither the negotiated quality of them nor their fragile or tentative character. In addition, the universalism of biological categories, sustained by the ideology of sex differences being constructed in nature, militates against an understanding of the actually experienced categories of male and female (masculinities and femininities).

While sex role theory has undoubtedly had some influence on criminological thinking in order to understand the maleness of crime, that influence has been limited not only by the failure of criminology and criminologists to reflect upon its value (the downgrading of gender over class, for example) but also by the limitations inherent within the sex role framework itself. Such limitations, as highlighted above, point to the need for a theoretical framework that can at least encompass an understanding of the power basis of gender relations. It is in developing an understanding of masculinity in this respect that the influence of both radical and socialist feminism may be found and has been drawn together in the work of Connell (1987) among others.

Categorical theory

The term 'categorical theory' has been used by Connell (1987) as a way of drawing together a number of different feminist perspectives on gender. Its use here is not intended to imply that Connell accepts the principles of categorical theory, but rather to reiterate some of the issues raised in Connell's work. It constitutes a valuable device for introducing the developments that have arisen from feminist-inspired work, in thinking about masculinity. As a way of understanding gender relations it matches the second option identified by Morgan (1992).

Categorical theory refers to a range of theoretical perspectives, emanating primarily from the feminist movement, that centre an understanding of gender relations by reference to two opposing categories: men and women. Understanding gender relations in these terms identifies both a theory and a politics for action. The categories, men and women, constitute both the units of analysis for understanding gender relations and the source of explanation for those relations. The key concepts of categorical theory are patriarchy, domination, oppression, exploitation. Within these concepts men are deemed the powerful and women are deemed the less powerful 'other'.

In criminology and victimology, categorical analysis has had its most profound effect in the study of sexual violence. In Chapter 4 we explore different ways of thinking about the nature and extent of sexual violence. The notion that all men keep all women in a state of fear, as articulated by radical feminism, was revolutionary not only in its public, personal and political implications but also in the avenue it provided for recognising a further dimension to the maleness of the crime problem. As discussed in Chapter 4, sexual violence is acknowledged as not exclusively a male activity and neither are all the victims of sexual violence exclusively female. Nevertheless, an ungendered understanding of sexual violence would only be a partial one and a criminology that failed to acknowledge the gendered nature and extent of sexual violence would be incomplete. However, an analysis of sexual violence couched in categorical terms is severely limited as a way both of understanding the nature and extent of that violence and as a way of understanding both the expression of masculinity and/or of femininity. This occurs for two reasons.

First, a concern with the category 'man' generates statements that characterise the behaviour of typical men. In the context of sexual violence, for example, such a typification equates the category 'man' with the potential for sexual violence. Hence the problematic statement that has arisen over time, 'All men are potential rapists'. Such a process does a disservice to any individual experience of being male and/or being female. As Connell states, it presents a 'false universalism' that does not resonate with lived social reality. In one sense, then, it could be said that categorical analysis takes us little further, theoretically, than sex role theory with the exception, of course, that biological universalism has been replaced by social universalism.

Second, a focus on the category 'man' equates that category with masculinity. This equation presumes that there is one universal form of masculinity (or, on the other hand, femininity) that is static. In one sense, of course, this tendency towards universalism and quiescence in understanding gender relations present in radical versions of feminism was designed as much to serve political purposes as it was to serve theories of gender relations. Such thinking does provide one way of constructing a policy agenda; however, politics are not always predicated on adequate theorising.

When taken together, these limitations should not serve to undermine the profound importance that feminist work, which has been loosely identified here as categorical, has had in our understanding of the nature of gender relations in general and the expression of masculinity in particular. Without this work it would not have been possible for theorists to recognise the need to connect the emphasis on patriarchally rooted power relations with both individually and collectively negotiated identities of masculinity and femininity. However, in a sense the question left unanswered by feminist work is the same as that posed by Brittain (1989) earlier in this discussion. He identified the problem of trying to understand the relationship between masculinism, the ideology which supports male dominance, and masculinity(ies), the individually negotiated and fragile identities constructed by men. This is the gap left by feminist work in this area that both Connell (1987, 1995) and Messerschmidt (1993, 1997) have attempted to bridge, the latter in the particular context of understanding crime and criminality.

Doing gender

This way of thinking about gender relations matches with Morgan's fourth option, which represents an attempt to explore the interdependent interconnections between power and difference. In some respects the problem of '*doing gender*' is the problem of understanding how any social action is constituted; how to find the balance between the impact of social structure and the choice of social action. In general sociological theory the work of sociologist Anthony Giddens (1987) has been particularly significant in finding a way to avoid the determinism inherent in a structuralist position on the one hand and the voluntarism inherent in a position which gives primacy to freedom of choice on the other. His work encourages us to think about the ways in which structure is constituted, reconstituted and changed by human actors through their everyday activities. These processes, which apply to the general construction of social action, also apply to the way in which gender relations are negotiated. Thus the theoretical question to answer, to paraphrase Connell (1987), is how gender is organised as an ongoing concern.

Connell's (1987) analysis focuses on three specific social structures underpinning gender relations: the gender division of labour, the gender relations of power, and sexuality. None of these are a constant entity. The specific form of each varies through time and space but, taken together, they define the conditions under which gender identities are constructed. In other words, these structures define the conditions under which expressions of masculinity and femininity are constructed and reconstructed. The interplay between, and impact of, these different structural relations has been defined by Connell (1987, 2000, 2005) as 'hegemonic masculinity' – referred to in later work as the 'most honoured way of being a man' (Connell and Messerschmidt 2005: 832).

Hegemony is a term borrowed from Antonio Gramsci, which he used to refer to the way in which one class or group can dominate a society by consent. Jefferson (2013: 216) defines 'hegemonic masculinity' as:

> The set of ideas, values, representations and practices associated with 'being male' which is commonly accepted as the dominant position in gender relations in a society at a particular historical moment.

According to Connell (1987), in the expressions of masculinity found in late modern societies, hegemonic power is possessed by those males who give expression to normative heterosexuality. This is achieved in the three domains of gender relations identified above in different but related ways. It is found in the dominant notion of the male as breadwinner (from the gender division of labour); it is found in the definition of homosexuality but not lesbianism as a crime (from the gender relations of power); and it is found in the objectification of heterosexual women in the media (from the arena of sexuality).

Normative heterosexuality is that form of masculinity which is most highly valued in all aspects of social life (as suggested by the examples offered above) and, in being so valued, it defines both the structure and the form of the struggle of any individual man to live up to the power of its expectations. At the same time it structures the lives of those who fail to, or choose not to, engage in such a struggle. As Messerschmidt (1993: 76) states, this notion of hegemonic masculinity 'defines masculinity through difference from, and desire for, women'. It also defines the kinds of possibilities available for variations in masculinity. If this version of masculinity (normative, white, heterosexual masculinity) possesses hegemonic power, then it follows that not only does this serve to provide individual men with a sense of themselves as more of a man or less of a man; it also serves to downgrade femininity as well as other versions of masculinity (homosexuality, for example).

This notion of 'hegemonic masculinity' also gives credence to a hierarchical structure underpinning the sense we have of ourselves as gendered subjects while simultaneously permitting an array of expressed masculinities and femininities. Such variations from the norm offer templates for individual action that are differentially valued and differently expressed in relation to normative heterosexuality for both men and women. In this sense, as Messerschmidt (1993: 79) states, 'gender is an accomplishment': something we are all required to work at, and to provide some account of, in our relationships with others. From this starting point in understanding gender relations, Messerschmidt (1993) goes on to offer one of the most thorough accounts of the relationship between masculinities and crime, which we will discuss briefly here.

Messerschmidt (1993: 119) states that:

> Research reveals that men construct masculinities in accord with their position in social structures and therefore their access to power and resources.

Messerschmidt (1993, 1997), following the work of Giddens and Connell, points to the importance of understanding the dynamic of not only the gendered nature of social structure but also its class and race dynamic. The complex way in which these three variables interact with one another is a key problem for those who would focus on only one of them, and is an issue to which we will return. Messerschmidt's view, however, leads him to analyse a variety of social contexts in which differential access to power and resources produces differently emphasised constructions of masculinity. In the context of crime this results in the consideration of three key locations: the street, the workplace and the home. In each of these locations Messerschmidt provides a detailed account of the variety of ways in which masculinity is given expression to; from the pimp on the street to the sharp business practice of the rising white-collar executive, to expressions of male proprietary and coercive control in the form of various violence(s) in the home.

All of these accounts are offered as a means of demonstrating the ways in which men display their manliness to others and to themselves. So while the business executive (or, in more contemporary examples, the film producer) may use his position and power to sexually harass his female colleague in perhaps more subtle ways than the pimp controls the women who work for him, the effects are the same. In this particular example, the women concerned are subjugated and the men concerned are affirmed as normatively heterosexual men. By extension their behaviour is normalised and accepted.

The 1997 work of Messerschmidt focused on how the lens of masculinities might provide us with a better picture of law-breaking behaviour and how class and ethnicity might differently focus that lens. Building on his own earlier work as well as that of Connell and Giddens, Messerschmidt (1997: 6) states that:

> Specific forms of gender, race and class are available, encouraged, and permitted, depending on one's position in these social relations . . . Accordingly, gender, race and class, must be viewed as structured action – what people do under specific social structural constraints.

Developing this further, Connell and Messerschmidt (2005) argue why we must move beyond one-dimensional understandings of gender and masculinity, a key part of which relies upon recognising the influence of 'the geography of masculinities' be it at local, regional and/or global level.

Thus recognising and emphasising the importance of the question of difference has emerged (see also the discussion of difference in Chapter 1). In other words, people routinely enact and re-enact social structures in their everyday activities; activities that are mediated by a number of different socio-structural variables, only one of which will be gender. They 'do' class and ethnicity as well. They may also be 'doing' or giving expression to other cultural values associated with 'fun', aggression and alcohol consumption (see also Graham and Wells 2003), none of which may necessarily in and of themselves be connected with or a reflection of their masculinity. By implication, this last comment draws our attention to one of a number of limitations inherent in this focus on the relationship between masculinity(ies) and crime.

Regardless of its recognised limits, the framing of hegemonic masculinity by Connell and Messerschmidt, the subsequent theorising of different constructs of masculinity and their use in explaining crime and criminality has been used as a springboard for scholars to examine the relationship between crime, masculinity and race, social class and power among other factors. This has led to a body of research which in taking violence as its focus has used differing constructions of masculinity as a means of making sense of the ways in which men use violence to perform or protest their masculinity (see, among others, Carrington and Scott 2008; Harland and McCready 2014; Polk 1994; Tomsen 1997; Treadwell and Garland 2011). Constructions of masculinity have also been used to examine the ways in which different layers of the legal system – police and courts – frame and represent men's violence (see for example, Collier 2010; Fitz-Gibbon 2016; Naffine 1990). Before exploring some of the critiques of this perspective it remains for us to consider one further dimension in this focus on difference within masculinity: that which draws upon biographical studies and psychoanalysis.

Biography and the psychoanalytical turn

The psychoanalytical focus within understandings of law-breaking behaviours has been much more concerned to use the notion of the 'masculine defended subject' (Jefferson 1993) to facilitate an understanding of men's recourse to the use of violence. Gadd (2000: 431) defends this turn to psychoanalysis by saying:

> By articulating the many emotional truths of men's 'experience' we expose the disparity between what violent men feel, say and do, the interface of men's psychic investment in social discourses and practices.

Exploring individual biographies through the use of the 'narrative interview method' (Hollway and Jefferson 1997) is the means through which these disparities are made visible. Biography and the concern to focus on men's 'psychic investment' is also pivotal to Jefferson's work on Mike Tyson (see, *inter alia*, Jefferson 1997).

However, this psychoanalytical turn within criminology is not without its critics. Hood-Williams (2001: 53), for example, argues:

> The psychic processes that psychoanalysis so cutely describe – projection, introjection, identification, cathexis, parapraxes, unconscious incorporation – are not, not one of them, 'gendered'. They are simply processes. They are certainly invested – cathected to – ideas about what it means, for the subject to be a woman/man, but masculinity and femininity are what the psyche deals with. It is not what psyches are. This means recognising that masculinity must be understood phenomenologically, that is not the exclusive property of men, that it has no essential underpinning in sex nor in the intrinsic character of what is to count as masculine.

This potentially damning critique is rescued in the recognition that the kind of work referred to here has forced a consideration of the subtly nuanced expression given to both masculinity and femininity in different contexts. Indeed, such nuanced understandings have led to a suggestion that it is the dualism inherent in the concept of gender relations itself that is problematic (see Miller 2002, and the reply by Messerschmidt 2002). Moreover, in a different way and suggesting a somewhat different agenda, Goodey (2000) has developed a cogent argument for a return to biographical studies within criminology.

These studies, however, would be concerned with 'epiphany', namely significant turning points in the lives of individuals that propelled them into crime against the structural backcloth of hegemonic masculinity. Nevertheless, as Hood-Williams (2001: 44) remarks: 'The question remains, however, why it is that only a minority of men need to produce masculinity through crime rather than through other, noncriminal means?'

Before further developing a critique of masculinity theory, we examine whether or not white, heterosexual men (or indeed any men) are always the beneficiaries of masculinity as it has been conceived of here. Putting this issue another way: Can men be victims?

Men as victims

Much victimological work implicitly leaves the impression that victims are unlikely to be male. This is particularly the case for interpersonal offences, such as sexual and intimate partner violence. The framing of such crimes largely renders female victimisation visible and male victimisation invisible (see, *inter alia*, Davies 2010; Newburn and Stanko 1994), aligning with Christie's (1986) notion of the ideal victim as a weak, powerless and passive individual – characteristics more stereotypically attributed to women. Yet as more recent, though still limited, work has suggested, men can be victims and, where they are, they often experience their victimisation as a key problem in their understandings of themselves as male (see for example, Stanko and Hobdell 1993; Goodey 1997). This is particularly the case for male victims of interpersonal violence, to which we turn our attention briefly here.

Given the high levels of under-reporting and the lack of specialised services for male victims of interpersonal violence, it is difficult to establish the prevalence of these kinds of experiences (for further details on under-reporting see Javaid 2015). One of the more recent explorations of male victimisation, completed as part of the Victorian (Australia) *Royal Commission into Family Violence*, found that men are more likely to be victims of violence from a parent, sibling or other family member than from a female intimate partner (RCFV 2016).

When one moves beyond family violence specifically, the victimisation profiles of males and females differ increasingly. Continuing with Australian research, it has been found that men are more likely to be physically assaulted by a stranger in a public location while women are more likely to be victimised by an intimate partner in a private residence (Bricknell *et al.* 2014). Patterns of violence may also differ, with male victims more likely to experience isolated incidents of physical violence as opposed to the ongoing nature of violence perpetrator upon female victims (Bricknell *et al.* 2014). Similar findings have been evidenced in other studies of male victimisation and prevalence foregrounding an emerging body of scholarship which points to the need for specialised responses, increased services and practitioner training (see for example, Javaid 2015, 2016; RCFV 2016).

Beyond prevalence, research has sought to examine how men *experience* victimhood. In their study of sexual violence, for example, Mezey and King (1992) reported that male victims found their experiences to be frightening, dehumanising, debasing and contaminating. To this end, the research suggests that male victims use all the terms in describing their experiences that a woman might use, suggesting that men face similar challenges of recognition to that traditionally encountered by women victims. These findings have been echoed in numerous studies on male sexual violence and intimate partner violence victimisation (see, *inter alia*, Brooks *et al.* 2017; Corbally 2015; Durfee 2011; Fisher and Pina 2013; Lees 1997; Stemple and Meyer 2014; Weiss 2010). Most recently, writing in the Canadian context, Brooks and others (2017) presented the findings of a small number of interviews completed with male victims of intimate partner violence. While illustrating the similarities in accounts of victimisation experienced by men and women, this research also highlighted the importance of power and control in understanding how men understand and respond to their own victimisation, connecting back to Connell's (1995, 2005) work on understanding control as a central feature of hegemonic masculinity. As such, it may be possible that the lens of masculinity, of being in control or out of control, helps our understanding of men's experiences of victimisation, but as yet this is a theoretical rather than an empirical assertion. How do we explain the continuities and discontinuities of experience alluded to here? In addition, how might those experiences be differently mediated not just by masculinity per se, but by masculinities; the subordinate or marginal masculinities commented on in the work of Connell and Messerschmidt?

What is also not yet fully understood is how and under what conditions *maleness* mediates the experience of victimisation. Anger (and the expression of aggression), for example, is one feeling more frequently reported on by men than by women when criminally victimised; but equally men report feelings of vulnerability, shame and powerlessness like those reported by women when sexually assaulted (see for example, Brooks et al. 2017; McMullen 1990; Lees 1997; Machado *et al.* 2016). Equally so, Australian research found that male victims experienced personal and social barriers to accessing support services, including feelings of shame and fear of 'being seen as "weak" and unmasculine' (Bricknell *et al.* 2014: xi; see also Weiss 2010). As Goodey (1997) notes, 'body don't cry'.

Doing gender: a critical assessment

In this chapter we have moved from understanding gender as the expression of behaviour learned through the socialisation process to a view of gender, not as pre-given by sexual attributes, but given by and negotiated through socio-structural locations. This position endows an individual with structured choice. Of course, this view also implies that individuals can, and often do, choose to behave outside of these structured choices; but such strategies do not necessarily afford them public or private acceptability. Scholars in this area have drawn heavily upon the work of Giddens in order to develop a framework for analysing not only gender relations in general, but also the specific relationship between masculinity(ies) and crime. This latter concern has produced some very provocative writing for criminology, as evidenced in the foregoing discussion. The question remains, however: What is left untouched by this way of thinking about the relationship between masculinity and crime?

The first question provoked by adopting a critical stance towards this kind of analysis arises out of the work of Jefferson (1993). Put simply, he asks: What about the individual? How do men choose to become what they become? This question is only partially answered by the assertion of a multiplicity of possible masculinities, structured under the influence of different socio-locations. Templates of appropriate action in different structural settings for men are evident, as the analysis offered by Messerschmidt (1993, 1997) suggests. Such templates still need to be played out, however; to be expressed or suppressed. In other words, they still need to be chosen and worked upon by individual men. Raising the question of what motivates individual men to choose one course of action as opposed to another, of course, raises areas that are conventionally problematic for sociological analysis.

For example, the questions of motivation and choice are illustrated in the perennial problematic assertion that 'all men are rapists'. Of course, while all men may be *potential* rapists, not all men commit rape. Why they choose to rape or not rape can only be understood in part by reference to the available, socially acceptable styles of masculine expression. Another part of the explanation for their choice must lie with understanding the contribution of motivations such as desire, pleasure and risk-seeking to their behaviour (see also Chapter 4). Asking this kind of question may, of course, take us down the highly individualistic route of psychoanalysis; but it may also lead us to reconceptualise our understandings of criminality in terms of what Katz (1988) called the 'seductions of crime'. As Jefferson (1993) argues, unless we understand the pleasures of crime as well as the opportunities for crime, we shall never really have a complete picture of criminal behaviour.

So there may be some value in situating our understanding of motivations for criminal behaviour within the framework of hegemonic masculinity; but to what extent and how? As Hood-Williams (2001) comments, the defence mechanisms alluded to by those who would have us go down the route of psychoanalysis are not in and of themselves gendered. So what are these researchers tapping into? Hood-Williams (2001) suggests that they are grasping a sense of the 'performative' aspects of masculinity, not the psychic. He goes on to suggest that this work leaves criminology with a puzzle which may lead to the erosion of the terms 'masculine' and 'feminine' in and of themselves.

This leads to a further and perhaps more fundamental question about the direction in which some of the more recent criminological debate is moving: Can the picture of crime be completed at all by constructing a framework for explaining crime through an understanding of masculinity? If the danger of psychoanalysis is that this may lead us down the route of celebrating individual difference to its ultimate, this second question poses a very different problem for the debate on masculinity and crime; the search for universalism.

As this chapter has indicated, the debate around masculinity and crime proceeded apace in the 1990s. It is possible, however, to detect an uneasy tension within this debate. That tension emerges when the fundamental characteristics of criminology discussed in Chapter 1 are reflected upon. In Chapter 1 it was argued that one of the dilemmas facing criminology was its implicit linkage with modernism through its acceptance of traditional masculinist concepts of science. This linkage has constantly resulted in the criminological search for a universal explanation of crime. This tendency is still present in the way in which the concept of masculinity has been explored thus far. In other words, while the concept of masculinity itself may have been tempered and modified, the actual debate which proceeds under its umbrella strains to fit all kinds of criminal behaviour occurring in all kinds of contexts within its terms. The maleness of crime, from state terrorism to joy-riding, though constituted differently and expressed differently, also becomes the source of its explanation. Thus not only does this reflect a failure to resolve fully the tendency towards universalism, it can also be read as tautological. This may be, of course, the resultant effect, of the 'doing gender' approach not having adequately addressed two remaining issues.

The first of these is, perhaps, rather more contentious than the second. This concerns the role of femininity and its relationship with masculinity. Much of the work on masculinity has presumed, if not explicitly, that masculinity exists as an expression of difference from femininity. The need to express that difference, however, should not be taken to mean that the two modes of 'doing gender' are not related. Indeed, in the expression of individual acts, as well as the expression of more collectively identifiable and understood modes of masculinity, what women want is an important feature. Put simply: Do women really want their men to stand apart from traditional structures and images of masculinity? And, if 'their man' does so, how do they deal with this? Raising this issue is not intended to imply that women are therefore to blame for men's behaviour; though it is quite clearly possible that it may be read in this way. Nevertheless, it is important to recognise the complexity of feminine expression. For example, where do we locate our understandings of females who identify more closely with traditionally masculine stereotypes (consider here Campbell's (1984) work on female street gangs)? These questions are raised merely to point up the complexities which exist between masculinities and femininities that cannot easily be resolved by privileging one framework over another.

The second issue focuses on the relationship between the state, masculinity(ies) and crime. This has been left relatively untouched by recent work on masculinity and crime (though see, *inter alia*, Connell 2016). This does not mean that the presence of the state and state politics has not been posed as a significant arena for the expression of masculinity(ies). This is evidently not the case. As MacKinnon (1989b: 170) has stated: 'However autonomous of class the liberal state may appear, it is not autonomous of sex. Male power is systemic. Coercive, legitimated, and epistemic, it is the regime.' Indeed, both Connell (1987), in understanding the relationship between gender and power, and Messerschmidt (1993), in analysing gender politics, posit not only the importance of the role of the state but go on to develop ways of thinking about the state as a mode of masculine expression. The argument here is that perhaps much more of this kind of work needs to be done. As MacKinnon (1989a) pointed out, the assertion by the state that it is objective and consequently gender neutral impacts upon all aspects of social life, including crime and its control.

There is, however, a third issue here which arises from the implicit acceptance and the powerful assertion of 'hegemonic masculinity'. This returns us to the presumption of normative heterosexuality contained within the notion of hegemonic masculinity. How this impacts upon the 'masculinity turn' within criminology has been fully explored by Collier (1998). In his view, not only does this turn result in the perpetuation of a false universalism, it also perpetuates the false dualism of sex/gender and, as a consequence, is rooted in heterosexism. The importance of such tendencies lies in what is made visible and invisible by them: what is given and named, how it is named, and how it is responded to. It is simply not enough to replace one agenda with another and assume that you have, as a consequence, dealt with each of them.

Finally, there is a political concern. At one level there has been much to commend the feminist and subsequent masculinist interventions in the academic and policy arena. However, as MacInnes (1998) argued, there are drawbacks to the 'personal is political' strategy. His concern is to 'reassert what politics is properly about: the collective struggle against material exploitation and inequality to achieve equal public rights for private citizens, using the sort of material which classic sociology provides' (MacInnes 1998: 136). Arguably one way to move in this direction is through a closer marriage of masculinity theory with state theory.

Conclusion

In this chapter we have explored different ways of thinking about masculinity and the way in which those differences have expressed themselves within criminology and to a lesser extent victimology. We have reviewed some of the work in this field and have suggested that some issues remain unresolved in the efforts to see all criminal behaviour through the lens of masculinity. A number of implications follow from the difficulties outlined above, several of which are returned to in the latter chapters of this book. How and under what circumstances masculinity is the key variable in committing crime, and how and under what circumstances social class may be the key explanatory variable, are questions which remain to be answered both from theoretical and empirical perspectives.

There is a tendency within some of the literature that centralises a concern with masculinity to seek to explain all kinds of criminal behaviour by reference to that masculinity; from state terrorism, to intimate partner violence, to joy-riding. This tendency runs the risk of being tautological and reflects the underpinning desire of many criminologists to produce a universal explanation of crime. However, we would argue that this desire betrays the discipline's inherent commitment to the modernist as opposed to the postmodernist project and its wish to generate a meaningful policy agenda implied by that commitment.

Scraton (1990) has observed that there is a 'pervasiveness of hegemonic masculinity' within the discipline, 'found covertly in the academic discourses which prevail within malestream criminology'. This statement sensitises us to understanding the discipline, not just as one peopled and dominated by men, but as one in which the very fabric of its structure has taken as given the views of men, women and crime. This has its origins in what Eagle-Russett (1989) has called the nineteenth-century 'sexual science' that laid the foundations for subsequent images of men and women. As Naffine (1987: 133) has stated:

> Feminist theory is likely to dismantle the long-standing dichotomy of the devilish and daring criminal man and the unappealing inert conforming woman. The threat it poses to a masculine criminology is therefore considerable.

This threat is still there. Criminology has, as yet, done little to dismantle it. So while the criminal and criminal activity may well be gendered, criminology is largely yet to be. However, another issue remains, as alluded to above and which is the recurrent theme of this book: What primacy should we give gender?

Messerschmidt (1997: 113) makes the point:

> Gender, race and class are not absolutes and are not equally significant in every social setting where crime is realised. That is, depending on the social setting, accountability to certain categories is more salient than accountability to other categories.

The work reported on by Walklate and Evans (1999) makes the same point about the mediating effect of community. The different ways in which researchers have endeavoured to conceptualise the sex/gender issue have been well summarised by Daly (1997). The point is well made, however. The complex ways in which different variables may interact with each other both in determining structural conditions for action and biographical responses of action demand critical reflection and examination.

By implication, this means exploring femininities as well as masculinities. It means exploring whiteness as well as 'blackness'. It means exploring class. It means exploring different sexualities and challenging normative heterosexuality (Collier 1998). It means exploring the real world as opposed to just the discursive one. Such a process may call into question all kinds of knowledge claims, including those made by feminists, and will certainly call into question any policy process which assumes that what works in one setting may work in another. So we are back to where we started: the variable that is taken to be the most important is most frequently decided upon theoretically. How and under what circumstances masculinity is the key variable in committing crime, or in experiences of criminal victimisation, and how and under what circumstances the key variable may be class, age or ethnicity, are questions that remain to be answered. Such answers may only be found within a theoretical and empirical agenda focused on the specificity of the relationship between particular crimes in particular contexts.

Recommendations for further reading

Those wishing to explore in greater detail an understanding of the relationship between masculinity and crime will find James W. Messerschmidt's (1993) *Masculinities and Crime* and (1997) *Crime as Structured Action* invaluable, as well as the seminal work of Raewyn Connell (1987, 2000, 2005). For a different kind of critique of the criminological enterprise from a gendered perspective, Richard Collier's (1998) *Masculinities, Crime and Criminology* is a good choice, as is Collier's more recent exploration of masculinity and its interaction with law in *Men, Law and Gender: Essays on the 'Man' of Law* (2010).

References

Bricknell, S., Boxall, S. and Andreski, H. (2014) Male victims of non-sexual and non-domestic violence: service needs and experiences in court. Research and Public Policy Series 126. Canberra: Australian Institute of Criminology.

Brittain, A. (1989) *Masculinity and Power*. Oxford: Blackwell.

Brooks, C., Martin, S., Broda, L. and Poudrier, J. (2017) 'How many silences are there?' Men's experience of victimization in intimate partner relationships. *Journal of Interpersonal Violence*, published online first: 1–24.

Campbell, A. (1984) *Girls in the Gang*. Oxford: Blackwell.

Carrington, K. and Scott, J. (2008) Masculinity, rurality and violence. *The British Journal of Criminology* 48(5): 641–666.

Christie, N. (1986) The ideal victim. In E.A. Fattah (ed.) *From Crime Policy to Victim Policy*. Basingstoke: Macmillan.

Cohen, A.K. (1955) *Delinquent Boys*. New York: Free Press.

Collier, R. (1998) *Masculinities, Crime and Criminology*. London: Sage.

Collier, R. (2010) *Men, Law and Gender: Essays on the 'Man' of Law*. Abingdon, Oxon: Routledge.

Connell, R.W. (1987) *Gender and Power*. Oxford: Polity Press.

Connell, R.W. (1995) *Masculinities*. Oxford: Polity Press.

Connell, R.W. (2000) *The Men and the Boys*. New South Wales: Allen and Unwin.

Connell, R.W. (2005) *Masculinities* (2nd edition). New South Wales: Allen and Unwin.

Connell, R. (2016) 100 million Kalashnikovs: gendered power on a world scale debate. *Feminista* 51: 3–17.

Connell, R.W. and Messerschmidt, J.W. (2005) Hegemonic masculinity: rethinking the concept. *Gender and Society* 19(6): 829–859.

Corbally, M. (2015) Accounting for intimate partner violence: a biographical analysis of narrative strategies used by men experiencing IPV from their female partners. *Journal of Interpersonal Violence* 30: 3112–3132.

Culley, J. (2017) 'Hello, I just killed my wife' 999 call of jealous hubby after stabbing mum 20 times. *Daily Star*, 19 January.

Daly, K. (1997) Different ways of conceptualising sex/gender in feminist theory and their implications for criminology. *Theoretical Criminology* 1(1): 25–52.

Davies, P. (2010) *Gender, Crime and Victimisation*. London: Sage.

Durfee, A. (2011) 'I'm not a victim, she's an abuser': masculinity, victimization, and protection orders. *Gender & Society* 25: 316–334.

Eagle Russett, C. (1989) *Sexual Science: The Victorian Construction of Motherhood*. Cambridge, MA: Harvard University Press.

Fisher, N.L. and Pina, A. (2013) An overview of the literature on female-perpetrated adult male sexual victimization. *Aggression and Violent Behavior* 18(1): 54–61.

Fitz-Gibbon, K. (2016) Constructions of masculinity and responsibility in the sentencing of children who commit lethal violence. In K. Fitz-Gibbon and S. Walklate (eds) *Murder, Gender and Responsibility*. London: Routledge, pp. 78–94.

Gadd, D. (2000) Masculinities, violence and the defended psychosocial subject. *Theoretical Criminology* 4(4): 429–450.

Giddens, A. (1987) *Social Theory and Modern Sociology*. Stanford, MA.: Stanford University Press.

Goodey, J. (1997) Boys don't cry: masculinities, fear of crime, and fearlessness. *British Journal of Criminology* 37(3): 401–418.

Goodey, J. (2000) Biographical lessons for criminology. *Theoretical Criminology* 4(4): 473–498.

Graham, K. and Wells, S. (2003) 'Somebody's gonna get their head kicked in tonight!' Aggression among young males in bars – a question of values? *British Journal of Criminology* 43(3): 546–566.

Harland, K. and McCready, S. (2014) Rough justice: considerations on the role of violence, masculinity and the alienation of young men in communities and peace building processes in Northern Ireland. *Youth Justice* 14(3): 269–283.

Hollway, W. and Jefferson, T. (1997) The risk society in an age of anxiety: situating fear of crime. *British Journal of Sociology* 48(2): 255–266.

Hollway, W. and Jefferson, T. (2000) The role of anxiety in the fear of crime. In T. Hope and R. Sparks (eds) *Crime, Risk and Insecurity*. London: Routledge, pp. 31–49.

Hood-Williams, J. (2001) Gender, masculinities and crime. *Theoretical Criminology* 5(1): 37–60.

Javaid, A. (2015) Police responses to, and attitudes towards, male rape. *International Journal of Police Science and Management* 17(2): 81–90.

Javaid, A. (2016) Male rape, stereotypes, and unmet needs: hindering recovery, perpetuating silence. *Violence and Gender* 3(1): 7–13.

Jefferson, T. (1993) Theorising Masculine Subjectivity. Plenary address, Masculinities and Crime Conference, University of Brunel, September.

Jefferson, T. (1997) The Tyson Rape Trial: the law feminism, and emotional truth'. *Social and Legal Studies* 6(2): 281–301.

Jefferson, T. (2013) Hegemonic masculinity. In E. McLaughlin and J. Muncie (eds) *The Sage Dictionary of Criminology* (3rd edition). London: Sage, pp. 216–218.

Katz, J. (1988) *The Seductions of Crime*. New York: Basic Books.

Lees, S. (1997) *Ruling Passions*. London: Sage.

Liddle, M. (1994) Gender, desire and child sexual abuse: accounting for the male majority. *Theory, Culture and Society* 10: 103–126.

Lion, P. (2016) Gang of five armed robbers who stole almost 250,000 over 15 heists targeting cash-in-transit vans jailed. *Mirror*, 10 October.

Machado, A., Santos, A., Graham-Kevan, N. and Matos, M. (2016) Exploring help seeking experiences of male victims of female perpetrators of IPV. *Journal of Family Violence* 1: 1–11.

MacInnes, J. (1998) *The End of Masculinity*. Buckingham: Open University Press.

MacKinnon, C. (1989a) *Feminism Unmodified*. Cambridge, MA: Harvard University Press.

MacKinnon, C. (1989b) *Towards a Feminist Theory of the State*. Cambridge, MA: Harvard University Press.

McMullen, R.J. (1990) *Male Rape: Breaking the Silence on the Last Taboo*. London: Gay Men's Press.

Messerschmidt, J. (1993) *Masculinities and Crime*. Maryland: Rowman and Littlefield.

Messerschmidt, J. (1997) *Crime as Structured Action*. London: Sage.

Messerschmidt, J. (2002) On gang girls, gender and structured action theory: a reply to Miller. *Theoretical Criminology* 6(4): 477–480.

Mezey, G. and King, M. (eds) (1992) *Male Victims of Sexual Assault*. Oxford: Oxford University Press.

Miller, J. (2002) The strengths and limits for 'doing gender' for understanding street crime. *Theoretical Criminology* 6(4): 433–460.

Morgan, D. (1992) *Discovering Men*. London: Routledge.

Naffine, N. (1987) *Female Crime*. Sydney: Allen and Unwin.

Naffine, N. (1990) *Law and the Sexes*. London: Allen and Unwin.

Newburn, T. and Stanko, E.A. (1994) *Just Boys Doing Business*. London: Routledge.

Parsons, T. (1937) *The Structure of Social Action*. New York: McGraw-Hill.

Polk, K. (1994) *When Men Kill: Scenarios of Masculine Violence*. Cambridge: Cambridge University Press.

RCFV (Royal Commission into Family Violence). (2016) *Final Report: Summary and Recommendations*. Victoria: Royal Commission into Family Violence.

Scraton, P. (1990) Scientific knowledge or masculine discourses? Challenging patriarchy in criminology. In L. Gelsthorpe and A. Morris (eds) *Feminist Perspectives in Criminology*. Buckingham: Open University Press, pp. 10–25.

Stanko, E.A. and Hobdell, K. (1993) Assaults on men: masculinity and male violence. *British Journal of Criminology* 33(3).

Stemple, L. and Meyer, I.H. (2014) The sexual victimization on men in America: new data challenges old assumptions. *American Journal of Public Health* 104(6): 19–26.

Sutherland, E.H. (1947) *Principles of Criminology*. Philadelphia, PA: Lippincott.

Therrien, A. (2017) One-punch deaths: how lives are devastated by a single blow. *BBC News Online*, 2 February.

Tolson, A. (1977) *The Limits of Masculinity*. London: Routledge.

Tomsen, S. (1997) A top night: social protest, masculinity and the culture of drinking violence. *British Journal of Criminology* 37(1): 90–102.

Treadwell, J. and Garland, J. (2011) Masculinity, marginalization and violence: a case study of the English Defence League. *The British Journal of Criminology* 51(4): 621–634.

Walklate, S. and Evans, K. (1999) *Zero Tolerance or Community Tolerance? Managing Crime in High Crime Areas*. Aldershot: Ashgate.

Weiss, K.G. (2010) Male sexual victimization: examining men's experiences of rape and sexual assault. *Men and Masculinities* 12(3): 275–298.

Part II

PRACTICE

FEAR, RISK AND SECURITY

Introduction

The first two chapters of this book have charted the intellectual origins and subsequent development of both criminology and victimology, and the ways in which assumptions about gender have been both embedded and deployed in both of these areas. These chapters have also illustrated the ways in which different thinking about gender, whether emanating from feminism and/or studies of masculinity, have endeavoured to challenge such gendered thinking. In this chapter the focus of attention shifts from the general influence of such thinking on criminology and victimology to a much more specific analysis of the ways in which the concepts deployed by them are illustrative of gender-saturated assumptions. The three concepts under consideration here are fear, risk and security. These concepts have been largely developed within Westo-centric or Northern theorising (referred to in Chapter 1), and this chapter will consider the extent to which that theorising impacts upon their value as relevant concepts for the global south. Against this backcloth this chapter also illustrates how these concepts may be differently understood and experienced in relation to other structural variables, such as class, ethnicity and faith. This affords an appreciation of the multi-faceted and multi-layered nature of each of these concepts.

These particular concepts frame this chapter not only because of their gendered assumptions and the controversy that such assumptions generate but also because they are concepts frequently employed in the policy arena. In addition, they inform two further ideas central to criminal justice policy agendas: responsibilisation and vulnerability. These ideas, as they are harnessed in criminal justice policy, further endorse gendered assumptions around fear, risk and security and serve to illustrate the importance of the modernist origins of both criminology and victimology (as discussed in Chapter 1). What follows provides an overview of the ways in which each of these concepts has informed criminology and victimology and the consequences this has had for *who* is considered fearful of what, *who* is thought to be risky from what, *who* it is assumed feels secure (or not), as well as *who* is and is not considered vulnerable and/or responsibilised along each of these dimensions. The chapter ends by reflecting on how some of these questions have impacted upon criminal justice policy.

Thinking about fear

Lee (2017) offers a succinct analysis of the genesis of thinking about fear within criminology and victimology. His analysis charts the growth and development of interest in fear of crime through its intimate connections with the emergence and increasing refinement of the criminal victimisation survey. As Lee notes, and as has been noted elsewhere (Walklate 2004), the purpose of those surveys and the ways in which they have endeavoured to operationalise the concept of fear has been subjected to considerable scrutiny. During the 1980s some of that scrutiny challenged the presumption that the fears expressed by women and the elderly as captured in such survey findings were somehow irrational (see, *inter alia*, Young 1987; Sparks 1992; Stanko 1990). Others have taken issue with the actual questions included within such surveys making the case for better formulated questions (see e.g. Farrall *et al.* 2009). Some have considered the ways in which a focus on the fear of crime is rooted in the wider governmentality project in which the politicisation of the victim has had an increasing presence (Lee 2007). Others have challenged the value of the concept of fear in and of itself (see e.g. Hollway and Jefferson 1997).

Despite these challenges, and the obvious difficulties associated with quantifying a feeling such as 'fear', the fear of crime industry has continued unabated. At the centre of this industry has been the criminal victimisation survey. Indeed, the reliance on this source of data remains paramount in informing understandings of who is and is not afraid (of crime). Over time, as intimated above, the fearful have variously included the elderly and women (constructed as both rational and irrational in their fears); men as fearful to express fear as being contra-indicated by their masculinity; and ethnic minority groups as being both the subjects of fear, the objects of fear, and both subjects and objects of fear simultaneously (Mythen *et al.* 2009). The salience of gender in each of these constructions of the fearful is complicated. Yet, as Kruttschnitt (2016) has observed, there is still a great deal of work to be done in understanding the place of gender in much criminological endeavour and the fear of crime debate is no exception to this. Moreover, if the measurement gaze on the fear of crime is reoriented from a focus on survey methodology to that which Lee (2017) highlights as the relationship between everyday violence and the fear of crime, there is an evident feminist legacy of thinking on fear which centres gender.

Feminist-informed work focuses on the nature of women's everyday lives and affords a different way of measuring and conceptualising fear and how it translates for women and men into what Stanko (1993) has called an 'ordinary fear'. Indeed, it is the potential normalcy of such experiences which radical feminism (as discussed in Chapter 1) takes as its starting point.

> Suddenly there are footsteps behind her. Heavy, rapid. A man's footsteps. She knows this immediately, just as she knows she must not look round. She quickens her pace in time to the quickening of her pulse. She is afraid. He could be a rapist. He could be a soldier, an harasser, a robber, a killer. He could be none of these. He could be a man in a hurry. He could be a man walking at his normal pace. But she fears him. She fears him because he is a man. She has reason to fear.
>
> (Morgan 1989: 23)

This quote captures many women's experiential response to a well-known situation. It taps into what radical feminists would argue is the root cause of women's fear of crime: the fear of male-perpetrated sexual danger. In this sense, the 'fear of crime' constitutes one end of a continuum of experiences (Kelly 1988) in which women routinely learn to manage their daily lives structured and informed by their relationships with the men in their lives: fathers, sons, partners, lovers, colleagues, co-workers. In these relationships women learn to deal with harassment, incest, violence and rape over the course of their lives. These learning experiences are not easily separable into a public and private domain, and, as will be illustrated in Chapter 4's examination of sexual violence, are not separable along the peacetime/wartime divide either. For example, the routine fears experienced by young mothers in Palestine, the associated surveillance of their bodies and their resistance to such oppression reported by Shalhoub-Kevorkian (2015) stands in stark contrast to the blinkered vision of the fearful engendered by criminal victimisation survey data. Indeed, if such fears (of sexual assault) in peacetime and in wartime are placed side by side, along with the fears named by Goodey (1994) as sub-legal, then the construction of women as fearful does not seem at all misplaced. However, the conceptual path taken in reaching this conclusion is quite a different one from that used by the criminal victimisation industry. The former path, however, may tempt us to ask how it is that we, as women, are not paralysed by such fears. Clearly this is not the case.

Women's lives are differently and differentially informed by the everydayness of ordinary fears. As Walklate (1997: 43) has commented:

> Thus while all women may not fear all men, some women have considerable knowledge about the men that they know, places they deem dangerous, and the potential for sexual danger from men that they know and do not know. Some may also be afraid of some women, as evidenced by the work on bullying in schools.

Of course, lurking in the background of the prominence of the criminal victimisation survey industry and its ungendered approach to fear is, as Young (2011: 79–81) has pointed out, criminology's love affair with the 'bogus of positivism' and its associated 'fetishism with number', as discussed in Chapter 1. Moreover, while feminist-informed work does not eschew number per se (on the contrary, see e.g. Russell's (1990) seminal survey work on rape in marriage), its desire to start in a different gendered conceptual space in understanding fear offers a different appreciation of who is fearful, when and from what. It certainly challenges the tendency to universalise women's fear. Simultaneously it is also important not to assume that those fears can be simply rendered as fears of men. As will be seen in Chapter 4 and as is developed later in this chapter, women's (and men's) negotiations of their everyday lives (in relation to violence) are considerably more subtly informed. Indeed, it is also important to note that men's fears may be equally constructed as ordinary, especially in relation to who they may be fearful of, where and when, and may equally comprise other men.

Also embedded in the criminal victimisation survey's understanding of fear is an:

> unreflective embrace of risk, a persistent assumption of what kind of crime there is to be feared and who might commit those crimes and an unwillingness to grapple with the situated fashion in which people make sense of, and negotiate crime risks for themselves.
>
> (Mythen and Walklate 2008: 221)

This unreflective embrace of risk is the next concept to be considered here.

Thinking about risk

In the wake of the seminal influence of the work of Ulrich Beck, whose book *The Risk Society* was published in English in 1992, and the increasing desire for politicians to seek ways of managing crime rather than preventing it, criminology along with other social sciences became enamoured with the promise of risk and risk theory. This promise was quickly translated into the development of risk-assessment tools as a means of managing offenders and has been refined more recently for informing responses to victims deemed at risk from (domestic violence) offenders. Yet this embrace of risk, intimately connected as it is with the modernist origins of both criminology and victimology (Walklate 1997) and its operationalisation within criminal victimisation surveys linked with fear, demands closer scrutiny from a gendered perspective both in terms of how risk is understood as well as how it is operationalised as an assessment tool.

Mythen (2014) has highlighted three limitations inherent in the social scientific embrace of risk: the limited visibility of power and power relations within risk theory, the partial view of human agency embedded within it, and the tendency towards catachresis (misapplying or overstretching the use to which the concept has been put). All of these limitations are relevant to the criminological and victimological embrace of risk. As one illustration of this embrace, as O'Malley (2006: 49) pointed out, 'crime prevention has succeeded in marrying risk with a more traditional social and behavioural form of criminology by translating the old causes of crime into risk factors'. This preoccupation with risk factors is evident from the local to the global illustrated by the adoption of the World Health Organisation's 'ecological model' of violence into national violence prevention programmes. This model assumes that violence can be prevented by reducing the violent characteristics of individuals. Thus individuals are 'sorted' (Feeley and Simon 1994) and responded to according to their respective risk factors for violence. Yet the question arises: Whose behaviour may be considered risky and whose behaviour not, and under what conditions? A further question may be: how is this concept being deployed when arguably violence and the recourse to violence exists in the folds of everyday life (to borrow a phrase from Das 2007) for many women, ethnic minority groups and indeed for some men? In other words, what risk actually means, for whom and under what conditions is often poorly articulated, is frequently partial and is equally likely to be eclectic.

The problematic nature of these issues is particularly well demonstrated by Shalhoub-Kevorkian (2003: 603), who, in discussing femicide, asks:

> What is the alternative if her male adult 'protector' abuses her (sexually, emotionally, physically), and how can she speak about her abuse if she has never learned that it is possible to voice personal matters? How can she speak out when she knows that customs and cultural codes may be used to cause her death? How can she ask for help when her protectors might also be her enemies? [.] What happens if the legal system supports her femicide?

Under these kinds of conditions what counts as risk and who counts as risky is arguably quite differently informed than a gender neutral conceptualisation of risk might lead us to believe. Indeed, O'Malley (2004) has argued that risk is structured: it is neither uniform nor unifying. Who is deemed at risk, and who is deemed risky is a multi-faceted phenomenon, mediated, for example, by global geo-political positions on the one hand (Aas 2012) and by locality on the other (Evans *et al.* 1996). It is also gendered, and the implicit acceptance of risk as a gender-neutral concept (within criminology and victimology) takes its toll on the respective disciplinary capacity for making sense of both men's and women's lives. Put simply, this hides the risk-seeking behaviour of women (or if such behaviour is recognised it is pathologised: Miller 2002) and hides the vulnerabilities of men (Walklate 1997), rendering their experiences of victimisation difficult to see, assess and respond to (Stanko and Hobdell 1993). Thus the conceptual implication is, as Chan and Rigakos (2002: 756) state:

> A recognition of risk as gendered relies on acknowledging that there can be no essential notion of risk; that risk is variable; risk itself is more than one type. [.] Risk is gendered on a continuum both in the sense of empirical potential harm and the recognition and the definition of that harm. Women, it may be argued, are required to engage in instrumental risk in order to interact socially, work, cohabitate with a man etc. However, this does not signal women's victimhood but rather their agency in flouting potential dangers in the general pursuit of material subsistence.

For example, Sanders' (2005) articulation of a 'continuum of risk' captures a highly subtle and active process for sex workers of making choices about where to work, how to work, alongside the need to manage questions of emotions, identity, health and relationships in their lives. Thus while 'risk burns in many different degrees' (Walklate and Mythen 2008: 215) when considered from individual perspectives, people's real lives are at the same time 'not about modernity and the ontological insecurity people experience: for women it is about misogyny and the continued perpetuation of women's oppression through fear of crime and blame for their situation' (Stanko 1997: 492).

Stanko's (1997) assertion of the ongoing powerful influence of misogyny and the connections this forges with the discussion of radical feminism in Chapter 1 notwithstanding, it is important to note that women are not passive agents in these processes (*qua* Sanders 2005 referenced above). Yet the criminological and victimological ungendered embrace of risk constitutes a categorical denial of women's agency straining towards uniform understandings in order to construct a unified individualised liberal (and fearful) subject (Walklate forthcoming). The intimate connections between conceptual constructions of fear and risk within criminological and victimological concerns take their toll in different ways in the capacity of these respective areas of analysis to make sense of men's and women's relationship with risk and fear, and it is worth spelling out the consequences of this in a little more detail. Of course, as noted elsewhere, such uniform and unifying understandings of fear and risk curtail understandings of other groups too (referred to in Chapter 1 as the problem of intersectionality). This is a limitation to which we return in the Conclusion of this book.

Women, fear and risk

Given some of the evidence already covered in this chapter, and those yet to come, it is not difficult to mount a convincing argument that women's 'fear' of crime is a reflection of their public and private experience of men (Warr 1985; Stanko 1985). This, of course, does not mean that all women are always afraid, or that all women are always or only afraid of men whom they know. The point is that these variously constituted threats of sexual danger permeate the public as well as private lives of women: their sense of well-being or ontological security, in ways which Stanko (1997) argues constitute a technology of the soul. If these threats are the backcloth against which to understand women's expressed 'fear' of crime, how may it be possible to make sense of them in such a way that resonates with their lived experiences? There are two issues here.

First, it is self-evident that all women are not afraid of all men. However, their sense of well-being will be informed by a range of factors – for example, the sex of the person(s) they are with at any one point in time, the place they are in and their structural location. This information then exists along a spectrum of experiences differently framed by culture, structure and other factors, as the citation from Shalhoub-Kervorkian (2003) aptly highlights. Thus, while women may not fear all men, they do have considerable knowledge about men whom they know, places they deem dangerous, and the potential for sexual danger from men whom they know and do not know. They may also be afraid of some women. This does not mean necessarily that there is a symmetrical relationship between women's fears of men and their fears of other women (see Dobash and Dobash 1992). The same, of course, may also be said of men in relation to men and women whom they know. The second question then is: to what extent are women's lives informed and influenced by such fears? Or is there a sense in which they challenge the presumptions of fearfulness and engage in risk-seeking behaviour, despite the conceptual construction of fear and risk rendering the notion of women as risk-seeking anomalous? Of course it is the case that when women do take risks they may be further 'othered', pathologised and/or victim-blamed as a result. However, this does not mean that risk-seeking is beyond their capacity as women. The early work of Carlen *et al.* (1985), highlighting risk and thrills as a motivation for crime, is just one illustration of the relevance of risk for making sense of women's criminal behaviour as well as their victimisation.

Taken together, it is evident that the ways in which both criminology and victimology have deployed risk and fear in relation to women have missed the mark in understanding the nature of women's real lives both as potential offenders and/or as victims of crime. Arguably this is a result of the valorisation of particular ways of knowing (discussed in Chapter 1) which have sustained the dominance of positivism in both areas of investigation. This sustenance has been further nourished by historically less visible conceptual architecture which underpins the exploration of fear and risk: namely the concepts of security, vulnerability and responsibilisation. Before we go on to consider the first of these concepts, a brief word is given on the consequences of an ungendered appreciation of fear and risk for understandings of men.

Men, fear and risk

It is perhaps worth making explicit that conventional criminal victimisation survey work clearly identifies young men as being at greater risk from street crime than any other category of people. Yet it is also the case that men remain far more unwilling to admit their victimisation or talk about their fears in general, let alone their fears of crime. The impact of this upon the discipline is well captured by Stanko and Hobdell (1993: 400), who state:

> Criminology's failure to explore men's experience of violence is often attributed to men's reluctance to report 'weakness'. This silence is, we are led to believe, a product of men's hesitation to disclose vulnerability.

Indeed, men's relationship with risk, fear and danger has been relatively under-explored. Lyng (1990: 872–873) suggests:

> Males are more likely to have an illusory sense of control over fateful endeavours because of the socialisation pressures on males to develop a skill orientation towards their environment. In so far as males are encouraged to use their skills to affect the outcome of all situations, even those that are almost entirely chance determined, they are likely to develop a distorted sense of their ability to control fateful circumstances.

Lyng's observations stem from ethnographic work carried out with a group of sky-divers. However, what Lyng has identified here, perhaps, is something much more deeply rooted than the experience of a different socialisation process. His insight also taps into readily available ideological and cultural images deeming males and females capable of different things. Such images emphasise a positive relationship between men and risk with the converse being the case for women. Stanko and Hobdell's (1993) work provides a somewhat different emphasis. The men in their study clearly proffered a range of responses to, relationship with and experience of violence which challenge any simplistic assumption about their relationship with risk from, in this example, personal violence. Of course the responses of Lyng's sky-divers and Stanko and Hobdell's victims of violence need to be understood as part of, and fundamentally connected to, these men's relationship with masculinity: 'hegemonic masculinity' in particular (as discussed in Chapter 2). So, while it is possible that Lyng's sky-divers may have being asserting control over the uncontrollable in a positive and ego-enhancing way, Stanko and Hobdell's victims may reflect how these men lost control in an ego-damaging way. The question of the motivation for and experience of each of these different types of behaviour and responses to it is, of course, a highly individual one. However, each of these responses captures some sense of what it is that is culturally expected of being a man, and the ways in which the variable responses to these cultural expectations may be rendered silent in the discourses which claim to be speaking about them.

By implication, then, it is necessary to locate men's relationship to fear and risk within a broader cultural context of the values associated with masculinity. That cultural context may not, however, provide the complete picture. While it is important to recognise that thrill and excitement frequently go alongside risk, fear and danger, and that all of these are frequently talked about in male terms, that 'talking' frequently not only silences women's experiences, as suggested above, but may also silence the experiences of some men. The interconnecting thread of masculinity between risk, fear, danger, excitement and control itself is neither uniform nor unifying at the level of the individual but, as Connell (2016) suggests, it does offer a sense of continuity between what might otherwise be deemed to be disconnected behaviours.

The capacity of criminology and victimology to perpetuate the kinds of conceptual blind spots intimated above reflects one of the main limitations of risk theorising in general expressed by Mythen (2014) as a partial view of agency. Within criminology this partial view of agency also translates into the policies and practices associated with risk, particularly those of risk assessment (discussed more fully below). All of this is further sustained by a similarly ungendered understanding of vulnerability and responsibilisation overlaid by a curtailed appreciation of security. Stanko's (1997) reference to the question of ontological security above connects understandings of risk with understandings of security namely leading us to ask: How, where and when do people feel safe? It is to that concept that we now turn.

Thinking about security

It is without doubt that the concept of security has become a key focus of the twenty-first century. Indeed, Crawford (2014) has argued that this concept has both paradoxical and precarious features which when operationalised can result in the opposite effect: heightened insecurity (see also Mythen and Walklate 2016). It is widely accepted that the study of security has been dominated by those concerned with international relations: a preoccupation with security as a 'big noun'. Such dominance notwithstanding, other disciplinary perspectives offer fertile ground for thinking about this concept. Bourbeau's (2015) edited collection imagines security in diverse ways: as being thick or thin, objective or subjective, strong or weak, always in the making (processual), operating at different levels and with different degrees of intensity. Indeed, security has been variously labelled as 'promiscuous' (Zedner 2009), 'sticky' (Fanghanel 2014), 'scalar' (Valverde 2014), 'polysemic' (Ranasinghe 2013) and 'stretched' (Mythen and Walklate 2016). Within criminology, security has tended to be discussed in terms of a zero-sum game – something that somebody has at someone else's expense (see. *inter alia*, Hudson and Ugelvik 2012). Despite this complexity and 'stretchiness' there has been a remarkable consistency in presuming security to be a 'big noun'. However, as Crawford and Hutchinson (2016) argue, security is also an everyday phenomenon: a 'small noun'. As captured in this brief overview, the criminological grasp on security reflects some of the tensions between its presence as a 'big noun' and the everyday experiences of security as a 'small noun'. It will be useful here to unravel the gendered aspects of these tensions.

Froestad *et al.* (2015) have suggested that security has always been the central focus of the discipline and, though the manifestation of this preoccupation has varied, central to it has been an understanding of security as freedom from interpersonal harms. Froestad *et al.* (2015) express this as a freedom from 'hitting and taking'. Feminist work has long been concerned with the 'hitting and taking' which men direct towards women. Voices from Power Cobbe (1878) to Russell and Rebecca Dobash (1980), to Genn (1988), Morgan (1989) and Pain (2012), as well as many others, confront the presumed safe haven of the 'home' as central in 'security experiences'. The routine, everyday violence experienced by women in private as well as in public was aptly expressed by Genn (1988: 95) three decades ago as 'just part of life'. The fears generated by these 'security experiences' and the impact they have, potentially, upon the nature of women's fears and their understandings of risk have already been referenced above and are further developed in Chapter 4. This kind of violence is often silenced: in the bedroom, on the street, in a children's home, in a prison, in the workplace and on a continent (Jordan 2011). It is sufficient at this juncture to reiterate that these feminist-informed interventions fundamentally challenge conventional thinking about what constitutes security in everyday life. They focus attention on security as a small noun.

Thus the knowledge generated by feminist-informed work has posed, and continues to pose, a serious challenge to those who may, for example, see the choice to stay in a violent relationship as irrational when evidence indicates that the point of separation, as women often know, is one of the most dangerous (see Dekeseredy and Rennison 2013; Mahoney 1991). The ways in which these experiences translate themselves into everyday practices are transcendent as well as culturally and geographically specific. For example, Lucashenko (1996) outlines how Australian indigenous women reject notions of 'traditional' law that support or allow violence against women. Shalhoub-Kevorkian (2015: 1202) documents how birthing mothers in Palestine find new ways to subvert colonial oppression and become more visible agents of liberation. These include breaking cultural taboos like unveiling, borrowing ID cards, driving without a licence, all whilst in pain, to enable them to cross borders and give birth safely.

In a similar vein Listerborn (2015) highlights how women, even in extreme conditions of othering while wearing the veil, find ways to negotiate and sustain their everyday lives as securely as they can. As Pain (2012: 6) reminds us, 'Keeping another person in a state of chronic fear does not require physical violence to be used all of the time, or at all.' Intimate knowledge of another person is sufficient.

This body of work speaks volumes about the everyday security practices and experiences of women as they negotiate the presence of violence in their everyday lives. Even these few examples on everyday security more than adequately illustrate the multi-faceted and multi-layered nature of security and its everyday manifestation for some women when seen through a gendered lens. Policy responses to security have been paradoxical and contradictory in the face of this evidence and have been subjected to critical scrutiny by Walklate *et al.* (2017). Nonetheless, for the purposes of this discussion, it is sufficient to note that the marginalisation of that work excavating the nature of security as a small noun and its gendered experience also detracts from the ability of both criminology and victimology as disciplines to fully appreciate, as with fear and risk, what security means as it is actually lived and experienced on a routine daily basis.

To summarise: the concepts of fear, risk and security have differently informed the debates emanating from criminology and victimology since the late 1960s. As this discussion has illustrated, the influence these concepts have had in framing how each of these areas think or fail to think about gender has been profound. A gendered perspective casts some considerable light on the contested nature of each of these concepts, not only for men and women but also for all kinds of groups and geographical locations, in which the Northern, white, heterosexual, masculine world carries different and differential resonances. The ways in which each of these concepts has informed criminal justice policy have also been equally profound: from generic crime prevention advice proffered to women on how to avoid sexual assault, to the presumption that national security advice only pertains to the threat of terrorism. In what follows we pay particular attention to the way in which risk and risk-assessment practices have unfolded within this policy setting.

This focus on risk assessment has been chosen for three reasons. First, reflections on risk assessment permit a consideration of how such practices have developed for use with both victims and offenders. Second, these practices have increasingly travelled the globe usually from North to South, so this discussion affords an opportunity to consider the implications of this trajectory and policy transfer, more broadly. Third, such practices more often than not make assumptions about responsibilisation and vulnerability, and therefore offer an opportunity to consider how these concepts are also harnessed in policy.

Risk assessment: policy and practice

In general terms risk-assessment tools, whether clinical or actuarial, focus attention on predicting future behaviour. Logically, of course, such tools can never provide anything more than a hypothesis about what might happen in the future, usually framed in terms of the presumed likelihood of serious violence or death. Indeed, their capacity for weak and/or modest prediction has been reported by Medina *et al.* (2016). Such weak findings stand in precise opposition to the purpose of risk management which is to minimise, in Bernstein's (1996: 334) words, the likelihood of 'wildness' breaking out. Thus the endeavour of risk management (of offenders), designed to deny the possibility of 'wildness', simultaneously denies human agency (*qua* Mythen 2014). This denial is captured in the conflation of prevention with prediction alluded to earlier and glosses what it is that professionals actually 'do' when assessing risk and what it is that those deemed 'at risk' may do in the light of having been assessed as risky.

On the question of professional practice, Kemshall (2010: 11) reveals that 'workers operate with subjective overrides where cases make them anxious or where subjective biases and organisational values do not "fit" actuarial results'. Broadhurst *et al.* (2010: 1052) describe an 'iterative process' between the 'demands of procedure' and the 'demands of the case' as comprising a range of values, including compassion, empathy and a sense of responsibility. Thus 'expert judgement' (Walklate 1999; Kemshall and Maguire 2001) is a significant component of risk assessment and, when the evidence conflicts, practitioners err on the side of precaution (Ansbro 2010), lending weight to Kemshall's (2010: 11) observation on the 'firewalls' to risk challenging the presumption of its 'inexorable logic'. So while such practices may mediate the effects of a uniform and unifying embrace of risk, characterised as 'risk crazed governance' by Carlen (2008), what does this logic nevertheless presume about gender? On this question there has been some considerable debate concerning whether or not risk assessments are appropriate for female offenders and how, if at all, they might inform practice. This debate ultimately exposes the tensions between viewing female offenders as risky or, alternatively, seeing them as women with needs. Both of these visions of the female offender bring to the fore quite different understandings of their offending behaviour: the former centring individual motivation and/or behavioural problems, the latter centring the importance of social context.

Risk-assessment tools foreground female offenders as risky rather than as women with needs (Hannah-Moffat 2006). Davidson and Chesney-Lind (2009: 222) go further. They add that risk-assessment tools distort the notion of risk for women in two ways. First, their preoccupation with the prediction of particular causes of crime (for example, those focusing on individual motivation) becoming inherent features of the instruments themselves. Second, by being based on male understandings of risk tools can distort the contextual meaning of risk for female offenders (what might have led them into crime in the first place including their relationship with their male partners: Barlow 2016). Taken together, these distortions have the potential to result in both an over-classification and an under-classification of women at risk all at the same time rendering them problematic as tools for practice. This result stems primarily from the inability of risk-assessment tools both to 'see' context (in this case the context of women's offending behaviour: for example, poverty, powerlessness, history of abuse: Chesney-Lynd and Pasko 2004) and to 'see' gender (that risk itself is gendered, as discussed above). These difficulties have informed a related debate on whether or not policy responses (for female offenders) should be framed as gender-specific or gender-responsive with these terms often used interchangeably.

Myers and Wakefield (2014) offer a useful overview of the different positions adopted in relation to prison policies and their capacity to capture gender-informed concerns. For example, a gender-specific approach to imprisonment recognises that many prisons and prison systems were built and developed with men in mind, and thus, by definition, those systems over-classify women as risky and incarcerate them accordingly. In light of these issues some prison policies have become much more aware of women's needs while in custody, offering support for the kinds of traumatic events (like abuse) that can propel some women into crime. However, such policy responses are not without their critics. On the one hand, some commentators point to the possible unintended consequences of such approaches insofar as a focus on the needs of individual offenders can mask the structural conditions that also propel some women into crime, particularly women from Indigenous populations. On the other hand, others point to the paucity of similar initiatives for male offenders.

This debate is marked by two further considerations. The focus on individual needs lends itself relatively easily to discourses of responsibilisation, while the lack of attention paid to men with gender-specific needs leaves them 'vulnerable to the collision of hegemonic masculinity and economic and social exclusion cycle through the justice system' (Myers and Wakefield 2014: 587). Both of these observations point to the ways in which the subtle deployment of responsibilisation and vulnerability has occurred through the vehicle of gender. Moreover, it is also important to remember that all of this 'promote[s] a homogeneous and unrealistic view of women [and men] and their needs ignoring more entrenched structural factors' (Bosworth and Fili 2013: 239). The strain towards not only ungendered but also uniform and unifying responses here is apparent.

A similar deployment of responsibilisation and vulnerability emerges in the use of risk-assessment tools for 'at-risk' victims.

The 'discovery' of the repeated nature of criminal victimisation from criminal victimisation survey data, especially in relation to intimate partner violence, has informed the development over time of different practices for responding to such violence. For example, initial responses in the UK 'flagged' such victims on police computer systems so that they could be dealt with appropriately. However, contemporarily a much more sophisticated range of risk-assessment tools are available, from the spousal risk-assessment guide (SARA), the Propensity for Abusiveness Scale (PAS); to the Partner Abuse Prognostic Scale (PAPS) (all cited in Hoyle 2008: 327). The DASH model is favoured by most police forces in the UK (Domestic Abuse, Stalking and Harassment, and Honour-based Violence). McCulloch *et al.* (2016) review a further nine tools (including DASH) designed to inform responses to intimate partner violence and used to assess the levels of risk judged to be present in individual cases (high, medium, low). Yet, as McCulloch *et al.* (2016: 58) state, 'there is a paucity of empirical research evaluating the outcomes of [international] risk assessments', with Westmarland (2011: 300–301) observing that the relationship between such risk-assessment exercises and subsequent incidents of femicide is somewhat arbitrary. Nonetheless, there seems to be some agreement on the key 'risk factors' for interpersonal homicide in the context of intimate partner violence. These are: prior interpersonal violence; age difference; cohabiting; estrangement; strangulation; and the presence of a child who is not biologically related to the abuser. Other high-risk factors include homes where there is mental illness, drug abuse, pregnancy and the presence of weapons (Campbell *et al.* 2009). However it is a moot point, as Westmarland (2011) intimates, how effectively an understanding of such risk factors informs professional practice, with Robinson *et al.* (2016) reporting that a small constellation of risk factors influence police officers' perceptions of risk veering towards the presence of physical injuries for these kinds of incidents.

Those risk assessment practices that endeavour to pay greater attention to the victim's voice in the assessment process are also subject to criticism. Hoyle (2008: 332) observes that such risk assessments typically include getting the victim to agree to 'safety plans' for which victims are made individually accountable – in part, at least – for minimising the risk of further violence. Moreover, 'Victims are encouraged to take seriously the recommendations of the domestic violence victim safety plan' while such plans simultaneously fail to 'take into consideration women's own assessments of the danger they are in, independent of other risk factors, even though most studies suggest it is highly predictive of serious domestic assault' (Hoyle 2008: 330; see also Campbell 2004; Heckert and Gondolf 2004). This analysis reveals much about who is being made responsible and for what. At the same time there are multiple examples of cases in which the failure to listen to women's own voices appropriately has resulted in their subsequent demise, from the Thurman Case in the United States in the early 1980s that led to the introduction of mandatory arrest policies in cases of domestic violence, to that of Kelly Thompson in Melbourne, Australia in 2015 who was killed by her partner after thirty-eight calls to police over a three-week period for breaches of intervention orders. In addition, the denial of structural variables as risk factors in incidents of intimate partner violence is inherent in the individualised focus of these tools. This also carries very specific consequences. For example, Robinson and Rowlands (2009) point to their inherent heterosexism of risk alongside the limited vision that risk assessment exercises offer of men as victims. Perhaps more importantly, this individualistic bias can also prove to be particularly problematic for Indigenous populations (see Cunneen 2014). Ultimately, as Walklate (2017) has argued, the difficulties of engaging in meaningful risk-assessment practices for at-risk victims amounts to conceptual failure (Lewis and Greene 1978), and exposes the faulty theoretical foundations of risk on which they are built.

This brief excursion into criminal justice policy, and the practices deployed to implement aspects of this policy, highlights the ways in which the lack of appreciation of gender at the level of theory poses similarly problematic assumptions (about gender) at the level of practice, the potential firewalls of 'expert' knowledge notwithstanding. This excursion has also afforded some insight into the creeping presence of additional conceptual devices in policies and practises, related to and arguably underpinning the concepts discussed so far, but which have nonetheless been subjected to somewhat less critical scrutiny, particularly through the lens of gender. These are responsibilisation and vulnerability.

Responsibilisation

Both O'Malley (2009) and Muncie (2013) agree that within criminology the concept of responsibilisation is associated with governmentality theory which emanates from the work of Foucault and the influence of that work on the discipline, particularly during the 1990s. Garland's (2001) *The Culture of Control* is noted for its use as one feature of a culture of control associated with criminal justice policy in the United States and the United Kingdom at that time. Largely connected with the wider neo-liberal turn in those Western governments (and elsewhere), this term captures the ways in which individuals and multi-agency partnerships are encouraged through criminal justice policy to assume responsibility for the problem of crime either by taking sensible precautions against crime and/or by sharing in the delivery of services and practices designed to respond to crime. However, as O'Malley (2009) points out, while this term appears to have some contemporary currency, the practices associated with it are on the one hand not new and on the other have built on the historical importance of the concept of responsibility in criminal law. These two observations are important and require further development.

In relation to the first observation, and recalling the discussion of victimology in Chapter 1, the concept of victim precipitation and its use within early victimological work provides a good example of the historical presence of responsibilisation. Chapter 1 noted the outcry from the feminist movement prompted by the publication of Amir's work on victim-precipitated rape in 1968. This study focused particular attention on the victim's own behaviour in contributing to what happened to them. The slippage between this, victim-blaming and the notion of responsibilisation is self-evident. Writ large, much crime prevention advice pays close attention to the need for everyone to take sensible precautions to avoid victimisation and in so doing we are all responsibilised for the problem of crime, from sexual assault to burglary. From this viewpoint the responsibility for crime is not only directed towards the individual; it is also directed to all of us as responsible citizens. Such strategies, of course, side-step the issues of what causes crime, who the criminal(s) might be, and the role of the criminal justice agencies themselves. They also elide the question of responsibility with the practice of responsibilisation and as a consequence the boundaries between the two become blurred. By implication, they also smooth out the ways in which such practices might be gendered.

To elucidate, feminists have long campaigned to bring traditionally silenced voices into the bounds of criminal law (for more on this, see Chapter 6). This has been the case particularly in those campaigns that have sought to bring to the fore the different ways in which the 'reasonable man of law' silences some voices (see Naffine 1990). In the context of homicide, the 'reasonable man of law' and its gendered presumptions takes its toll on the capacity of the law to think differently about the question of responsibility, in law, for what transpired. One feature of the campaigns trying to address this issue has been to seek ways to ensure that the law actually reflects and can respond to what is known about lethal violence occurring between intimate partners. This has often focused attention on changing the law to better address such lethal violence. However, gender and gendered assumptions about masculinity and femininity thread their way through the law and its practices in this regard, and this is particularly manifested in how the concept of responsibility is operationalised (see the edited collection by Fitz-Gibbon and Walklate (2016) for a fuller explication of this). At the level of individual cases, understandings of responsibility reflect gendered assumptions while simultaneously denying the wider structural context in which these assumptions are constructed as being a factor in such cases. In other features of the law the reverse occurs.

For example, the introduction of 'Clare's Law' (The Domestic Violence Disclosure Scheme) in England and Wales is marked by a concern to take seriously the repeat patterning of domestic violence by male offenders towards their female partners. It offers members of the public and partners in a relationship both the 'right to ask' and the 'right to know' whether or not their current partner has a history of domestic abuse. Fitz-Gibbon and Walklate (2017: 286) identify three objectives in this process:

> to strengthen the ability of the police and other multi-agency partnerships to provide appropriate protection and support to victims at risk of domestic violence; to reduce incidents of domestic violence through prevention; and to reduce the health and criminal justice-related costs of domestic violence.

These would appear to be laudable aims and some commentators have complimented these efforts as a way of enabling women to 'make informed choices' (Bessant 2015: 118). However, Fitz-Gibbon and Walklate (2017) point out that requiring the victim to request access to information about their current partner and to act on that information transfers responsibility for what transpires between the two to the victim, simultaneously detracting from the responsibility of the offender. At the same time the victim is required to engage with criminal justice professionals in order to do this in the face of a body of research on the reluctance of victims living with violence to do so. It also presents the victim with a dilemma. Armed with the knowledge of her partner's previous violence, the onus is on her to do something on the basis of this knowledge. If she does nothing then the question is raised as to how the criminal justice system will subsequently treat her should any proceedings ensue. The capacity for victim-blaming as a consequence is clear.

So, even in this legislation where some effort has been made to take account of the patterning of abuse and its gendered features, it is nevertheless the individual victim (the woman) who is rendered responsible for acting out the consequences of this legislation. In other words, she is responsibilised. Thus the boundaries between responsibility and responsibilisation are blurred and gender is hidden from view. As O'Malley (2009) intimates, practices such as those are one feature of the ways in which risk management on the part of the legislator or the criminal justice system has become deeply embedded within criminal justice practice. A further characteristic embedded in such practices is the concept of vulnerability.

Vulnerability

Green (2007) suggests that the concept of vulnerability has rarely been explored in its own right, particularly in the context of criminology. Yet Sparks (1982), for example, commented that vulnerability refers to a state in which the victims themselves do nothing to put themselves at special risk but find themselves vulnerable because of the attributes they possess: being frail, very young and so on. According to Killias and Clerici (2000), such physical vulnerability contributes to the fear of crime. Indeed, as Pain (2003) has pointed out and building on Christie's seminal work, presumptions of physical vulnerability fuel stereotypical views of the elderly and their experience of crime, even though not all older people are frail. The 'injurability' of the body (Butler 2009: 34) captures one dimension of the experience of feeling vulnerable which Walklate (2011) has called 'inherent vulnerability'. Much policy response has taken inherent vulnerability, especially that characterised by age, or mental capacity, as the grounds for special treatment. For example, this is evident in various courtrooms worldwide where partial and complete defences to murder have been designed and implemented to allow the courts to directly consider and account for those individual characteristics.

Sparks (1982) goes on to link vulnerability to those who may be harmed, and those who put themselves at risk. Vulnerability is not physical in his analysis, but rather is informed by who is considered to be at risk and who is considered to be harmed. Such a view is apparent in criminal victimisation survey questions addressing people's routine activities (for example, going out alone at night, using public transport) as measures of risk from crime. Such criminal victimisation survey data calculates vulnerability by measuring who is at most risk from crime and then linking that data with other information about those upon whom crime has the most impact. The relationship between these two variables determines who is the most vulnerable: alluding to patterns of structural vulnerability. Borrowing from the implication of the statement made by Das (2007: 63) that 'To be vulnerable is not the same as to be a victim', Walklate (2011), drawing upon feminist-informed work on victimisation, adds to this by suggesting a further dimension to vulnerability: the experiential.

Each of these dimensions to vulnerability (inherent, structural and experiential) is differently informed by structural variables, including gender, and is suggestive of a hierarchy of vulnerability overlaying the hierarchy of victimisation identified by Carrabine *et al.* (2004). At the bottom of this hierarchy of vulnerability would be the homeless, the drug addict, the street prostitute: all those for whom their lifestyle renders them prone to victimisation (vulnerable but denied true victim status); and nearer the top would be the elderly female victim of violent crime (the least prone to such crime, but assumed to be vulnerable and readily assigned legitimate victim status). Hidden from view, but nonetheless illuminating the power of this hierarchy, would be, for example, young offenders who find themselves incarcerated: invisible, victims and vulnerable (Goldson and Cole 2005), and men for whom the cultural expectations associated with masculinity (as explored in Chapter 2) make it difficult for them to think of themselves either as victims or as vulnerable.

Thus vulnerability, rather like responsibility, is informed by structural processes, including gender. This renders the relationship between victimisation, responsibility and vulnerability complex. It is clear that there is neither a simple nor a linear relationship between these concepts and their capacity to make sense of people's everyday lives. The ways in which these concepts are manifested in policy along gendered and other dimensions is also not simple. However, it is evident from the discussion here that their presence in criminal justice policy, criminology and victimology is intimately connected with the rising recognition of the nature of the fear of crime, the embrace of risk (particularly within the development of the criminal victimisation survey and risk assessment practices), the contemporary preoccupations with security as a 'big noun', and the increasing creep of vulnerability found within and across all of these domains.

Conclusion

This chapter has sought to illustrate the complex ways in which gender frames some of the key concepts with which criminologists and victimologists work. As has been suggested here, gender is not the only variable that may inform these concepts and practices, and there is still some considerable work to be done to understand how and under what circumstances gender is the *salient* variable. Moreover, much of the work referred to here is also illustrative of the theoretical and conceptual preoccupations of those working within the Northern hemisphere. Indeed, Cunneen and Rowe (2015: 27) point out that (in addition to developing a much more subtle appreciation of the salience of gender):

> there is a need for a much deeper understanding of Indigenous ontologies and the way in which the 'self' is understood in connectivity to the social, physical and spiritual world. The centrality of interrelationality to Indigenous worldviews means that the understandings of particular situations and contexts, and the decisions which people make, are formed from within a worldview that is in strong contrast to colonising assumptions regarding individual decision making based on autonomous self-interest.

The questions posed by these authors require more than a greater sensitivity to difference, and/or modifying existing (criminal justice) systems and practices to take account of the complex relationship Indigenous people may have with such systems (see e.g. Marchetti and Daly 2016). They also require more than 'simply' inserting women's voices into the process and/or improving criminal justice policies and practices, though there is without doubt much that could be achieved on each of these fronts. The questions here (as alluded to in Chapter 1) are epistemological: What kind of knowledge counts and who can speak and be heard on that knowledge? This question re-emerges in the chapters that follow.

Recommendations for further reading

The suggestions below are intended to stretch the reader's understanding of the concepts introduced and interrogated in this chapter. It may be worth reflecting on the extent to which gender features in any of them and if so to what extent it is visible or invisible as a concept.

Garland, D. (2001) *The Culture of Control*. Oxford: Oxford University Press.

Green, S. (2007) Crime, victimisation and vulnerability. In S. Walklate (ed.) *Handbook of Victims and Victimology* (1 edition). Cullompton, Devon; Willan, pp. 91–118.

Kelly, L. (1988) *Surviving Sexual Violence*. Oxford: Polity Press.

Lee, M. (2007*) Inventing Fear of Crime*. Cullompton, Devon: Willan.

Mythen, G. (2014) *Understanding The Risk Society*. London: Palgrave.

References

Aas, K.F. (2012) 'The Earth is but one but the world is not': criminological theory and its geopolitical divisions. *Theoretical Criminology* 16(1): 5–20.

Ansbro, M. (2010) The nuts and bolts of risk assessment: when the clinical and actuarial conflict. *Howard Journal of Criminal Justice* 49(3): 252–268.

Barlow, C. (2016) *Coercion and Women Co-offenders*. Bristol: Policy Press.

Bernstein, P.L. (1996) *Against the Gods: The Remarkable Story of Risk*. New York: Wiley.

Bessant, C. (2015) Protecting victims of domestic violence: Have we got the balance right? *Journal of Criminal Law* 79(2): 102–121.

Bosworth, M. and Fili, A. (2013) Corrections, gender-specific programming and offender re-entry. In C. Renzetti, S. Miller and A. Gover (eds) *Routledge International Handbook of Crime and Gender Studies*. London: Routledge, pp. 231–242.

Bourbeau, P. (ed.) (2015) *Security: Dialogue Across Disciplines*. Cambridge: Cambridge University Press.

Broadhurst, K., Hall, C., Wastell, D., White, S. and Pithouse, A. (2010) Risk, instrumentalism and the humane project in social work: identifying the informal logics of risk management in children's statutory services. *British Journal of Social Work* 40(4): 1046–1064.

Butler, J. (2009) *Frames of War: When Is a Life Grievable?* London: Verso.

Campbell, J. (2004) Helping women understand their risk in situations of intimate partner violence. *Journal of Interpersonal Violence* 19(12): 1464–1477.

Campbell, J., Webster, D.W. and Glass, N. (2009) The danger assessment: validation of a lethality risk assessment instrument for intimate partner femicide. *Journal of Interpersonal Violence* 24(4): 653–674.

Carlen, P. (2008) Imaginary penalities and risk crazed governance. In P. Carlen (ed.) *Imaginary Penalities*. Cullompton, Devon: Willan Publishing, pp. 1–25.

Carlen, P., Hicks, J., O'Dwyer, J., Christina, D. and Tchaikovsky, C. (1985) *Criminal Women*. Oxford: Blackwell.

Carrabine, E., Inganski, P., Lee, M., Plummer, K. and South, N. (2004) *Criminology: A Sociological Introduction*. London: Routledge

Chan, W, and Rikagos, G. (2002) Risk, crime and gender. *British Journal of Criminology* 42(4): 743–761.

Chesney-Lind, M. and Pasko, L. (2004) *The Female Offender: Girls, Women and Crime*. London: Sage.

Cobbe, F. Power (1878) Wife torture in England. *The Contemporary Review* 32: 55–87.

Connell, R. (2016) 100 million Kalashnikovs: gendered power on a world scale debate. *Feminista* 51: 3–17.

Crawford, A. (2014) Thinking about sustainable security; metaphors, paradoxes and ironies. In M. Schuillenberg, R. van Steden and B. Oude Brueil (eds) *Positive Criminology: Reflections on Care, Belonging and Security*. The Hague: Eleven Publishing, pp. 33–56.

Crawford, A. and Hutchinson, S. (2016) Mapping the contours of 'everyday security': time, space, and emotion. *British Journal of Criminology* 56(6): 1184–1202.

Cunneen, C. (2014) Access to justice for Aboriginal people in the Northern Territory. *Australian Journal of Social Issues* 49(4): 219–242.

Cunneen, C. and Rowe, S. (2015) Decolonising indigenous victimisation. In D. Wilson and S. Ross (eds) *Crime, Victims and Policy: International Contexts, Local Experiences.* London: Palgrave, pp. 10–32.

Das, V. (2007) *Life and Words; Violence and the Descent into the Ordinary.* Berkeley: University of California Press.

Davidson, J. and Chesney-Lind, M. (2009) Discounting women: context matters in risk and need assessment. *Critical Criminology* 17: 221–245.

Dekeseredy, W.S. and Rennison, C.M. (2013) Comparing female victims of separation/divorce assault across geographical regions. *International Journal for Crime, Justice and Social Democracy* 2(1): 65–81.

Dobash, R. and Dobash, R. (1980) *Violence against Wives.* Shepton Mallet: Open Books.

Dobash, R.E. and Dobash, R. (1992) *Women, Violence and Social Change.* London: Routledge.

Evans, K., Fraser, P. and Walklate, S. (1996) Whom can you trust? The politics of grassing on an inner city estate. *Sociological Review* 44(3): 361–380.

Fanghanel, A. (2014) Approaching/departure: effacement, rasure and 'undoing' the fear of crime. *Cultural Geographies* 21: 323–341.

Farrall, S., Jackson, J. and Gray, E. (2009) *Social Order and the Fear of Crime in Contemporary Times.* Oxford: Oxford University Press.

Feeley, M. and Simon, J. (1994) Actuarial justice: the emerging new criminal law. In D. Nelken (ed.) *The Futures of Criminology.* London: Sage, pp. 173–201.

Fitz-Gibbon, K. and Walklate, S. (eds). (2016) *Homicide, Gender and Responsibility: An International Perspective.* London: Routledge.

Fitz-Gibbon, K. and Walklate, S. (2017) The efficacy of Clare's Law in domestic violence law reform in England and Wales. *Criminology and Criminal Justice* 17(3): 284–300.

Froestad, J., Shearing, C. and Van der Merwe, M. (2015) Criminology: reimagining security. In P. Bourbeau (ed.) *Security: Dialogue Across Disciplines.* Cambridge: Cambridge University Press, pp. 177–195.

Garland, D. (2001) *The Culture of Control.* Oxford: Oxford University Press.

Genn, H. (1988) Multiple victimisation. In M. Maguire and J. Ponting (eds) *Victims of Crime: A New Deal?* Buckingham: Open University Press, pp. 88–98.

Goldson, B. and Cole, D. (2005) *In the Care of the State? Child Deaths in Custody in England and Wales.* London: Inquest.

Goodey, J. (1994) Fear of crime? What can children tell us? *International Review of Victimology* 3: 195–210.

Green, S. (2007) Crime, victimisation and vulnerability. In S. Walklate (ed.) *Handbook of Victims and Victimology* (1st edition). Cullompton, Devon: Willan Publishing, pp. 91–118.

Hannah-Moffatt, K. (2006) Pandora's box: risk/need and gender responsive corrections. *Criminology and Public Policy* 5(1): 183–191.

Heckert, D.A. and Gondolf, W. (2004) Battered women's perceptions of risk versus risk factors and instruments in predicting repeat reassault. *Journal of Interpersonal Violence* 19(7): 778–800.

Hollway, W. and Jefferson, T. (1997) The risk society in an age of anxiety: situating fear of crime. *British Journal of Sociology* 48(2): 255–266.

Hoyle, C. (2008) Will she be safe? A critical analysis of risk assessment in domestic violence cases. *Children and Youth Services Review* 30(3): 323–337.

Hudson, B. and Ugelvik, S. (2012) Introduction: new landscapes of security and justice. In B. Hudson and S. Ugelvik (eds) *Justice and Security in the 21st Century*. London: Routledge, pp. 1–5.

Jordan, J. (2011) Silencing rape, silencing women. In J. Brown and S. Walklate (eds) *Handbook on Sexual Violence*. London: Routledge, pp. 253–286.

Kelly, L. (1988) *Surviving Sexual Violence*. Oxford: Polity Press.

Kelly, L. (2011) Preface. In J. Brown and S. Walklate (eds) *Handbook on Sexual Violence*. London: Routledge, pp. xvii–xxvi.

Kemshall, H. (2010) Risk rationalities in contemporary social work policy and practice. *British Journal of Social Work* 40(4): 1247–1262

Kemshall, H. and Maguire, M. (2001) Public protection, partnership, and risk penality: the multi-agency risk management of sexual and violent offenders. *Punishment and Society* 3(2): 237–264.

Killias, M. and Clerici, C. (2000) Different measures of vulnerability and their relation to different dimensions of fear of crime. *British Journal of Criminology* 40(3): 437–450.

Kruttschnitt, C. (2016) The politics, and place, of gender in research on crime. *Criminology* 54(1): 8–29.

Lee, M. (2007) *Inventing Fear of Crime: Criminology and the Politics of Anxiety*. Cullompton, Devon: Willan Publishing.

Lee, M. (2017) Fear, vulnerability and victimisation. In P. Davies, P. Francis and C. Greer (eds) *Victims, Crime and Society: An Introduction* (2nd edition). London: Sage, pp. 127–145.

Lewis, R. and Greene, J.R. (1978) Implementation evaluation: a future direction in project evaluation. *Journal of Criminal Justice* 6: 167–176.

Listerborn, C. (2015) Geographies of the veil: violent encounters in urban public spaces in Malmö, Sweden. *Social & Cultural Geography* 16(1): 95–115.

Lucashenko, M. (1996) Violence against Indigenous women: public and private dimensions. *Violence Against Women* 2(4): 378–390.

Lyng, S. (1990) Edgework: a social psychological analysis of voluntary risk taking. *American Journal of Sociology* 95(4): 851–886.

Mahoney, M. (1991) Legal images of battered women: redefining the issue of separation. *Michigan Law Review* 90(1): 1–94.

Marchetti, E. and Daly. K. (2016) Indigenous partner violence, Indigenous sentencing courts and pathways to desistance. *Violence Against Women* online first. doi: 10.1177/1077801216663241.

McCulloch, J., Maher, J.M., Fitz-Gibbon, K., Segrave, M. and Roffee, J. (2016) Review of the Family Violence Risk Assessment and Management Framework (CRAF) Final Report. Available at www.monash.edu Melbourne.

Medina, A.J., Robinson, A. and Myhill, A. (2016) Cheaper, faster, better: expectations and achievements in police risk assessment of domestic abuse. *Policing*. Advance access. doi:10.1093/police/paw023.

Miller, J. (2002) The strengths and limits for 'doing gender' for understanding street crime. *Theoretical Criminology* 6(4): 433–460.

Morgan, R. (1989) *The Demon Lover: On the Sexuality of Terrorism*. New York: Norton Books.

Muncie, J. (2013) Responsibilization. In E. McLaughlin and J. Muncie (eds) *The Sage Dictionary of Criminology*. London: Sage, pp. 382–383.

Myers, R.R. and Wakefield, S. (2014) Sex, gender and imprisonment: rates, reforms, lived realities. In R. Gartner and

B. McCarthy (eds) *The Oxford Handbook of Sex, Gender and Crime*. Oxford: Oxford University Press, pp. 572–593.

Mythen, G. (2014) *Understanding the Risk Society*. London: Palgrave.

Mythen, G. and Walklate, S. (2008) Terrorism, risk and international security: the perils of asking what if? *Security Dialogue* 39(2–3): 221–242.

Mythen, G. and Walklate, S. (2016) Counterterrorism and the reconstruction of (in)security: divisions, dualisms, duplicities. *British Journal of Criminology* 56(6): 1107–1124.

Mythen, G., Walklate, S. and Khan, F. (2009) 'I'm a Muslim, but I'm not a terrorist': victimization, risky identities and the performance of safety. *British Journal of Criminology* 49(6): 736–754.

Naffine, N. (1990) *Law and the Sexes*. London: Allen and Unwin.

O'Malley, P. (2004) *Risk and Uncertainty*. London: Glasshouse Press.

O'Malley, P. (2006) Criminology and risk. In G. Mythen and S. Walklate (eds) *Beyond the Risk Society*. London: McGraw-Hill, pp. 43–58.

O'Malley, P. (2009) Responsibilisation. In A. Wakefield and J. Fleming (eds) *The Sage Dictionary of Policing*. London: Sage, pp. 276–278.

Pain, R. (2003) Old age and victimisation. In P. Davies, P. Francis and V. Jupp (eds) *Victimisation: Theory, Research and Policy*. London: Palgrave, pp. 61–78.

Pain, R. (2012) Everyday terrorism: how fear works in domestic abuse. Centre for Social Justice and Community Action, Durham University and Scottish Women's Aid.

Ranasinghe, P. (2013) Discourse, practice and the production of the polysemy of security. *Theoretical Criminology* 17(1): 89–109.

Robinson, A. and Rowlands, J. (2009) Assessing and managing risk among different victims of domestic abuse: limits of a generic model of risk assessment. *Security Journal* 22(3): 190–204.

Robinson, A.L., Pinchevsky, G.M. and Guthrie, J. (2016) A small constellation: risk factors informing police perceptions of domestic abuse. *Policing and Society*. doi: 10.1080/10439463.2016.1151881.

Russell, D. (1990) *Rape in Marriage*. Indiana: Indiana University Press.

Sanders, T. (2005) *Sex Work; A Risky Business*. Cullompton, Devon: Willan Publishing.

Shalhoub-Kevorkian, N. (2003) Reexamining femicide: breaking the silence and crossing 'scientific' borders. *Signs* 28(2): 581–608.

Shalhoub-Kevorkian, N. (2015) The politics of birth and the intimacies of violence against Palestinian women in occupied East Jerusalem. *British Journal of Criminology* 55(6): 1187–1206.

Sparks, R.F. (1982) *Research on Victims of Crime: Accomplishments, Issues, and New Directions.* Rockville, MD: US Department of Health and Human Services.

Sparks, R. (1992) Reason and unreason in 'left realism': some problems in the constitution of the fear of crime. In R. Matthews and J. Young (eds) *Issues in Realist Criminology.* London: Sage, pp. 119–135.

Stanko, E.A. (1985) *Intimate Intrusions: Women's Experience of Male Violence.* London: Virago.

Stanko, E.A. (1990) *Everyday Violence.* London: Verso.

Stanko, E. (1993) Ordinary fear: women, violence and personal safety. In P. Bart and E. Moran (eds) *Violence against Women: The Bloody Footprints.* London: Sage, pp. 155–164.

Stanko, E.A., (1997) Safety talk; conceptualising women's risk assessment as a technology of the soul. *Theoretical Criminology* 1(4): 479–499.

Stanko, E.A. and Hobdell, K. (1993) Assaults on men; masculinity and male violence. *British Journal of Criminology* 33(3): 400–415.

Valverde, M. (2014) Studying the governance of crime and security: space, time and jurisdiction. *Criminology and Criminal Justice* 14(4): 379–391.

Walklate, S. (1997) Criminal victimisation and risk: a modernist dilemma? *British Journal of Criminology* 37(1): 35–45.

Walklate, S. (1999) Is it possible to assess risk? *Risk Management: An International Journal* 1(4): 45–53.

Walklate, S. (2004) *Gender, Crime and Criminal Justice* (2nd edition). Cullompton, Devon: Willan Publishing.

Walklate, S. (2011) Reframing criminal victimization: finding a place for vulnerability and resilience. *Theoretical Criminology* 15(2): 179–194.

Walklate, S. (2017) Criminology, gender, and risk: the dilemmas of Northern theorising for Southern responses to intimate partner violence. Paper presented to the Crime and Justice in Asia and the Global South Conference, Cairns, July.

Walklate, S. (forthcoming) Women as fearing subjects? In G. Mythen and M. Lee (eds) *The Routledge International Handbook on Fear of Crime.* London: Routledge.

Walklate, S. and Mythen, G. (2008) How scared are we? *British Journal of Criminology* 48(2): 209–225.

Walklate, S. and Mythen, G. (2011) Risk beyond calculability and theory: experiential knowledge and 'knowing otherwise'. *Criminology and Criminal Justice* 11(2): 99–113.

Walklate, S. McCulloch, J., Fitz-Gibbon, K. and Maher, J.M. (2017) Criminology, gender and security in the Australian context: making women's lives matter. *Theoretical Criminology* online first. doi /10.1177/1362480617719449.

Warr, M. (1985) Fear of rape among urban women. *Social Problems* 32(3): 238–250.

Westmarland, N. (2011) Co-ordinating responses to domestic violence. In J. Brown and S. Walklate (eds) *Handbook of Sexual Violence*. London: Routledge-Willan, pp. 287–307.

Young, J. (1987) The tasks of a realist criminology. *Contemporary Crises* 2: 337–356.

Young, J. (2011) *The Criminological Imagination*. Cambridge: Polity Press.

Zedner, L. (2009) *Security*. London: Routledge.

Chapter 4

GENDERING (SEXUAL) VIOLENCE

Introduction

What is understood as violence is highly contested. As a concept it has been differently defined to foreground its structural characteristics (Galtung 1969), its symbolic features (Zizek 2008) alongside the more commonly understood physical harm caused by one person to another. How violence is defined, identified, understood and accounted for is also contested within criminology and victimology. Within criminology, violence in the street, as opposed to violence in the home, as opposed to the violence(s) of the state, have each been viewed conventionally as separate and separable arenas of inquiry. Perhaps more importantly, as Barberet (2014) has pointed out, criminology and victimology have assumed for the most part that their respective concerns with violence and its victims have been with the violence(s) of peacetime rather than with the violence(s) of war. Yet it is increasingly evident that whether in times of peace or in times of war, sexual violence and the recourse to violence has commonly recurring features. This is particularly the case when consideration is given to who the perpetrators of sexual violence are (mostly men) and who its victims are (mostly women and children).

The purpose of this chapter is to centre these commonly recurring features of sexual violence as one way of bringing to the fore the extent to which sexual violence, whether occurring in peacetime, wartime or in post-conflict situations, is highly gendered. It is important to note that the focus on sexual violence adopted here needs necessarily to be situated in the light of the recourse to violence more generally. In addition, in thinking about the relationship between these two features of violence, this chapter also points to the complex relationship between sex, gender and violence more broadly. Thus, for the purposes of this discussion, it is neither assumed that all males are by definition violent, nor is it assumed that all females by definition cannot be violent. In addition, following the lead of Barberet (2014), this chapter will both transgress and blur the traditional boundaries informing the more conventional consideration of the relationship between gender and sexual violence within criminology and victimology.

Blurring the boundaries: criminology, victimology and sexual violence

Many of the voices associated with the emergence of second-wave feminism (as discussed in Chapter 1) transgressed the conventional criminological focus on what Froestad *et al.* (2015) have referred to as 'hitting and taking'. That conventional focus confined the criminological gaze to the interpersonal harms of the street and, while the violence(s) of rape, for example, were included in that gaze it was a vision which presumed the assailant to be a stranger and the victim to be complicit in her attack (or why else would she be out unescorted on the street at night). Those second-wave feminist voices did much to challenge this vision and to direct the criminological gaze to the sexual violence(s) occurring behind closed doors between people known to each other. These voices by implication challenged the presumptions of victim-blaming implied in the notion of complicity. Much of this work is now well established in the criminological and the victimological canon. However, it is also important to note that some of these same feminist voices placed the violence(s) of war, especially sexual violence(s), in the same frame as those on the street and/or behind closed doors. Notable in this regard is Susan Brownmiller's (1975) seminal work, *Against our Will*. It has taken some time for her vision of violence to reappear on the criminological and victimological horizons.

There are two conceptual devices which enabled radical feminists in particular to place these assumed different spheres of violence in the same plane: the concept of patriarchy and the concept of a continuum. While the concept of patriarchy has been subjected to significant refinement since the 1970s, its assertion led both criminology and victimology to a far more nuanced understanding of men, masculinities, and the maleness of the crime problem and its patterns of criminal victimisation (see Chapter 2). Yet at the same time, as Connell (2016: 15) has observed, the presence of patriarchal social relations remain telling:

> Not just a power-oriented masculinity but also a cultivated callousness is involved in organizing abductions of girls, suicide

bombings, femicide, beheadings, and mass addiction. It seems close to the callousness involved in drone strikes, mass sackings, structural adjustment programmes, nuclear armaments, and the relentless destruction of our common environment.

Similarly, the concept of a continuum, implied in the quote from Connell above, facilitates the connections she outlines. This concept has been deployed by different writers in different ways. In the context of criminology, Kelly (1988) introduced the concept of a 'continuum of sexual violence' which emanated from listening to women's voices. Listening to women's voices and their experiences of sexual violence and its impact centred those experiences in how to make sense of such violence(s) in ways not previously acknowledged within the discipline. Kelly's concept put women's experiences from 'flashing' to murder, from those occurring in public to those occurring in private, from single offences to multiple offences, from single offenders to multiple offenders, all in the same conceptual plane. This was violence as experienced by women over and through time. Kelly's work has fundamentally challenged conventional thinking preoccupied by thinking about these 'offences' as separate and separable. In a parallel vein, Cockburn (2013) offers a further transgressive challenge to traditional bounded thinking on violence. She suggests thinking of continua rather than a single continuum:

> For instance, a continuum of scale of force: so many pounds per square inch when a fist hits a jaw; so many more when a bomb hits a military target. A continuum on a social scale: violence in a couple, in a street riot, violence between nations. And place: a bedroom, a street, a police cell, a continent. Time: during a long peace, pre-war, in armed conflict, in periods we call 'postconflict'. And then type of weapon: hand, boot, machete, gun, missile.
>
> (www.cynthiacockburn.org)

Again, Cockburn (2013), like Kelly (1988), challenges the conventional criminological and victimological presumption that the violence(s) reflected in each of these continua involve analytically separate and separable phenomena.

Taken together, these interventions comprise a continuum of violence (*qua* Bourke 2015), and in gendering sexual violence they point to the importance for both criminology and victimology to consider a wide range of places and contexts in which such violence(s) might occur. Barbaret (2014), as alluded to above, suggests this means encompassing wartime and post-conflict situations as a constituent part of, and important extension to, the criminological and victimological preoccupation with peacetime violence(s) against women. Importantly, this approach also demands the inclusion of a wider range of violent behaviours than usually embraced by conventional criminology and victimology. Barbaret (2014) argues that this means taking the 1993 *United Nations Declaration on Eliminating Violence against Women* on board.

Article 2 of the 1993 Declaration states:

> Violence against women shall be understood to encompass, but not be limited to, the following:
>
> (a) Physical, sexual and psychological violence occurring in the family, including battering, sexual abuse of female children in the household, dowry-related violence, marital rape, female genital mutilation and other traditional practices harmful to women, non-spousal violence and violence related to exploitation;
>
> (b) Physical, sexual and psychological violence occurring within the general community, including rape, sexual abuse, sexual harassment and intimidation at work, in educational institutions and elsewhere, trafficking in women and forced prostitution;
>
> (c) Physical, sexual and psychological violence perpetrated or condoned by the State, wherever it occurs. (United Nations A/RES/48/104, 20 December 1993)

Noting that this Declaration was made in 1993, criminology and victimology have been slow to follow in its wake in recognising a number of these issues as legitimate areas of their respective disciplinary concerns, particularly in relation to item (c). Moreover, the agenda set by this declaration blurs the traditional bounded thinking within each of these disciplines in relation to these kinds of behaviours and their consequences, and lends some weight to the observation made by Connell (2016) quoted above. This agenda also serves to remind us that much of this behaviour and its consequences are not only gendered, they are also sexual, and can be directed towards children in general and female children in particular. Its sexual nature is an important feature of the issues addressed in this chapter and requires further explication.

Heberle (2014: 59) has commented:

> Violence in itself is a particularly egregious harm that in most criminal justice systems warrants harsher punishments than other kinds of harm (against property or reputation). [.] Modify violence with the term *sexual* and questions of consent, desire, identity in relationship to gender, sex, and sexuality are invoked.

Thus she points to the complex interplay between gender, sex and sexuality in making sense of sexual violence. This is an interplay that is differently nuanced in different cultures at different historical moments. For example, the contributions of D'Cruze (2011), McGregor (2011) and Bell *et al.* (2011), when taken together, suggest that despite evolving understandings of sexuality and sexual norms, the historical traces of being 'thrown down' (a historical reference to being sexually assaulted) remain intractable and resonate down the centuries. Indeed, it is to be noted that in some parts of the world certain historical practices and laws have re-emerged in the name of religious purity (see e.g. Carrington 2015). Indeed, MacKinnon (1989: 92) has similarly noted the salience of sex in terms of the motivations for and carrying out of sexual assaults, commenting:

> Battery as violence denies its sex-specific nature. I think that it is done sexually to women. Not only in where it is done – over half the incidents are in the bedroom, or in respect of the surrounding events – the precipitating sexual jealousy.

Other complexities come to the fore in considering different socio-economic and cultural contexts. For example, the 'Delhi rape case', which received wide media coverage and animated political reform debate in 2012, demands to be understood in relation to religion, caste, demography and changing socio-economic processes as well as gender relations (Sharma and Bazilli 2014). At the same time it is also well recognised that male sexual propriety features as a characteristic of intimate partner homicide across a wide range of different cultural contexts (Wilson and Daly 1992; Polk 1994), as does the thrill of sexual conquest associated with rape (see Cameron and Fraser 1987; Scully and Marolla 1993). Rape is like 'riding the bull at Gilley's', as one of Scully and Marolla's respondents said (Scully and Marolla 1993: 41), intimating both power and sex as underpinning the act (see also Yllö and Torres (2016) on marital rape).

In recognising the kind of complexity underpinning sexual violence, it is possible to appreciate how such violence becomes 'folded into everyday life': an 'intertwining of the descent into the ordinary' in which 'ordinary people become scarred' (Das 2007: 14). The ordinariness of violence of this kind is captured in the United Nations' 1993 Declaration which brings to the fore taken-for-granted cultural practices (for example, female genital mutilation, forced sterilisation and female infanticide) as well as implying the important role that state-sponsored violence(s) play in harming women (and children). This is the ordinary violence of conflict and post-conflict contexts. In explicitly noting such acts, the Declaration provides an important framework through which the harms of intimate partner violence can be better recognised and responded to. This is an ordinariness that also includes men, not solely as perpetrators but also as victims of sexual violence(s).

Once such ordinariness is recognised, the enormity of the challenge such an agenda poses for criminology and victimology becomes transparent. This challenge not only poses questions for how both areas of investigation conceptualise what may count or not count as sexual violence, it also poses questions about how to count such violence and, once counted, how to make sense of what such counting reveals. Put another way, it asks both areas of investigation to reflect upon how their knowledge is gathered (methods) and what theories help make sense of that knowledge (explanation), both of which are invaluable in terms of information prevention and response initiatives. Each of these contexts of sexual violence have been differently interrogated by the different feminisms discussed in Chapter 1. Each of these issues will be briefly outlined here.

Measuring (sexual) violence(s): whose gaze counts?

One of the most contested issues in relation to sexual violence(s) is the ability to assess the size of the problem. It is well established that official statistics, as in those incidents recorded by the police and to an even greater extent the courts, massively under-represent the extent of rape and/or sexual assault. This is the case regardless of jurisdiction or geographical location. The introduction, development and refinement of the criminal victimisation survey from the late 1960s to date sought to offer a better indicator of the extent of such incidents for those countries where this kind of survey is used. However, even that does not overcome the limits of official statistics and, as such, the survey is still subject to a range of problematic issues (see Walklate 2014). The import of such issues relates in part to the tendency within such surveys to measure incidents over a particular time period (as opposed to the feminist preference for prevalence measures offering figures over a lifetime) and in part to the tendency to smooth out cultural differences (Machado *et al.* 2010). Moreover, even when such surveys endeavour to address these issues, Kelly (2011: xxi) observes:

> [Few surveys] ask about the everyday intrusions in which women's personal space and being with their self is intruded upon: what is measured counts, and not counting means that the everydayness of violence is again hidden, minimised and trivialised.

Indeed, the United Nations' (2010: 127) own statistical report states:

> Current statistical measurements of violence against women provide a limited source of information, and statistical definitions and classifications require more work and harmonization at the international level.

Walby *et al.* (2017) subject the implications of this lack of harmonisation around definition and measurement practices to serious interrogation, suggesting the need for a wide range of international, regional, national and other organisations to come to an agreement of what counts as violence and how to count it.

The possibility for such moves notwithstanding, the World Health Organisation (WHO 2013), reporting on intimate partner violence as a health issue, suggests that, overall, 35 per cent of women worldwide have experienced either physical and/or sexual intimate partner violence or non-partner sexual violence. Globally, intimate partners commit as many as 38 per cent of all murders of women. The WHO report goes on to suggest that the impact of this kind of violence may be discerned in other health problems, with 16 per cent of women in violent relationships more likely to have a low-birth-weight baby, are twice as likely to have an abortion and almost twice as likely to experience depression, all of which carry economic costs (see further Walby 2004). These figures, despite their narrow focus, provide a useful indicator of the nature and extent of sexual violence more generally picked up in the themes developed later in this chapter.

Of course, it should be noted that the issues highlighted above have so far only been discussed in relation to the kinds of violence(s) criminology and victimology have increasingly recognised: the violence(s) of the street and the violence(s) behind closed doors. Indeed, even in these well-established areas of criminological and victimological investigation some gazes have counted more than others. Historically this has been particularly the case in those gazes minimising and/or trivialising the nature and extent of sexual violence which is all too often reflected in stereotypical beliefs that share much in common across the globe (see e.g. the UN Report on Thailand and Vietnam 2017). Nevertheless, when conflict and post-conflict situations are added in, what counts as sexual violence and how it is counted can be compounded by different though no less problematic issues associated with how to establish the evidence. Buss (2014) discusses these issues in some detail. The desire to render women's experiences of sexual violence in conflict and post-conflict situations visible (largely emanating post the events in Rwanda in 1994 and the former

Yugoslavia in 1993) has left some problematic lacunae in the capacity to appreciate the gendered nature of such violence(s). Buss (2014) suggests that the focus on rendering sexual violence visible in such events has facilitated the elision of conflict and post-conflict violence with the rape of women by men. This has resulted in a lack of appreciation of both women's involvement in such violence and the use of sexual violence as a means of humiliating men. The relatively small body of feminist work which has emerged in this arena has brought the sexual violence(s) of conflict and post-conflict situations squarely to the political table (see e.g. True 2012). Criminological voices have lagged behind somewhat and in some respects the tardiness of criminology to come to this particular table is in part explicable by the marginalisation of war more generally from its agenda.

Nonetheless, some criminological and victimological work has endeavoured to embrace conflict and post-conflict situations as important for each of their respective disciplinary concerns with sexual violence. Using a range of methods of data collection, Hagan and Rymond-Richmond (2009), Mullins (2009), 2011), Mullins and Visagaratnam (2015) and Houge (2016) have made important interventions in the criminological domain in recognising sexual and sexualised violence(s) in these situations. Mullins and Visagaratnam (2015) in particular point to the use of such violence(s) against men. Moreover, the collection edited by Letschert *et al.* (2011) offers a significant agenda in this regard for victimology. Yet, this work notwithstanding, as Barbaret (2014) and Buss (2014) observe, much remains to be done in appropriately documenting the nature and extent of these kinds of violence(s) and their relationship with those more conventionally accounted for in peacetime. The relative absence of an appreciation of the sexual violence(s) associated with conflict situations is particularly interesting in relation to victimology, since as an area of investigation its origins are to be found in the aftermath of World War II. Arguably such relative silences (the earlier voices of people like Frances Power Cobbe likening marital violence to torture being exceptional) is intimately connected with the wider social and cultural silences surrounding sexual violence(s) more generally. These silences are not only associated with the global north; they have a strong presence in other parts of the world as well. Directing a global gaze at the question of the nature and extent of sexual violence in peace, conflict and post-conflict situations is indeed challenging particularly when faced with the nature, extent and role of conflict in the global south. For example, in Nigeria the activities of Boko Haram on the one hand and women's role in insurgency on the other (Oriola 2012) are particularly telling for Northern criminological and victimological agendas.

The summary offered here on the question of measurement highlights how that gaze has been directed and what it has been directed towards. As Buss (2014) has commented, the attention paid to Africa in much of this work can distort the bigger picture and hints at some deep intellectual 'fault lines' in thinking around these issues. These fault lines carry very real and practical consequences for *who* is recognised as a victim and *what kinds* of entitlements and responses will follow from such recognition. Thus this brief overview suggests that counting is not only problematic for all practical purposes; it is also problematic politically in relation to whose voices are heard and when. Similar observations can be made concerning the criminological and victimological explanatory gaze.

Explaining sexual violence(s): contesting the gaze

The conventional framing of violence(s) in the street, violence(s) in the home, and the violence(s) of war as separate and separable has not only facilitated their measurement and exploration as separate areas of specialist expertise but it has also facilitated the dominance of particular ways of explaining such violence(s). Conventionally these explanations have privileged the individual as the unit of analysis, as opposed to the institutional, collective and/or the structural. It will be useful to develop the nature of this privileging in a little more detail.

Much of the criminological work from the early 1950s to the late 1970s deployed what Scully (1990) called the 'disease model' of the sexually violent offender (in her particular study, the rapist) which assumed the offender to be in some way mentally or sexually disordered. A decade later this model was revisited in the widely commented on and highly contested views of Thornhill and Palmer (2000) explained as the need to appreciate the nature of male sexual desire. This disease model of explanation was also to be found in the growing concern with parent-to-child sexual abuse in the 1980s, referred to by Parton (1985) as the disease model of parenting. More recently, increasing recognition of paedophilia has reflected similar tendencies. A parallel focus on the individual may be found in that work which has addressed excessive and sexual violence committed by soldiers: a focus on the deviant soldier or the question of the 'spill-over effect' (see, *inter alia*, Walklate and McGarry 2016). All of this work makes differential presumptions about 'stranger danger' with the role of victim classically translated as victim precipitation (as in the highly contested work of Amir 1971) or in the question still frequently asked of women who choose to continue to live with violent partners: Why doesn't she leave? (This is a question that has produced a wealth of research pointing to a range of variables by way of explanation, including personality problems, psychopathology, social isolation, dependency and the cycle of violence thesis: see, *inter alia*, Gelles 1987: 40). Of course the focus on the deviant and/or diseased offender and/or a less than capable victim serves to support widely held cultural myths about sexual violence that have been, and continue to be, sustained over time. Arguably this has been contributed to in the bounded (criminological and victimological) approach to thinking about sexual violence(s) under scrutiny here.

In part as a response to this disease/psychologically deranged individual explanatory focus, in understanding sexual violence the feminist gaze turned its attention in the question of explanation towards the power wielded by all men over all women. For Brownmiller (1975), for example, rape was the weapon by which all men kept all women in a state of fear. A statement like this turns the explanatory focus away from the individual to the structural and asks the question: Who holds power over whom and how is this power expressed? In so doing, it removes the psychologically deranged individual from the equation and puts in its place patriarchal social relationships. As

Chapter 2 has illustrated, this change of direction promoted a wide range of research in criminology (and to a lesser extent victimology) on the maleness of (sexual) crime and its relationship with differently endorsed expressions of normative hegemonic masculinity. Kersten (1996), for example, offered an interestingly nuanced and comparative analysis of the different ways in which masculinity was achieved (or not) in different social contexts in which rape may be seen as a resource for the expression of masculinity. In the context of understanding violence(s) in the home, the focus on male power shifted the explanatory question from why doesn't she leave to why does she stay. The latter question draws attention to the economic and physical constraints of many women's lives in which, socially isolated by their partner, they often believe what their partner says about them, and what will happen to their children should they choose to leave. This has been conceptualised by Stark (2007) and others as 'coercive control' and nonetheless ultimately forces a recognition of 'love matters' (Kuennen 2014).

As was intimated earlier, the exclusive focus on the act of rape by men in much of this work has resulted in some significant exclusions in endeavours to gender sexual violence(s) across the different domains under consideration here. Importantly it denudes sexual violence from its sexual content (however that may be expressed) and hides from view the role of women as perpetrators and men as victims (on this, see Chapter 2), within which of course there is also the question of children. Moreover, despite the significant intervention by much feminist work in foregrounding male power, as Messerschmidt (1993) came to observe, the particular ways in which the expression of gender is accomplished are done so differently across different contexts. This has led to a third explanatory framework focusing attention on the different institutional contexts in which gendered sexual violence(s) are facilitated.

Placing an understanding of sexual violence(s) within their institutionally expressed context permits a more nuanced consideration of 'doing gender'. Thus across peacetime, war and post-conflict situations, in different socio-geographical locations, the gendered nature of sexual violence(s) will be more or less visible depending upon the institutional setting in which it occurs. Moreover, research findings suggest that different institutional values can endorse or challenge the gendered deployment of such violence(s). For example, in many Western societies the institution of the family, and the associated role expectations within the family, has changed markedly over the past fifty years. In the 1950s many women remained silent and were silenced by family and friends on the question of violence in the home. In the twenty-first century such silence is frowned upon, even if still not necessarily adequately dealt with within the criminal justice system (see Chapter 6). However, such changes are not manifested across the globe and are variously mediated by class, caste and religion. Moreover, from this example it is also worth noting the efforts within Western criminal justice systems as institutions to reorient attitudes towards such violence(s) away from responses trivialising violence in the home as 'just a domestic' to taking such incidents more seriously, however inadequate this may still be. Other examples illustrating the importance of the institutional level of explanation relevant to the focus of this chapter may be found, for example, in the ways in which the sexually abused victims of the UK celebrity, Jimmy Savile, were 'hiding in plain sight' (Leavitt 2013: 6) and denied by the British Broadcasting Company. Similar observations concerning the physical and sexual abuse of children in church- and state-run homes (see, *inter alia*, Stanley 2014; Death 2015) are also evident. In the context of wartime sexual violence(s) scholars have pointed to the institutional recognition of such violence(s) as a weapon of war (Mullins 2009), the role of military command systems in endorsing their use, or what Collins (2012: 87) has called 'the emotional tunnel of violent attack'. In all of these examples, the expression of 'doing gender' is hidden, heightened or endorsed within different institutional settings in different ways. What still remains less visible is the role of the state itself in framing the different ways in which these violence(s) are or are not recognised and responded to.

To summarise, these different explanatory gazes focus attention on different levels of analysis and make different kinds of assumptions about sexual violence victims, offenders, and the relationship between the two. Each pays different attention to the import of gender in their explanations and in so doing each offers a different way of making sense of the available empirical evidence. By implication it is easy to discern how contested explanations of sexual violence(s) emerge and what the role of gender may be in those explanations. By way of furthering the analysis of gender offered in this chapter, three substantive areas of concern will be developed in a little more detail in what follows. These areas of concern loosely echo the different levels of analysis discussed here, reflect the central importance of placing an understanding of sexual violence in the context of the continua discussed at the beginning of this chapter, and shift that understanding beyond the bounded thinking found in much contemporary criminological and victimological thought. The three areas to be discussed further are: intimate partner homicide, child sexual abuse in the Catholic Church, and genocide.

Intimate partner homicide

The question of 'domestic' violence and/or intimate partner violence, like many of the other issues addressed in this chapter, has been and still is, highly contested. The nature of this contestation ranges from how this kind of lethal violence is defined (over the decades this has ranged from wife battering, to 'domestic' violence, to intimate partner violence and, in recognition of different cultural contexts, family violence), and how to measure such violence (from the deployment of the conflicts tactics scale developed by Murray Straus and his colleagues in the late 1970s, to prevalence surveys, to criminal victimisation surveys, to research 'by women, with women, for women'). This contestation has generated different answers to the question of who does what to whom and has resulted in an ongoing debate on whether or not men are just as victimised as women in the use of such violence. All of these questions are prompted by the different presumptions framing work in this area. This work often sits uncomfortably among community myths and misconceptions surrounding understandings of sexual violence, including the ever-present question of 'why does she stay' or 'why doesn't she leave'. Such debates notwith-standing when consideration is given to the statistics on the deaths that result from such violence, the evidence is stark.

Set against the bigger picture of homicide statistics in general (which indicate that, overall, men kill each other with the greatest frequency), homicide marking the end of an intimate partner rela-tionship is also a common feature of these same statistics. While as Corradi and Stockl (2014) point out, it is difficult to trace the links between violence in relationships and intimate partner homicide especially comparatively (largely because of different definitional and recording practices), intra-jurisdiction statistics suggest that such links are present. For example, Dobash *et al.* (2004) reported that 76 per cent in their sample of male murderers had experience of rela-tionship breakdown, with 56.9 per cent reporting previous use of violence against their partners (as compared with 60.8 and 34.9 per cent respectively for the men in their sample who murdered other men). Indeed, it is almost a truism of the feminist literature that a woman is at greatest risk when attempting to leave a relationship (see, *inter alia*, Hanmer and Itzin 2000; Dekeseredy and Rennison 2013; Mahoney 1991). The interconnections referred to above are particularly evident in specific cases. A report by Fitz-Gibbon (2016: 7) examining the Australian case of Kelly Thompson clearly demon-strates the significance of this at the individual level:

> In February 2014 43-year-old Kelly Thompson was killed by her former partner, Wayne Wood. At the time of her death, Thomp-son had an intervention order taken out against Wood, a 'jeal-ous and possessive man', which had been breached on at least two occasions (Coronial Inquest 2016: 77). In the months prior to her death, Wood made repeated threats of violence, strangled Thompson and stalked her (Spooner 2015). In the three weeks prior to her death, Thompson called the police on at least 35 occasions, disclosed the violence she was experiencing to friends, neighbours and work colleagues, and made contact with a family violence outreach service (Percy 2015, Coronial Inquest 2016). Three hours before she was killed, Thompson's neighbour called

the police to report that she had seen Wood at the house acting strangely (Davey 2016). Despite the intervention order in place, a police response was not sent to the house (Coroner Inquest 2016). Three hours later Kelly Thompson had been stabbed to death by her former partner, Wayne Wood, who then committed suicide.

Individual cases such as these form part of the story behind the evidence forthcoming from systematic death reviews, which point to histories of abuse, prior threats of strangulation and relationship separation as clear indicators of high risk of homicide and/or very serious injury (Bugeja *et al.* 2013; Dearden and Jones 2008; Virueda and Payne 2010).

Indeed, the number of intimate partner homicides has remained at a consistent level over the past three decades in many Western jurisdictions and in some cases has increased (see e.g. Brennan (2016) in the United Kingdom; Cussen and Bryant (2015) in Australia; Smith *et al.* (2014) in the United States). Crime statistics for England and Wales (Flatley 2016) show that 332 women and 78 men were killed by their partners/ex-partners between March 2012 and March 2015, and the English Femicide Census, published for the first time in 2016, revealed that 598 women had been killed by a current or former partner in the six-year period between 2009 and 2015, a similar rate to that reported in Australia by Cussen and Bryant (2015). Moreover, studies have found that intimate partner violence contributes to more death, disability and illness for women aged 15 to 44 than any other preventable risk factor (VicHealth 2004; WHO, 2013; Webster 2016). These high prevalence rates have led to calls for governments to orient their focus from the public to the private, and to take the safety and security of women more seriously (see e.g. Walklate *et al.* 2017). The question remains: What lies behind these statistics?

In analysing thirty-three intimate partner homicides reported in 2014 to 2015, a Home Office Report on Domestic Homicide Reviews found that just under half (fifteen cases) included dependent children in the family structure; the presence of mental health issues (twenty-five of the thirty-three intimate partner homicides); and in just over half of all domestic homicides (n = 21), substance use was mentioned. Further, in twenty-four of the thirty-three intimate partner homicides the perpetrator had a history of violence; and in six cases the victim had a history of violence towards the perpetrator (Home Office 2016: 3). Not only do these findings support the interconnections commented on above, they also lend some weight to what psychologists working in this field might call the 'toxic trio': that is, the presence of drugs and/or alcohol (probably subsumed by the term 'substance abuse') and mental health problems. While this may lend itself to the psychologically deranged/deviant offender explanation, this small sample does not offer an understanding of the complete picture. In an earlier Australian study Polk (1994) noted the presence of male propriety in cases of homicide involving partners and/or other family; a concept developed by Wilson and Daly (1998) in their use of both sexual jealousy and sexual rivalry to explain the patterning of homicide statistics more generally. The predominant maleness of intimate partner homicide is self-evident and this is the case even in societies that enjoy relatively high levels of gender equality such as Sweden where gendered violence and intimate partner violence and homicides persist (Fundamental Rights Agency 2014).

The concept of a continuum has facilitated an appreciation of the interconnections between the routine and mundane recourse to violence on an everyday basis, as Genn (1988: 97) has said, as being 'just part of life' and the extent to which such violence(s) have gendered characteristics and outcomes. Debates concerning whether the recourse to violence in intimate relationships is equally deployed and experienced by men and women or is a disproportionate response on behalf of men aside, it is the case that women die disproportionately as a result of such violence. The murderer in these cases is not some pathological monstrosity. He is (potentially) any man (Young 1987). In continuing the theme of violence as being 'just part of life', the next example considers what may be learned about the gendered nature of sexual violence by reflecting on the institutional level of analysis. The importance of this level of analysis became particularly prominent at the turn of the twenty-first century implied in the child abuse claims made against the Catholic Church.

Institutional child abuse

At the outset it is important to note that the issue of child abuse, either physical or sexual, is not a new phenomenon. Specific cases have repeatedly brought this issue to the attention of the media, resulting in inquiries of various kinds in a wide range of jurisdictions. It is also important to note that such abuse may occur in a wide range of different settings (from the family, to the school, to the orphanage, to the care home, to the juvenile detention centre) and may involve a wide range of actors (from parents, guardians, siblings and other relatives, to a wide range of individuals charged with the care and protection of the child and/or juvenile) (for a general discussion of these issues see Petrie 2011).

From the mid-1980s onward, increasingly persistent claims concerning the abuse of children in a wide range of institutional settings came to the fore (for a thorough analysis of a substantial number of the cases arising in Canada and Australia see Daly 2016). Earlier work on this issue focused on accounting for and understanding child abuse primarily within the familial setting. This work generated four explanations for the abuse characterised by Morris (1987) as children fantasising, children as seducers, mothers as complicit, and the view that because children were deemed 'innocent' no real harm was done. This focus on the role of the child in their capacity as victim drew attention away from the perpetrator and the power relationships underpinning such abuse. However, when the nature and extent of such abuse came to light (in the context of the UK in particular as a result of the Cleveland Inquiry (Butler-Sloss 1988; Walklate 1989) and elsewhere prompted by the kinds of cases discussed by Daly (2016) and Swain (2015), it became increasingly apparent that such explanations fell short of the mark when placed against the systemic and patterned abuse occurring within institutional settings.

Of course, institutional abuse can be perpetrated on groups of people wider than children and juveniles: for example, the elderly and those in prison. Moreover, in these settings such abuse can be both gendered and sexualised (for example, the widely reported treatment of prisoners held in Abu Graib). Space dictates that not all of these contexts can be discussed here. Nonetheless, because the institutional abuse of children within the Catholic Church had an international reach, and has been subjected to a wide range of inquiries and processes for seeking redress, for analytical purposes it offers some useful insights into furthering an understanding of the gendered nature of sexual violence(s).

Analysing the claims made to the Australian Royal Commission into Institutional Responses to Child Sex Abuse (2017: 12), the Commission's report states that 90 per cent of the claims made were against Catholic Church authorities with only male members and, of the alleged perpetrators, 90 per cent were male and 10 per cent female (ibid.: 15). Moreover, where the gender (the term used by the Commission) of the complainant was known, 78 per cent were male and 22 per cent female (ibid.: 12). All claimants were between 10 and 12 years old at the time of the alleged offence (ibid.: 13) and most incidents occurred within a school or residential setting. As the summary of this data implies, many of these incidents occurred some time ago. In a similar attempt to assess the nature and extent of child sexual abuse in the Catholic Church in the United States, a report by John Jay College of Criminal Justice (2004) reviewed evidence on cases from 1950 to 2002 indicating that 80.9 per cent of the complainants were male (compared to 19.1 per cent female), the majority of whom lived at home at the time of the incident. This report assumes the maleness of the priesthood over this period of time with the majority of those complained about being unmarried.

These two examples serve to illustrate the wider, recurring patterning of institutional child sex abuse, both pointing to the maleness of this behaviour and importantly the mostly male victims. This patterning adds a significant nuance to understanding the gendered nature of sexual violence under consideration here. Moreover, from the data gathered in the reports referred to above, the nature and extent of the complaints recorded and offered redress challenges explanations that might point to a vision of a pathological or paedophilic offender. This view is certainly challenged in a follow-up study in the United

States conducted by Terry *et al.* (2011), who found that few priests exhibited serious pathological or developmental disorders.

Thus the brief overview given above not only complicates assumptions about the victims and offenders of sexual violence (for example, females were also named as perpetrators in the Australian report); it also complicates understandings of the circumstances under which such violence(s) may be perpetrated: not only in intimate personal relationships associated with the home but also in those private spaces of institutional settings. In these settings the trust imbued between them is violated and the power afforded to individuals working in those settings abused. Arguably, this is particularly problematic when compounded by religious belief. In terms of explanation these examples draw attention to the gendered and sexual nature of both victims and perpetrators with the added appreciation of the enhanced power afforded to such behaviours in organisational and cultural contexts which compound the vulnerability of the victims (see Munro and Fish 2015). When taken together, alongside the evident denial of such a phenomenon in order to secure institutional reputation, Death (2015: 204) points out:

> The central message of this work is that the Catholic Church has resisted responsibility for CSA [child sexual abuse], that power and privilege have been used to facilitate cover up of abuse, and that this has relied on institutional power, thus causing direct harm to victims of CSA and, accordingly, should be understood and discussed as institutional abuse.

Thus an appreciation of institutional abuse leads inexorably to an appreciation of the practices of the institution itself above and beyond the behaviour of individuals comprising that institution and to a consideration of the interconnections between the two. Indeed, Stanley (2014) pushes this kind of analysis further, encouraging a consideration of the role of the state. For the purposes of this chapter, this is taken to mean the role of the gendered state. Recognition of this leads indirectly to the third example to be explored here: genocide.

Chapter 4

Genocide

As was intimated earlier in this chapter, understandings of gendered sexual violence(s) in conflict and post-conflict situations have, until recently, been marginalised in much criminological and victimological endeavour. Nonetheless, as some of the work highlighted in that earlier discussion has demonstrated, the question of gender remains a salient feature of violence in these contexts. For the purposes of furthering an understanding of sexual violence(s) in these situations, this discussion will take a brief look at the gendered nature of violence(s) associated with genocide.

Alvarez (2010) has indicated that different genocides arise in different ways and are differently motivated. However, what they have in common is a planned and organised rationale in which people are exterminated for who they are rather than for what they have done (Jamieson 1999). That this rationale is also gendered – that is, it differently targets men and women – was captured by Jones (2000) in his particular concept of gendercide. This interpretation conjures sex-selectivity in terms of victims, perpetrators and behaviours. For example, in some genocides there is evidence that young men were singled out to be 'disappeared' (as in Kosovo or East Timor). Yet other women were singled out for rape to ensure spoiling the heritage of a particular ethnic group (as in Serbia). In one of the most thorough and far-reaching analyses of genocide written from a criminological perspective, Rafter (2016: 170) concludes:

> Genocide, my data show, is *always* a gendered activity. Symbolically rape feminizes the victim group (including men who are raped or otherwise sexually violated), demonstrating its powerlessness, while at the same time it masculinizes the victors.

These processes are not replicated in exactly the same way in all genocides, as the examples discussed by Rafter (2016) illustrate, but they do contribute to the reordering of society in the interests of the perpetrators. The behaviours that contribute to these processes are also sexual. They involve not only a wide variety of sexual acts but also include violating those parts of the body associated with sexual identity or humiliation in the insistence on committing a wide range of sexual acts (often in public) or demanding the nakedness of those so targeted. These include fathers being forced to rape sons and/or daughters, or sons their fathers, the witnessing of sexual torture of family members and so on, some of which was evidenced and documented in the Bosnian context. There is evidence that women also engage in these acts of despoliation towards other women as well as men under these kinds of conflict conditions. These kinds of violence(s) can also be perpetrated and evidenced in more 'conventional' war contexts in which mass killings and atrocities can take on a gendered and sexualised character (see e.g. Altinay and Petö 2016). In terms of explanation, the example of genocide endorses the importance of centring a structural and cultural level of analysis in any understanding of the gendered nature of sexual violence. As Rafter (2016: 180) comments, 'Gender colors the conduct of genocide from start to finish irrespective of whether the event involves genocidal rape.'

Conclusion

This chapter has illustrated how far criminology and victimology have travelled in understanding the nature and extent of sexual violence(s) and its gendered features. In so doing, how much further there is to go. The feminist challenges posed for each of these areas of investigation (highlighted in Chapter 1) are self-evident. Yet it is also evident that these challenges are not simple or straightforward. While feminist input has clearly placed the 'cultivated callousness' of masculinities (Connell 2016: 15) on the agenda, such callousness (as the examples discussed in this chapter have illustrated) is not the sole preserve of men. Men are not always and only the perpetrators of such violence(s). They can also be victims, as women can also be perpetrators of all kinds of violence(s), including sexual violence. Thus the challenge for criminology and victimology is not only to look across their respective domains of investigation to examine the continuities and interconnections between the violence(s) of peacetime and the violence(s) of conflict and post-conflict situations. It is also to examine much more carefully their own use and understanding of the terms sex, gender, masculinity and femininity, the complex interplay between these differing facets of an individual's identity and their variable expression in different socio-cultural contexts. In doing so, it is also important to recognise that there are patterns in the issues discussed here. In analysing these issues it is necessary to take heed of Buss' (2014) observations on the intellectual 'fault lines' in how such analyses are done: to reflect upon what behaviours are being centred and why. Such complexities are important not only intellectually but also in informing policy. This is discussed in Chapter 5.

Recommendations for further reading

It is well worth looking at Susan Brownmiller's (1975) *Against our Will*. This was a ground-breaking book and affords one way into the issues addressed in this chapter. Joanna Bourke's (2015) *Deep Violence* puts the question of violence into the wider context of war and peace, and the edited collection by D. Buss, J. Lebert, B. Rutherford and others, *Sexual Violence in Conflict and Post-conflict Societies* (2014), offers a deep and insightful analysis of the nature of sexual violence in conflict and post-conflict societies. Finally, the seminal works of Liz Kelly's (1988) *Surviving Sexual Violence*, Jan Jordan's (2008) *Serial Survivors: Women's Narratives of Surviving Rape* and Nicole Rafter's (2016) *The Crime of all Crimes: Towards a Criminology of Genocide* provide both theoretically and critical complexity for a criminological and/or victimological analysis of the issues discussed here.

References

Altinay, A.G. and Peto, A. (eds) (2016) *Gendered Wars, Gendered Memories: Feminist Conversations on War, Genocide and Political Violence*. London: Routledge.

Alvarez, A. (2010) *Genocidal Crimes*. London: Routledge.

Amir, M. (1971) *Patterns of Forcible Rape*. Chicago, IL: University of Chicago Press.

Barberet, R. (2014) *Women, Crime, and Criminal Justice*. London: Routledge.

Bell, L.M., Finelli, A. and Wynne-Davies, M. (2011) Sexual violence in literature: a cultural heritage? In J. Brown and S. Walklate (eds) *Handbook of Sexual Violence*. London: Routledge, pp. 52–68.

Bourke, J. (2015). *Deep Violence*. University of California: Counterpoint Press.

Brennan, D. (2016) *Femicide Census Profiles of Women Killed by Men: Redefining an Isolated Incident*. London: Women's Aid.

Brownmiller, S. (1975) *Against our Will*. New York: Bantam Books.

Bugeja, L., Butler, A., Buxton, E., Ehrat, H., Hayes, M., McIntyre, S. and Walsh, C. (2013) The implementation of domestic violence death reviews in Australia. *Homicide Studies* 17(4): 353–374.

Buss, D. (2014) Seeing sexual violence in conflict and post-conflict societies: the limits of visibility. In D. Buss, J. Lebert, B. Rutherford *et al.* (eds) *Sexual Violence in Conflict and Post-conflict Societies*. London: Routledge, pp. 3–27.

Butler-Sloss, E. (1988) *Report of the Inquiry into Child Abuse in Cleveland 1987 Short Version*. London: HMSO.

Cameron, D. and Fraser, E. (1987) *The Lust to Kill*. Oxford: Polity Press.

Carrington, K. (2015) *Feminism and Global Justice*. London: Routledge.

Cockburn, C. (2013) Towards a different common sense. Available at www.cynthiacockburn.org.

Collins, R. (2012) C-escalation and D-escalation: a theory of time-dynamics of conflict. *American Sociological Review* 77(1): 1–20.

Connell, R. (2016) 100 million Kalashnikovs: gendered power on a world scale debate. *Feminista* 51: 3–17.

Corradi, C. and Stockl, H. (2014) Intimate partner homicide in 10 European countries: statistical data and policy development in cross-national perspective. *European Journal of Criminology* 11(5): 601–618.

Cussen, T. and Bryant, W. (2015), Domestic/family homicide in Australia. Research in Practice no. 38, Australian Institute of Criminology.

Daly, K. (2016) *Redressing Institutional Abuse of Children*. Basingstoke: Palgrave-Macmillan.

Das, V. (2007) *Life and Words; Violence and the Descent into the Ordinary*. Berkeley: University of California Press.

D'Cruze, S. (2011) Sexual violence in history: a contemporary heritage? In J. Brown and S. Walklate (eds) *Handbook on Sexual Violence*. London: Routledge, pp. 23–51.

Dearden, J. and Jones, W. (2008) *Homicide in Australia: 2006–07*. National Homicide Monitoring Program, Annual Report, Australian Institute of Criminology.

Death, J. (2015) Bad apples, bad barrel: exploring institutional responses to child sexual abuse by Catholic clergy in Australia. *International Journal for Crime, Justice and Social Democracy* 4(2): 94–110. doi: 10.5204/ijcjsd.v3i2.229.

Dekeseredy, W. and Rennison, C.M. (2013) Comparing female victims of separation/divorce assault across geographical regions. *International Journal for Crime and Justice* 2(1): 65–81.

Dobash, R.E., Dobash, R.P., Cavanagh, K. and Lewis, R. (2004) Not an ordinary killer – just an ordinary guy: when men murder an intimate woman partner. *Violence Against Women* 10(6): 577–605.

Fitz-Gibbon, K. (2016) *The Peter Mitchell Churchill Fellowship to Examine Innovative Legal Responses to Intimate Partner Homicide*. Canberra: Winston Churchill Memorial Trust.

Flatley, J. (2016) *Crime in England and Wales*. London: Home Office Statistical Bulletin.

Froestad, J., Shearing, C. and Van der Merwe, M. (2015) Criminology: reimagining security. In P. Bourbeau (ed.) *Security: Dialogue Across Disciplines*. Cambridge: Cambridge University Press, pp. 177–195.

Fundamental Rights Agency (2014) *Violence against Women: An EU-wide Survey*. Vienna: European Union Agency for Fundamental Rights.

Galtung, J. (1969) Violence, peace, and peace research. *Journal of Peace Research* 6(3): 167–191.

Gelles, R. (1987) *Family Violence*. London: Sage.

Genn, H. (1988) Multiple victimisation. In M. Maguire and J. Pointing (eds) *Victims of Crime: A New Deal?* Buckingham: Open University Press, pp. 90–100.

Hagan, J. and Rymond-Richmond, W. (2009) *Dafur and the Crime of Genocide*. Cambridge: Cambridge University Press

Hanmer, J. and Itzin, C. (2000) *Home Truths about Domestic Violence: Feminist Influences on Policy and Practice: A Reader*. London: Routledge.

Heberle, R. (2014) Sexual violence. In R. Gartner and B. McCarthy (eds) *The Oxford Handbook of Gender, Sex, and Crime*. Oxford: Oxford University Press, pp. 59–79.

Home Office (2016) *Domestic Homicide Reviews: Key Findings from Analysis of Domestic Homicide Reviews*. London: Home Office.

Houge, A.B. (2016) 'He seems to come out as a personally cruel person': perpetrator re-presentations in direct murder cases at the ICTY. In K. Fitz-Gibbon and S. Walklate (eds) *Homicide, Gender and Responsibility: An International Perspective*. London: Routledge, pp. 113–129.

Jamieson, R. (1999). Councils of war. *Criminal Justice Matters* 34(1): 25–29.

John Jay (2004) *The Nature and Scope of Sexual Abuse of Minors by Catholic Priests and Deacons in the United States 1950–2002*. New York: John Jay College of Criminal Justice.

Jones, A. (2000) Gendercide and genocide. *Journal of Genocide Research* 2(2): 185–211.

Kelly, L. (1988) *Surviving Sexual Violence*. Oxford: Polity Press.

Kelly, L. (2011) Preface. In J. Brown and S. Walklate (eds) *Handbook on Sexual Violence*. London: Routledge, pp. xvii–xxvi.

Kersten, J. (1996) Culture, masculinities and violence against women. In T. Jefferson and P. Carlen (eds) *Masculinities, Social Relations and Crime*. Special Issue of the *British Journal of Criminology* 36(3): 381–395.

Kuennen, T. (2014) Love matters. *Arizona Law Review* 56(4): 977–1015.

Leavitt, Q.C.A. (2013) *In the matter of the Late Jimmy Savile. Report to the Director of Public Prosecutions*. London: Crown Prosecution Service.

Letschert, R., Haveman, R., de Brouwer, A-M. and Penberton, A. (eds) (2011) *Victimological Approaches to International Crimes: Africa*. Cambridge: Intersentia.

Machado, C., Dias, A. and Coehlo, C. (2010) Culture and wife abuse: an overview of theory, research and practice. In S.G. Shoham, P. Knepper and M. Kett (eds) *International Handbook of Victimology*. Boca Raton, Fl.: CRC Press, pp. 639–668.

MacKinnon, K. (1989) *Towards a Feminist Theory of the* State. Cambridge, MA: Harvard University Press.

Mahoney, M. (1991) Legal images of battered women: redefining the issue of separation. *Michigan Law Review* 90(1): 1–94.

McGregor, J. (2011) The legal heritage of the crime of rape. In J. Brown and S. Walklate (eds) *Handbook on Sexual Violence*. London: Routledge, pp. 69–89.

Messerschmidt, J. (1993) *Masculinities and Crime*. Maryland: Rowman and Littlefield.

Morris, A. (1987) *Women, Crime and Criminal Justice*. Oxford: Blackwell.

Mullins, C.W. (2009) 'He would kill me with his penis': rape during the Rwandan genocide as a state crime. *Critical Criminology: An International Journal* 17(1): 15–33.

Mullins, C.W. (2011) War crimes in the 2008 Georgia–Russia conflict. *British Journal of Criminology* 51(6): 918–936.

Mullins, C. and Visagaratnam, N. (2015) Sexual and sexualised violence in armed conflict.

In S. Walklate and R.McGarry (eds) *Criminology and War: Transgressing the Borders*. London: Routledge, pp. 139–157.

Munro, E. and Fish, A. (2015) Hear no evil, see no evil: understanding failure to identify and report child sexual abuse in institutional contexts, Royal Commission into Institutional Responses to Child Sexual Abuse, Sydney.

Oriola, T. (2012) The Delta Creeks, women's engagement and Nigeria's oil insurgency. *British Journal of Criminology* 52(3): 534–555.

Parton, N. (1985) *The Politics of Child Abuse*. London: Macmillan.

Petrie, S, (2011) Violence, sex and the child. In J. Brown and S. Walklate (eds) *Handbook of Sexual Violence*. London: Routledge, pp. 331–352.

Polk, K. (1994) *When Men Kill: Scenarios of Masculine Violence*. Cambridge: Cambridge University Press.

Rafter, N. (2016) *The Crime of all Crimes: Towards a Criminology of Genocide*. New York: New York University Press.

Royal Commission into Institutional Responses to Child Sexual Abuse (2017) *Analysis of Claims of Child Sexual Abuse Made with Respect to Catholic Church Institutions in Australia*. Sydney: Royal Commission.

Scully, D. (1990) *Understanding Sexual Violence*. London: Unwin Hyman.

Scully, D. and Marolla, J. (1993) 'Riding the bull at Gilleys': convicted rapists describe the rewards of rape. In P.B. Bart and E.G. Moran (eds) *Violence Against Women: The Bloody Footprints*. London: Sage, pp. 26–46.

Sharma, R. and Bazilli, S. (2014) A reflection on gang rape in India: what's law got to do with it? *International Journal for Crime, Justice and Democracy* 3(3): 4–21.

Smith, S.G., Fowler, K.A. and Niolon, P.H. (2014) Intimate partner homicide and corollary victims in 16 states: National Violent Death Reporting System, 2003–2009. *American Journal of Public Health* 104(3): 461–466.

Stanley, E. (2014) The victimisation of children in state-run homes in New Zealand. In D.L. Rothe and D. Kauzlarich (eds) *Towards a Victimology of State Crime*. London: Routledge, pp. 46–65.

Stark, E. (2007) *Coercive Control*. New York: Oxford University Press.

Swain, S. (2015) Why sexual abuse? Why now? In S. Sköld and S. Swain (eds) *Apologies and the Legacy of Abuse of Children in 'Care': International Perspectives*. Basingstoke: Palgrave-Macmillan, pp. 83–94.

Terry, K., Smith, M.L., Schuth, K. *et al.* (2011) The Cause and Context of Sexual Abuse of Minors by Catholic Priests in the United States 1950–2010. United States Conference of Catholic Bishops, Washington, DC.

Thornhill, C. and Palmer, R. (2000) *A Natural History of Rape: Biological Bases of Sexual Coercion*. Cambridge, MA: MIT Press.

True, J. (2012) *The Political Economy of Violence Against Women*. Oxford: Oxford University Press.

United Nations (2010) The World's Women 2010. Downloaded 23 April 2013.

United Nations (2017) The Trial of Rape: Understanding Criminal Justice System Response to Sexual Violence in Thailand and Viet Nam, November. Downloaded 8 December 2017.

VicHealth (2004) The Health Cost of Violence: Measuring the Burden of Disease Caused by Intimate Partner Violence. Available at www.vichealth.vic.gov.au/search/the-health-costs-of-violence (accessed 12 February 2016).

Virueda, M. and Payne, J. (2010), *Homicide in Australia: 2007–08 National Homicide Monitoring Program, Annual Report*. Australian Institute of Criminology.

Walby, S. (2004) *The Cost of Domestic Violence*. London: DTI.

Walby, S., Towers, J., Balderston, S., Corradi, C., Francis, B.J., Heiskanen, M., Helweg-Larsen, K., Mergaert, L., Olive, P., Palmer,

C.E., Stockl, H. and Strid, S. (2017) *The Concept and Measurement of Violence against Women and Men.* Bristol: Policy Press.

Walklate, S. (1989) *Victimology: The Victim and the Criminal Justice Process.* London: Unwin Hyman.

Walklate, S. (2014) Sexual violence against women? Still a controversial issue for victimology? *International Review of Victimology* 20(1): 71–84.

Walklate, S. and McGarry, R. (2016) Murderousness in war: from Mai Lai to Marine A. In K. Fitzgibbon and S. Walklate (eds) *Gender, Homicide and Responsibility: An International Perspective.* London: Routledge, pp. 97–112.

Walklate, S., McCulloch, J., Fitz-Gibbon, K. and Maher, J.M. (2017) Criminology, gender and security in the Australian context: making women's lives matter. *Theoretical Criminology,* Online First. doi: 10.1177/1362480617719449.

Webster, K. (2016). *A Preventable Burden: Measuring and Addressing the Prevalence and Health Impacts of Intimate Partner Violence in Australian Women* (ANROWS Compass, 07/2016). Sydney: ANROWS.

WHO (World Health Organisation). (2013) *Global and Regional Estimates of Violence against Women: Prevalence and Health Effects of Intimate Partner Violence and Non-partner Sexual Violence.* Geneva: World Health Organisation.

Wilson, M. and Daly, M. (1992) Till death us do part. In J. Radford and D. Russell (eds) *Femicide: The Politics of Woman Killing.* Buckingham: Open University Press, pp. 83–98.

Wilson, M., and Daly, M. (1998) Sexual rivalry and sexual conflict; recurring themes in fatal conflicts. *Theoretical Criminology* 2(3): 291–310.

Yllö, K. and Torres, G. (eds) (2016) *Marital Rape Consent, Marriage, and Social Change in Global Context.* Oxford: Oxford University Press.

Young, J. (1987) Murder most English. *Time Out,* 14–21 January.

Zizek, S. (2008) *Violence: Six Sideways Reflections.* London: Profile Books.

Part III

POLICY

Chapter 5

POLICING GENDER-BASED VIOLENCE

Introduction

The purpose of this chapter is to explore the extent to which questions relating to gender pervade the work of the police generally, and policing of gender-based violence specifically. As noted in earlier chapters, while some gains are evident, there continues to be an uneven distribution of employment patterns between different arms of the criminal justice system with respect to sex. For example, while voluntary and administrative work associated with the criminal justice system is often taken up fairly evenly between the sexes (or in the latter case often has a higher representation of female employees) policing and the judiciary continue to be male-dominated workforces. Other branches of the criminal justice system (for example, prosecution units) fall somewhere between the two extremes. It also continues to be the case in many jurisdictions that the further one moves up the criminal justice process as an employee, the more likely the workforce is to be male dominated. While we acknowledge that this does not make the criminal justice system particularly unique in that similar sexed patterns are replicated across other workforces, it is important to keep in view when analysing the differential ways in which men and women experience the criminal justice system in practice.

Over the past two decades the efforts that have been made to overcome sexed patterns in workforces within the criminal justice system have been varied in their success. The focus in the first half of this chapter is on the gendered nature of police work and in the second half of the chapter the policing of gender-based violence is examined in some detail. In order to do so, examples of policies and policing strategies are examined, including the spread of mandatory arrest policies, the emergence of women-only police stations, debates surrounding whether the policing of gender-based violence should be specialised work, and finally, the move towards private security. While it takes as its central focus the police, the areas explored are relevant to parallel debates that emerge at the prosecution, court and penal branches of the criminal justice system.

What is policing about?

Much of this chapter is centrally concerned with policing – be it the individual officer, the role of the police service as a whole as well as the ability of the police to adequately respond to situations of gender-based violence. As such, and while we acknowledge that there are taken-for-granted presumptions about the work of the police, at the outset it is important to step back and consider a broad question: What is policing about?

'Blue uniform' policing – the focus of much of this chapter – carries with it a specific mandate, specific powers and a specific form of accountability that sits within a wider system of criminal justice. The powers granted to officers to undertake 'blue uniform' policing are extremely varied and are often carried out on a discretionary basis. As Brogden *et al.* (1988: 2, emphasis in original) have described:

> '[B]lue-uniform' policing or *state* policework implies a range of functions, namely, enforcing (and sometimes defining) the criminal law, maintaining order, intelligence gathering, and securing consent, all directed towards a singular end: upholding the general framework of the *state* – by persuasion if possible, violently if necessarily.

When considered together, these features are what equip an officer to uphold law and order. When this is centred on the day-to-day routine this can involve a wide range of roles. As Uglow (1988: 1) observes:

> We all recognise contrasting, even contradictory images of the police – the officer on the beat courteously directing tourists; the patrol car, blue light flashing, speeding in pursuit of a stolen vehicle; massed ranks of policemen clad in helmets, wielding truncheons, confronting demonstrates or strikers; officers talking to school children about road safety or the dangers of glue sniffing; Special Branch officers tapping telephones or opening mails; incident rooms coordinating house-to-house enquires; the village

bobby pushing a bicycle and chatting to customers at the local shop.

These contrasting images of piecework continue to be ever present, despite nearly three decades passing since Uglow's writing. The wide range of roles highlighted illustrate the difficulty faced by officers in making sense of their day-to-day work as well as the difficulties faced by anyone on the receiving end of these different tasks in making sense of the policing role.

The discretion associated with the policing role, and in carrying out each of the duties listed above, equips police officers with (potentially) a high level of personal and structural power. Research suggests that police officers deal with this discretion, and the confusion it sometimes generates, through the construction of collectively understood and often taken-for-granted norms and values, frequently referred to in academic literature as 'cop culture' (see for example, Fielding (1994) and Chan (1996) for a critique of the notion of 'police culture'). Given the focus of this book on *gender* it is worth spending a moment examining this notion of 'cop culture' and its influence on the gendering of policing broadly and police decision making more specifically (see also Hoyle and Sanders 2000).

Reiner (1992) identifies the following as key characteristics of 'cop culture': a sense of mission, suspicion, isolation/solidarity, conservatism, machismo, pragmatism and racial prejudice. These characteristics inform specific policing actions under specific circumstances. The phenomenon of the 'high-speed car chase', for example, may be seen as a by-product of both the sense of mission and the machismo identified by Reiner; an activity which his imbued with the same excitement and thrill for the police officer as for those being chased. As such, these subcultural characteristics provide a useful framework through which to understand how the central task of policing is practically managed and discretionary decisions carried out. Moreover, it is also particularly useful in providing an insight into one way of constructing an understanding of the gendered nature of police work and the ongoing salience of a masculinist culture within the policing context (see also Loftus 2009; Westmarland 2001).

Understanding the gendered nature of police work

As has already been noted, policing has traditionally been a male-dominated workforce within which the recruitment of females into all ranks has been slow, the promotion of females into leadership positions arguably slower, and the challenging of gendered practices cumbersome. Research has found that as the number of women in the policing profession increases there is an ongoing need to challenge gendered attitudes and stereotypes towards female officers and long-term inequity issues in the profession (Prenzler *et al.* 2010). Other research, which points to the ongoing presence of gendered attitudes among police, has found that the longer an officer has been in the force the more likely they are to hold negative perceptions of women officers (Chu 2012) and that the differential treatment of officers by sex creates an environment whereby women are kept in the lower ranks of policing organisations (Garcia 2003). These findings are examples of a wide body of research that has documented the gendered nature of police administration.

In 1993 the release of the final report and recommendations of the *Inquiry into Police Responsibilities and Rewards* (hereinafter known as the 'Sheehy Report') represented a key opportunity for change in how the UK police 'service' was structured, including how various levels of police ranking were renumerated. While the report's recommendations failed to gain favour with the Home Office at the time, the findings, while not explicitly acknowledging the gendered nature of police administration and conditions of service, do provide a blueprint for the need to ensure that the 'police service is seen as a service rather than a "race apart"' (Sheehy Report 1993, Executive Summary: 5). Within this, the Sheehy Report emphasised the importance of ensuring quality day-to-day interactions between police officers and the public, including the need to recognise the central importance of front-line police work. To incentivise officers to ensure 'good' front-line practice, the Sheehy Report recommended that officers be rewarded, beyond the promotion route, for the provision of good routine service. In doing so it re-emphasised the notion of the police as a 'service' rather than as a 'force' per se.

What the 'service model' – as proposed in the Sheehy Report and by others – fails to acknowledge however is the deep history of a militaristic model of management that has historically underpinned policing. Militaristic influences are evidence in the historical practice of police marching on parade, the use of the police salute, the routine reference to senior officers as 'sir', among other practices. While we acknowledge that some of the more militaristic practices may be waning in contemporary policing practices, the legacy of these are still ever apparent in the continued need for discipline that runs throughout policing practices. As Wiles (1993: 55) has pointed out, 'some policing jobs require obedience to command, and all policing requires a high level of accountability for individual actions, then only a discipline service can fulfil these two requirements'.

While this alignment of militaristic practices and the need for discipline may appear at face value to be a happy marriage, the extent to which a militaristic model of policing achieves accountability has been heavily critiqued and arguably represents only one interpretation of what an 'accountable' police service may look like. What this model also does is privilege a form of policing – that being militaristic – which is heavily gendered. As Hearn (1987: 94) states:

> Those parts of the state that are more concerned with repression and violence are more fully male-dominated and male-membered than those parts which are concerned with caring, welfare and reproduction which are usually male-dominated and female-membered.

Hearn's reflections here are important, as they serve to remind us about who occupy positions of power in the community. When combined with the knowledge that policing also offers the opportunity for the legitimate use of violence and force, the relationship between gender, power, the state and the role of the police becomes a particularly significant one (reiterating an issue raised in Chapter 4 and commented on in the Conclusion). The influence of gender in the role of the police is further cemented when the risky and action nature of police work is also taken into account. However it is also important to recognise more the subtle forms of power that are present in the policing role. As Lukes (1974) pointed out more than three decades ago, the exercise of force is only one face of power. The ability to control agendas, information flow and self-perception are also crucially important and powerful actions.

Given the influence of the militaristic model, the common feature of 'power' in the nature of police work and police access to the legitimate use of force, it is perhaps unsurprising that policing has historically been, and in many jurisdictions continues to be, gendered in nature. We refer again to Hearn (1992: 133) who recognised:

> Policing has itself always been gendered, and no less so in criminal work [.] in the policing of crime, one set of men work against, and something with, another set of men.

As such, the management of policing has been traditionally far more concerned with ensuring a hierarchal adherence to authority and the demonstration of solidarity than it was with developing the best expertise and skills of individual officers.

Acknowledging this and establishing the masculinist and militaristic nature of policing is important, since it highlights why merely recruiting more female officers, or appointing more senior female managers, may not in and of itself impact positively upon the gendered management and practice of policing. As Silvestri (2003: 184) states:

> Recruitment of more female officers and of more female senior management will not in and of itself impact upon the deep-rooted gendered assumptions on which policing, more generally, and management practice more specifically, are based. To achieve meaningful change within policing, we need to think beyond the numerical.

As such, and as Silvestri points out, calls to address gendered practices within the police require more than a quantitative exercise of discerning sex patterns for the workforce. Rather it highlights the need for understanding the need for cultural change at all levels of management and leadership.

It is perhaps opportune here, before we move to an examination of policing practices for gender-based violence, to consider the presence, role and influence of policewomen in these debates. As acknowledged earlier, policing has long been considered an inherently masculine role; however, when considering the reform of policing to better serve responses to gender-based violence, the role of policewomen has featured heavily. An optimist may suggest that this is because, influenced by feminism, it is assumed that women in general, and women in vulnerable circumstances in particular, prefer talking to other women. At face value this proposition is appealing; however, responses to this feminist-informed view have been somewhat ambivalent, highlighting the need for wider cultural and practice changes if women police officers are to meaningfully improve policing responses to gender-based violence. We return to this question later in this chapter in our exploration of the emergence of women-only police stations in Latin America.

Policing gender-based violence: from the 1980s up until today

The move towards a service delivery model of policing in the wake of the Sheehy Report and other movements internationally demanded that policing take seriously the private 'safe haven' of the personal home. While traditionally police work had focused on the public domain of the street this represented a significant shift in attention, albeit one that has been slow to gain traction in many areas and at many levels. Reflecting on a quote from over thirty years ago, Radford and Stanko (1991: 192) state:

> [I]n 1984 Sir Kenneth Newman attempted to shed police responsibility for what he considered to be 'rubbish' work, or nonpolice matters, namely domestic violence and stray dogs are two such

examples. By 1990 police forces compete with each other to find the most creative policy to deal with domestic violence.

While the intervening decades have clearly evidenced a change of direction in how police and police services view intimate partner violence, there remains a question as to the extent to which the traditional view of domestic violence as not real police work lingers (Bittner 1990; Faragher 1981; see also Segrave *et al.* 2016). Confirming this suspicion in 2014 the report of the HMIC Inquiry into the policing of domestic abuse concluded:

> Domestic abuse is a priority on paper but, in the majority of forces, not in practice. Almost all police and crime commissioners have identified domestic abuse as a priority in their Police and Crime Plans. All forces told us that it is a priority for them. This stated intent is not translating into operational reality in most forces. Tackling domestic abuse too often remains a poor relation to acquisitive crime and serious organising crime.
>
> (HMIC 2014: 6)

Reflecting this view, since the rise of feminist advocacy in the 1970s there has been a growing body of research that has critiqued police responses to intimate partner violence. Scholars have argued that there is a lack of understanding of the nature of domestic violence, a hesitance to view domestic violence as a criminal offence in the same way as that committed between strangers, and a reluctance to arrest the perpetrator (Douglas 2008; Lewis 2004; Meyer 2011; Stewart 2001). Compounding this further, scholars have argued that when police do respond, their response is often to minimise the harm of the violence perpetrated, a factor subsequently cited by victims as decisive in their decision not to engage police in future incidents (Douglas 2012). As described by Douglas in her Australian-based study, 'the descriptors of violence [by police] as "not that serious" or as "annoying" trivialise the experience of women and push it outside of the law'. Other barriers cited by domestic violence victims as reasons not to engage with the police include fear of gender bias and discrimination, perceived loss of support from the police and a fear that the violence will escalate following criminal justice intervention (Meyer 2011; Stewart 2001).

Low levels of reporting, combined with negative attitudes and the proliferation of gendered myths and misunderstandings have long hampered policing efforts in relation to gender-based violence. This is particularly evident in the case of rape and intimate partner violence. Jordan's (2001) research with women victims of sexual violence, for example, detailed the ways in which New Zealand police officers respond to reports. Women interviewed as part of Jordan's research described experiences of belittling, a lack of empathy from the police and a dissatisfaction with the initial response received. As two women in Jordan's research (2001: 687) described:

> He talked to me like I was dirt. [.] He said he wanted to get the truth out of me. They [the police] asked me so many questions *I* felt like the bad person. They really made me feel so stink. I just wanted to cry. They should be more sensitive. He was like a pig to me [.] they should be more direct and up front, and say they have to sort out the truth for court. It made me very angry.

Similar findings have been documented elsewhere in research examining police responses and attitudes towards rape victims (Adler 1987; Du Mont *et al.* 2003; Temkin 1987) and victims of intimate partner violence (Segrave *et al.* 2016; Stephens and Sinden 2000).

When a report does occur, one of the legacies of the perception that intimate partner violence did not constitute real police work was a hesitancy among officers to make an arrest and then later to pursue a prosecution. As such, traditionally, arrests were rarely made in intimate partner violence cases (Edwards 1986), and in cases where an arrest was made, achieving a prosecution were fraught with barriers, including the police' perceived unwillingness of a 'reluctant victim' (Stanko 1989). Indeed, research by Dobash and Dobash (1979) found that even in cases where the woman was keen to support prosecution, often the police were not. Police failure to arrest and to support prosecution cumulated in low levels of police satisfaction among members of the general community. It is to some of the flowing initiatives introduced to address these issues that our attention turns in the second half of this chapter.

Prior to doing so, it is important to acknowledge that calls to do 'more' or to operate 'differently' in this space do not always necessitate an action for more punitive responses. As such, a changing policy stance on intimate partner violence should not necessarily equate with arresting the offender in all cases (particularly given that the evidence supporting the effectiveness of arrest is ambivalent to say the least). What it does require however is a reorientation of policing to view gender-based violence, including, for example, intimate partner violence, as a real threat to an individual's health and safety, and to prioritise it in practice as such. The following section examines several of the reform initiatives that have been introduced in an attempt to achieve this and to challenge the militaristic and masculine values of the police.

The changing nature of policing gender-based violence

While changes have occurred in policing policy over the past two decades, the impact of those changes in practice is not always clearly identified and/or remains contested. It also depends upon the variables used to measure 'success'. For example, in some cases an increase in the number of police-recorded incidents of gender-based violence (e.g. rape or intimate partner violence) are attributed to an increased willingness of victims to engage police services (that is, higher confidence in the police); however, such a change could just as easily be associated with a change in police practice or wider socio-political factors. For example, in relation to the latter, in Victoria (Australia) an increase in police-reported incidents of family violence in the twelve months following the establishment of a state-based *Royal Commission into Family Violence* was attributed by some to an awakening among victims that this was behaviour they *could* report to the police. Regardless of the cause of an increase in police-recorded incidents – and a combination of several factors may be attributable up to a point – the question emerges as to whether an increase in police reports suggests a positive impact upon the persons (often women) in receipt of police services. Within criminology and victimology there is a growing body of research that has sought to deal with this question in one way or another (see for example, Gregory and Lees 1999; Fitz-Gibbon and Walklate 2016).

Mandatory arrest policies

Arguably one of the defining moments in community and political shifts to 'take domestic violence seriously' was the introduction in the 1980s in the United States of mandatory (or in some cases presumptive or pro-) arrest policies for domestic violence offenders. In the three decades since, several other countries, including Canada and Australia, have also introduced mandatory arrest policies for intimate partner violence incidents (Braaf and Sneddon 2007; Hirschel *et al.* 2007; Walklate and Fitz-Gibbon forthcoming). While the policies of each jurisdiction vary slightly according to the level of discretion afforded to the individual police officer and the extent to which a victim's desire not to charge is taken into consideration, these policies represent a definite shift in policing towards removing the decision-making responsibility from the victim. Broadly speaking, mandatory arrest policies sought to address concerns surrounding police inaction in domestic violence cases while simultaneously recognising that many victims of intimate partner violence may be unwilling to pursue charges against their abusive partner for a range of reasons. As such, and regardless of victim support, the policy was based on the idea that increased arrests and mandatory police powers would better protect women victims from intimate partner violence and act as a deterrent for would-be abusers (see, *inter alia*, Braaf and Sneddon 2007; Lewis 2004; Stewart 2001).

Some feminists have supported the symbolic power of an 'arrest', arguing that it implies a strong legal response to private violence.

However, research from a range of different jurisdictions has suggested that policies which provide for mandatory or pro-active arrest may not in practice benefit the very category of victim for whom they are designed to protect. Indeed, there is a mounting body of evidence that documents the limits of this approach (see for example, Chesney-Lind 2012; Miller and Meloy 2006), however, and in spite of this as a policing strategy it has continued to gain favour in both the global north and south (for more on the problems of this, see Walklate and Fitz-Gibbon forthcoming).

Regardless of its use in the context of private or public violence, the use of 'arrest' as a policing strategy is rooted in assumptions regarding its effectiveness. Numerous academics have argued that arrest should never be the automatic outcome of policy involvement in any incident and that to do so automatically presumes a strong causal relationship between arrest and deterrence. The latter reflects a problematically uncritical acceptance of the findings of earlier research, largely US based, which suggested a relationship between the two but which the authors themselves have since added caveats to (see Sherman *et al.* 1991).

Women-only police stations

Moving away from policing initiatives founded in the global north, since 1985 countries in Latin America have introduced 'women-only' police stations as a way of improving police responses to gender-based violence. First introduced in Brazil, as of March 2015 there were 485 women-only police stations in Brazil alone and similar stations have been introduced in other countries, including Argentina, Peru, Uruguay, South Africa, the Philippines and India, among others (Carrington 2015). While there are some variances in the model adopted in each country, as the name suggests women-only police stations are made up of female police officers (although not exclusively in all instances) with specialist training in responding to women's experiences of sexual and domestic violence. In most countries, the station is located away from 'standard' police stations and in some cases it is co-located with other specialist services for female victims of sexual and domestic violence (United Nations Women 2011).

A 2011 case study by the United Nations Women highlighted the positive impact of this approach, finding that women-only police stations increase women's willingness to report violence, increase the likelihood of subsequent convictions, and enhance service and referral pathways for victims who engage the police. Other reviews have found that while it is difficult to quantify the impact of the stations upon preventing death and serious injury, the presence of a women-only station may lead to a reduction in the femicide rate (Perova and Reynolds 2017) and may lead to an increased understanding of gender-based violence as criminal behaviour (Kavanagh 2011). Described by the United Nations Women (2011) as 'one of the most important entry points for accessing the justice system and specialized services in general', positive findings emitting from these stations have led to calls for this approach to be adopted elsewhere, including in Australia (see Carrington 2015).

General duties or a specialised skill?

Recognition of the inadequacies of police responses to intimate partner violence to date has led in many instances to calls for a specialised response. Essentially there is mounting recognition of the complex nature of policing intimate partner violence and the need for those who do so to possess specialised knowledge, skills and experience. This has been particularly apparent in the wake of successive reviews that have pointed to the lack of skills and knowledge among officers sufficient to carry out the day-to-day duties associated with responding to domestic violence (see for example, HMIC 2014; RCFV 2016).

Proponents of a specialised approach to the policing of intimate partner violence argue that specialisation overcomes organisational culture challenges in the policing of intimate partner violence (IPV) while also addressing known deficits in the policing response, including the failure of the police to understand the context with which IPV occurs, a lack of awareness of victim behaviour, and the problematic reliance upon evidence of neatly distinguishable victim/offender categories. Specialisation also provides the opportunity to embed knowledges, including for officers to better understand the difference between scenarios of violence that are reactive and incident based, as opposed to the cumulative and often ongoing nature of intimate partner violence. As Segrave *et al.* (2016: 13) have argued, family violence 'requires a very different policing response in comparison to other significant aspects of general duties policing'; the benefits could be:

> specialisation that involves a clear and significant demarcation of dedicated police working exclusively on IPV cases enables greater efficiency in policing and, we would argue such specialisation has the potential to increase satisfaction with police work as those who find this work rewarding can commit the time and resources necessary to respond appropriately, while those who prefer the cut and thrust of general duties responsive work can largely do away with the responsibilities and intensity of IPV cases.
>
> (Segrave *et al.* 2016: 13)

In their review of policing domestic abuse, the HMIC (2014: 23) report stopped short of suggesting that such knowledge should be specialised, instead finding that policing domestic abuse is 'core policing business' and recommending that all officers be trained to understand the dynamics of domestic abuse, including coercive control. One of the arguments in favour of viewing the policing of domestic violence as a general duty is the frequency with which the police are required to respond to a domestic violence incident. In the UK, the police receive an emergency call relating to an incident of domestic abuse on average every thirty seconds (HMIC 2014). In Australia, on average police deal with a domestic violence case every two minutes, equating to approximately 5,000 cases each week (Blumer 2016).

As such, a tension emerges between how to provide opportunities to specialised officers with the goal of improving response quality while simultaneously ensuring that the number of officers is retained to meet the demands of call-outs. In considering this tension in recent years, the majority of Australian state and territory jurisdictions have moved to establish – to varying degrees – specialised police responses to family violence. In Victoria (Australia), for example, a range of specialisation approaches have been adopted, beginning with the 2004 introduction of Family Violence Advisors (FVA) in each police region across the state and culminating most recently in the establishing of thirty specialised Family Violence Units across Victoria (Victoria Police 2015). Supporting such moves at the state level, in a national review of legal responses to family violence the Australian Law Reform Commission (2010: 32.124) concluded that there is 'substantial merit in the use of specialised police in family violence, sexual assault and child protection matters'.

This trend towards specialisation is neither new nor unique to the Australian context. In England and Wales between 1986 and 1990 the London Metropolitan Police set up dedicated Domestic Violence Units (DVUs). The dedicated unit model sought to model police responses to domestic violence incidents, to offer support to the victim, to ensure that women are aware of the range of options available to them, and to liaise with other relevant agencies (Edwards 1989; Friedman and Shulman 1990). Beyond intimate partner violence, a similar trend in specialisation is evident in the sexual violence space and in some jurisdictions in responses to child protection. There are also connections to be made here in the move towards specialisation in other branches of the criminal justice system. Over the past two decades several jurisdictions – including the USA, Canada, Australia, England and Wales, and Spain – have to varying degrees introduced specialist criminal prosecution units, as well as specialist domestic violence courts. Underpinned by similar goals, specialisation at later stages of the justice process has sought to increase the prospects of conviction and in acknowledgement of the difficulties that victims experience in court, to better support victims throughout the justice process.

While there are definite benefits of specialisation (see further Segrave *et al.*, 2016), a concern arises if – or perhaps when – specialised units become heavily female dominated. Arguably there is a risk that male officers may view the work of their female colleagues as 'just' working in domestic violence units. Returning to the notion of domestic violence as not 'real' police work (or as 'soft' policing: see

Foster 2003), policewomen deployed as part of specialised units may be confronted with day-to-day feelings of inadequacy in the face of a long-held culture that has failed to take the policing of women's domestic security seriously.

The move towards private security

Having examined the various ways in which the police, as the gate-keeper branch of the criminal justice system, identify, respond to and manage gender-based violence; this chapter finishes by questioning the extent to which private security companies may have a valuable service to offer in this space. Essentially the question arises: Given the recognised inadequacies of police action in this space, could private security officers provide a more effective response? If so, what would that look like? Would it bring with it many of the concerns that have arisen through the emergence of private security in other areas of the criminal justice system?

But first let us consider a recent example and one of the world's first instances of private security presence in 'policing' intimate partner violence. In Victoria (Australia), a private security company, Protective Services Pty Ltd, has begun offering services directly to victims of family violence since 2013 (see Schultze 2015). Services offered include victim risk assessments, court chaperoning, police liaison, family violence staff training, and providing advice to individuals about home security and technology. The range of services offered focus on providing personal 'security' to victims as opposed to a promise of the attainment of 'justice' (see further Harkin and Fitz-Gibbon 2017). A victim can approach the company directly for service or the more common route is through referral by a female violence service.

This emerging presence of private security in responding to intimate partner violence raises interesting questions from the perspectives of victims – for those that desire security but not justice, is this a more effective response? And for the system – how will such companies be held to account? And what challenges does this pose for information sharing and multi-agency responses to intimate partner violence? These questions come with the possibility of risks. For example, if private security is seen to be operating in this space, will this mean that intimate partner violence is again relegated to the bottom of the police priority list, harking back to the days of its 'not real' policing image? (This point is made further by Harkin and Fitz-Gibbon 2017).

Given the infancy of private security's involvement in this space, empirical evidence of its impact is largely yet to emerge, and while the body of critical scholarship on the operation of private security should not be ignored, such initiatives have been cautiously welcomed by some scholars provided that the necessary regulations are put in place (see for example, Harkin 2017; Prenzler and Fardell 2016). One area where promising results have been noted is in relation to the provision of 'home fortification' or 'home security enhancement' approaches, whereby a private security officer provides advice on security systems and technology packages that can be harnessed by the individual to minimise their personal risk and enhance safety. Describing this as an example of a 'victim-centred program', Prenzler and Fardell (2016: 3) set out that the programmes will allow a victim to remain safely in their home (in some cases with children) and reduces the reliance on refuges and emergency accommodation initiatives. Beyond the Australian example provided above, Prenzler and Fardell (2016) list home security enhancement initiatives that have been trialled in New Zealand and the United Kingdom. As such, and given the speed with which intimate partner violence policy and practice initiatives have tended to travel (on this, see Walklate and Fitz-Gibbon 2018), it would appear that private security may be a new response branch to watch in future years.

Conclusion

This chapter, building on the material already presented in this book, has explored the gendered nature of policing and the implications of different approaches to policing gender-based violence. While differences in the employment rates of men and women in policing roles and other criminal justice agencies are closing, it remains the case that criminal justice work has historically and to a degree continues to be men's work. This is not however to diminish the importance of those initiatives that have sought to challenge the masculine nature of policing or to undermine the impact that reforms in this space have had. As the discussion in this chapter has illustrated, it is often difficult to measure the impact of changes in practice but, in recognition of the significant challenges that the police have faced in securing just outcomes for women victims of gender-based violence, it is essential that policy makers do not tire of the challenge. A gendered lens can help us think more critically and maybe more constructively about different ways in which, in this case, policing and justice may be conceptualised and carried out. Some of the questions generated by such a discussion are considered in Chapter 6's exploration of the criminal law and the criminal justice system.

Recommendations for further reading

For those seeking a deeper appreciation of the traditional nature of police work, read Reiner's (1992) *The Politics of the Police* as well as McCulloch's *Blue Army* (1997) for a critical analysis of the paramilitarisation of the police, using Australia as a case study example. For scholarship focused on women and policing, see Westmarland's (2001) *Gender and Policing* as well as Silvestri's (2003) *Women in Charge: Policing, Gender and Leadership*.

References

Adler, Z. (1987) *Rape on Trial*. London: Routledge and Kegan Paul.

Australian Law Reform Commission. (2010) *Family Violence – A National Legal Response*. ALRC Report 114. Canberra: Australian Law Reform Commission.

Blumer, C. (2016) Australian police deal with domestic violence every two minutes. *ABC News*, 21 April.

Bittner, E. (1990) *Aspects of Police Work*. Boston, MA: Northeastern University Press.

Braaf, R. and Sneddon, C. (2007) *Arresting Practices: Exploring Issues of Dual Arrest for Domestic Violence*. New South Wales: Australian Domestic & Family Violence Clearinghouse.

Brogden, M., Jefferson, T. and Walklate, S. (1988) *Introducing Police Work*. London: Unwin Hyman.

Carrington, K. (2015) Women's only police stations to combat violence against women. QUT Crime and Justice Research Centre blog, 8 March. Available at https://blogs.qut.edu.au/crime-and-justice-research-centre/2015/03/08/womens-only-police-stations-to-combat-violence-against-women/.

Chan, J. (1996) Changing police culture. *British Journal of Criminology* 36(1): 109–134.

Chesney-Lind, M. (2012) Criminalizing victimization: The unintended consequences of pro-arrest policies for girls and women. *Criminology & Public Policy* 2(1): 81–90. doi: 10.1111/j.1745–9133.2002.tb00108.x.

Chu, D.C. (2012) Gender integration in policing: a comparison of female police officers' perceptions in Taiwan. *International Journal of Comparative and Applied Criminal Justice* 37(2): 143–157.

Dobash, R. and Dobash, R. (1979) *Violence against Wives*. Shepton Mallet: Open Books.

Douglas, H. (2008) The criminal law's response to domestic violence: what's going on? *Sydney Law Review* 30: 438–469.

Douglas, H. (2012) Battered women's experiences of the criminal justice system: decentring the law. *Feminist Legal Studies* 20(2): 121–134.

Du Mont, J., Miller, K-L. and Myhr, T.L. (2003) The role of 'real rape' and 'real victim' stereotypes in the police reporting practices of sexually assaulted women. *Violence against Women* 9(4): 466–486.

Edwards, S. (1986) *The Police Response to Domestic Violence in London*. London:Polytechnic of Central London.

Edwards, S. (1989) *Policing 'Domestic' Violence*. London: Sage.

Faragher, T. (1981) The police response to violence against women in the home. In J. Pahl (ed.) *Private Violence and Public Policy*. London: Routledge, pp. 110–124.

Fielding, N. (1994) Cop canteen culture. In T. Newburn and E.A. Stanko (eds) *Just Boys doing Business? Men, Masculinities and Crime.*. London and New York: Routledge, pp. 46–53.

Fitz-Gibbon, K. and Walklate, S. (2016) The efficacy of Clare's Law in domestic violence law reform in England and Wales. *Criminology and Criminal Justice*. Published Online First. doi: 10.1177/1748895816671383.

Foster, J. (2003). Police cultures. In T. Newburn (ed.) *Handbook of Policing*. Cullompton, Devon: Willan, pp. 196–227.

Friedman, L. and Shulman, M. (1990) Domestic violence: the criminal justice support. In A.J. Lurigi, W.G. Stanko and R.C. Davies (eds) *Victims of Crime: Problems, Policies and Progress*. London: Sage, pp. 87–103.

Garcia, V. (2003) 'Difference' in the police department: women, policing, and 'doing gender'. *Journal of Contemporary Criminal Justice* 19(3): 330–344.

Gregory, S. and Lees, S. (1999) *Investigating Sexual Assault*. London: Sage.

Harkin, D. (2017) Regulating private security sector provision for victims of domestic violence. *Theoretical Criminology*. Published online first. doi: 10.1177/1362480617737760.

Harkin, D. and Fitz-Gibbon, K. (2017) Private security companies and domestic violence: a welcome new development? *Criminology and Criminal Justice* 17(4): 433–449.

Hearn, J. (1987) *The Gender of Oppression*. Brighton: Harvester Wheatsheaf.

Hearns, J. (1992) *Men in the Public Eye*. London: Routledge.

HMIC (Her Majesty's Inspectorate of Constabulary). (2014) *Everyone's Business: Improving the Police Response to Domestic Abuse*. London: HMIC.

Hirschel, D., Buzawa, E., Pattavina, A. and Faggiani, D. (2007) Domestic violence and mandatory arrest laws: to what extent do they influence police arrest decisions. *Journal of Criminal Law and Criminology* 98(1): 255–298.

Hoyle, C. and Sanders, A. (2000). Police response to domestic violence: from victim choice to victim empowerment? *British Journal of Criminology* 40(1): 14–36.

Jordan, J. (2001) Worlds apart? women, rape and the police reporting process. *British Journal of Criminology* 41: 679–706.

Kavanagh, P. (2011) Seeking justice: women's police stations in Latin America. *International Development Research Centre*, 24 January. Available at www.idrc.ca/en/article/seeking-justice-womens-police-stations-latin-america.

Lewis, R. (2004) Making justice work: effective legal interventions for domestic violence. *British Journal of Criminology* 44: 204–224.

Loftus, B. (2009). *Police Culture in a Changing World*. Oxford: Oxford University Press.

Lukes, S. (1974) *Power: A Radical View.* London: Macmillan.

McCulloch, J. (1997) *Blue Army: Paramilitary Policing in Australia.* Melbourne: University of Melbourne.

Meyer, S. (2011) Seeking helping for intimate partner violence: victims' experiences when approaching the criminal justice system for IPV-related support and protection in an Australian jurisdiction. *Feminist Criminology* 6(4): 268–290.

Miller, S.L. and Meloy, M.L. (2006) Women's use of force: voices of women arrested
for domestic violence. *Violence Against Women* 12(1): 89–115.

Perova, E. and Reynolds, S.A. (2017) Women's police stations and intimate partner violence: evidence from Brazil. *Social Science and Medicine* 174: 188–196.

Prenzler, T. and Fardell, L. (2016) *Role of Private Security in Supporting Policy Responses to Domestic Violence.* Report to the Australian Security Industry Association Limited, University of Sunshine Coast, Queensland.

Prenzler, T., Fleming, J. and Boyes, A. (2010) Gender equity in Australian and New Zealand policing: a five year review. *International Journal of Police Science and Management* 12(4): 584–595.

Radford, J. and Stanko, B. (1991) Violence against women and children: the contradictions of crime control under patriarchy. In K. Stenson and D. Cowell (eds) *The Politics of Crime Control.* London: Sage, pp. 188–202.

RCFV (Royal Commission into Family Violence). (2016) *Report and Recommendations.* Victoria: Royal Commission into Family Violence.

Reiner, R. (1992) *The Politics of the Police* (2nd edition). Hemel Hempstead: Harvester Wheatsheaf.

Schultze, S. (2015) Witness statement to the Royal Commission into Family Violence. Victoria, 22 July. Available at www.rcfv.com.au/ MediaLibraries/RCFamilyViolence/Statements/WIT-0079-001-0001-Schultze-9.pdf.

Segrave, M., Wilson, D. and Fitz-Gibbon, K. (2016) Policing intimate partner violence in Victoria (Australia): examining police attitudes and the potential of specialisation. *Australian and New Zealand Journal of Criminology.* Published online first. doi: 10.1177/0004865816679686.

Sheehy Report. (1993) *Inquiry into Police Responsibilities and Rewards: Report.*

Sherman, L., Schmidt, J., Regan, D., Gartin, P. and Cohn, E. (1991) From initial deterrence to long-term escalation: short custody arrest for ghetto poverty violence. *Criminology* 29(4): 821–849.

Silvestri, M. (2003) *Women in Charge: Policing, Gender and Leadership*. Cullompton, Devon: Willan.

Stanko, E.A. (1989) Missing the mark? Policing battering. In J. Hamner., J. Radford and E. Stanko (eds) *Women, Policing and Male Violence*. London: Routledge, pp. 58–84.

Stephens, B.J. and Sinden, P.G. (2000) 'Victims' voices: domestic assault victims' perceptions of police demeanor. *Journal of Interpersonal Violence* 15(5): 534–547.

Stewart, A. (2001) Policing domestic violence: an overview of emerging issues. *Police Practice and Research: An International Journal* 2: 447–460.

Temkin, J. (1987) *Rape and the Legal Process*. London: Sweet and Maxwell.

Uglow, S. (1988) *Policing Liberal Society*. Oxford: Oxford University Press.

United Nations Women. (2011) *Women's Police Stations in Latin America Case Study: An Entry Point for Stopping Violence and Gaining Access to Justice (Brazil, Peru Ecuador and Nicaragua)*. Security Sector Module, December.

Victoria Police. (2015) *Victoria Police Submission to the Royal Commission into Family Violence*. Melbourne, Australia: Victoria Police.

Walklate, S. and Fitz-Gibbon, K. (2018) The violence of 'Northern' theorising for policy responses to intimate partner violence. In K. Carrington, M. Sozzo, R. Hogg and J. Scott (eds) *Palgrave Handbook on Criminology and the Global South*. London: Palgrave.

Westmarland, L. (2001) *Gender and Policing: Sex, Power and Police Culture*. Cullompton, Devon: Willan.

Wiles, P. (1993) Policing structures, organisational change and personnel management. In R. Dingwell and J. Shapland (eds) *Reforming British Policing: Missions and Structures*. Sheffield: Faculty of Law.

6

GENDER, LAW AND CRIMINAL JUSTICE POLICY

Introduction

Chapters 1 and 2 focused on feminist interventions and theories of masculinity, and their influence on the disciplines of criminology and victimology. Thus far we have considered the extent to which these theoretical perspectives are useful in developing an understanding of the nature of criminal behaviour and its impact upon victims and wider community understandings about crime. This chapter extends that analysis to a new sphere – the criminal courtroom – and considers the extent to which criminal law has historically been able to provide justice for victims of gendered harm, the degree to which gender influences the practice of the law and experiences of reform.

Questions surrounding the adequacy of criminal justice system responses to incidents of gender-based violence have prompted over three decades of feminist, socio-legal and criminological study (see, among others, Smart 1989; Naffine 1990; Morris and Gelsthorpe 2000; Walklate 2008). Much of this work has considered the extent to which women, as victims, offenders and participants in the criminal justice system, are framed as 'the other' and the influence of this framing in practice (Currie 1995; Walklate 2008). Writing over twenty years ago, Currie (1995: 14) described:

> The realities of women's lives have been invisible in the law because women have not been able to tell their stories, because they have not been listened to and because they have not been believed.

In recognising the work that has been undertaken to illuminate the stories of women and to ensure that women are believed, this chapter examines the extent to which thinking around 'gender' and 'sex' has been influential in the operation and reform of criminal law and criminal justice policy. In order to do so this chapter is structured into three main sections. The first considers the importance of terminology in criminal law and criminal justice policy, and how the labels applied to gendered violence and its related legislation have changed over time. The second section looks specifically at the question of gender and the role of the courts. Beyond merely questioning the impact of the sex of the judge, it considers the schools of thought on whether there is a need for a feminist jurisprudence while also charting the emergence of the international Feminist Judgments movement. Finally, the chapter concludes by examining the efficacy of law reform in this space, specifically (following on from the focus of Chapter 4) in relation to sexual violence and homicides committed in the context of self-defence. Noting the limits of law in effecting change, the chapter engages with the reasons why the law has failed to meet the needs of victims of gendered violence and how this has influenced the reform of criminal justice policy in these areas.

Terminology in law and policy

Violence against women and girls has escalated up the political agenda in recent years both globally led by the United Nations and in a wide range of different national jurisdictions. Parallel concern has risen over the importance of terminology and the need to appropriately *name* the problem. Contestations exist around whether labels and legislation should be gender specific, how best to identify the range of violence that occurs across familial structures and how to acknowledge differences across diverse communities. Fehlberg *et al.* (2015: 134) argue that the label prescribed by law is not itself important but rather that the importance lies in ensuring that whatever label chosen does not 'suggest the behaviour is somehow less serious than violence that occurs in other contexts'.

Take, for example, debates surrounding the labelling of men's violence against a female intimate partner. There are a range of terms preferred internationally and across policing, legal and practice sectors (MacDonald 1998; National Domestic and Family Violence Bench Book 2017). In England and Wales, for example, the term 'domestic abuse' is preferred, as it is seen as broad enough to encapsulate physical as well as coercive and controlling behaviours (on this, see also Fisher 2012). In Australian states and territories, recent years have seen a preferred term to describe such abuse as 'family violence', as it is broad enough to encapsulate the wide range of familial relationships within which violence can be perpetrated. However, both of these terms may be critiqued for failing to acknowledge the gendered nature of such violence (see Behrens 1996). Other terms that are often used, sometimes interchangeably, include intimate partner violence, violence against women, domestic harm, domestic control and domestic violence (National Domestic and Family Violence Bench Book 2017). Differences in terminology complicate counting exercises in that comparability across jurisdictions becomes difficult (for more on the challenges of counting, see Chapter 4).

In the labelling of legislation, there has also been a continued trend in some instances to name legislation 'in honour' of individual victims of gendered violence. A recent high-profile example is 'Clare's Law' in England and Wales, which was introduced nationally in 2014 following the high-profile killing of Clare Wood by her former male intimate partner (for further details on Clare's Law, see Fitz-Gibbon and Walklate 2016). Beyond Clare's Law other examples of legislation named after victims of domestic and sexual violence include Sarah's Law, introduced in England and Wales following the 2000 paedophilic murder of 8-year-old Sarah Payne, and Jessica's Law, introduced in Florida (United States) following the abduction, sexual assault and murder of Jessica Lunsford. Since the early 2000s these 'victim-focused laws' (Fitz-Gibbon and Walklate 2016: 4) have often been introduced following a heavily politicised and emotive-based campaign for law reform. Drawing mixed responses, these laws have heightened visibility around the assumed needs of victims of crime and are symptomatic of a broader trend towards bringing victims into focus in criminal justice system responses to gender-based violence (see further Duggan 2012).

Understanding the law: for men, by men

One of the central foundations of the rule of law is the notion of equality, the ideal that all persons who come before the law should be treated equally regardless of class, race and, of greatest relevance here, gender. While this is an important ideal, what it fails to recognise is the inherently masculine tradition and make-up of the criminal law and operation of the criminal justice system. Thus an understanding of the law requires first an understanding of the historical foundations of the criminal law – a law made for men, by men. Referred to as 'white man's justice' by Hudson (2006), the subject and object of the criminal law – being that of the rational 'man' – creates a criminal justice response that has often been criticised for its inability to respond to the diverse circumstances within which criminal offending and victimisation occurs. Such diversity needs to be understood as inclusive of and extending beyond sex and gendered violence, to race, ethnicity, religion and so on. Beyond acknowledging the masculine nature of the law, it is also important to understand how the law operates in practice, essentially the processes by which some behaviours and persons are labelled criminal while others are not. In other words, to understand the reasons why not all guilty persons who are brought before the criminal courts are either found guilty or necessarily punished for their actions. To do so is to grasp two (often problematic) issues: the adversarial tradition of the law (for the most part in the Anglo-speaking world) and the influential role of case law. (The inquisitorial system of some European countries and/or the 'confession'-based system of traditional Chinese justice have different practices associated with them but in some respects some of the processes are informed by similar gendered assumptions.) Each is briefly examined here in turn.

The adversarial tradition of the law, embraced in the UK, Australia, New Zealand and the United States, places primacy on establishing, beyond reasonable doubt, and on the basis of admissible evidence, that the defendant is guilty of the offence for which they have been charged. Truth seeking sits as a subservient concern to this priority. Consequently, the process by which evidence is tested and interpreted, a judge rules upon evidence and a judge or jury decides upon guilt or innocence, become crucial features of the adversarial criminal trial. The interpretation of evidence by decision makers within the justice system – be it judge or jury – allows for variance within the bounds of the law. While one is directed not to make decisions based on personal prejudices, it is within the space of evidence gathering and interpretation that gendered presumptions concerning both victims and offenders are often evidenced.

In addition to the crucial role of evidence in the adversarial system, the role that case law plays in both setting precedents for understanding particular issues at law as well as acting as a catalyst for changing those precedents is a critical area of inquiry. It is through the practice and implementation of the law, as shown via case law, that different ways of understanding and interpreting the intent of pieces of legislation is constituted. While significant changes in the law often occur via law reform, it is possible for changes to occur in practice and interpretation without any change in legislation but rather through emerging case law in any given area. This lends to the conclusion that while the law may appear to be steeped in tradition and its masculinist nature set in stone, case law provides some flexibility in the law's interpretation.

However, where evolving case law has not been deemed sufficient, concerns surrounding the traditionally masculine nature of the law have led to calls for its reform. Writing over twenty years ago, Laster and O'Malley (1996) called for better inclusion of the stories of the powerless within criminal law through a transformation of the legal subject of the law – the white male (see also Walklate 2008). Similar calls have been made elsewhere in the two decades since. And while such reform has aimed at transforming areas of the law to better accommodate the circumstances within which women experience victimisation and perpetration are meritorious, short-term gains in the law have not always resulted in effective long-term change. For example, as was examined in the previous chapter, mandatory domestic violence police charging has unintentionally negatively impacted upon the very category of victim they were designed to better protect (see also Douglas and Fitzgerald 2013; Chesney-Lind 2006). It is to the operation of the court system in cases of gendered violence and attempts at its reform that we now turn.

Gender in court

Since the 1986 publication of Mary Eaton's *Justice for Women: Family, Court and Social Control*, followed not long after by Helena Kennedy's 1992 *Eve was Framed*, the gendered operation of the criminal court system has been placed under the microscope by feminist, socio-legal and criminological scholars. Over three decades later there is now an ever-growing body of scholarship which critically documents the extent to which gendered assumptions permeate and influence the operation of criminal court proceedings and their outcomes.

One of the ways in which the gendered nature of the criminal courts has been examined is to compare and contrast the experiences of male and female defendants. At one level this has been done through a quantitative analysis of differences in sentencing outcomes dependent on sex. For example, Australian research by Bond and Jeffries (2014) found that when 'sentenced under statistically similar circumstances' domestic violence perpetrators were less likely than persons convicted for an offence outside the context of a domestic relationship to receive a term of imprisonment. Where a term of imprisonment was imposed upon a domestic violence offender, comparatively it was significantly shorter than those imposed for crimes outside of a domestic context. Similar results have been reported elsewhere. In the Canadian context, Dawson's (2015) analysis of four decades of sentencing outcomes in femicide cases evidenced that homicides involving a victim who was a family member or intimate partner of the offender were treated more leniently than those involving a non-related victim.

Beyond sentencing outcomes, research also suggests that the differential treatment of intimate partner violence may be evident from the outset of the court's response. For example, in his study on the management of domestic violence cases and the role of prosecutorial decision making in two English magistrates' courts, Cammiss (2006) found that domestic violence cases were more likely to be resolved at the lower level of the magistrates' court rather than in the English Crown Court system. As such, and while there have undoubtedly been some gains made in ensuring that the legal system takes domestic violence seriously, there remain real concerns over the degree to which courts are complicit in promulgating the notion that criminal harm committed against an intimate partner is less serious than that committed against a stranger (essentially the public versus private violence debate).

At another level, scholars, including Eaton (1986), Allen (1987), Hedderman and Gelsthorpe (1997), among others, have examined the qualitatively different ways in which the decision makers of the criminal courts respond to male and female defendants and/or victims. This body of research has been particularly interested in discourse and the descriptors used to frame the characters, behaviours and actions of male versus female defendants. Within this the actions of female defendants charged with violent crimes are often interpreted and framed through the lens of traditional presumptions of femininity. Worrall (1990) describes this as the 'compassion trap' – a view that a woman cannot separate herself from the presumptions of femininity that prescribe her to be caring, nurturing and domestic. From this vantage point women who commit violent crimes are judged first as bad mothers, wives and carers before they are judged as offenders.

Conversely it is unsurprising that the same gendered scripts are applied in understanding male perpetration and victimisation in that males become bound by their own set of stereotypical assumptions. Male defendants are judged according to their ability to abide by the script of the family provider, the breadwinner and the good father. This can work in favour of men who come before the law in the interpretation of emotions broadly and expressions of male anger specifically. For example, the historical operation of the partial defence of provocation has been seen to favour men who commit homicide in response to a threat to their masculine honour or as a 'crime of passion'. The latter most typically occurs where a man kills his female intimate partner upon finding out that she intends to leave him or that she has been unfaithful to the relationship. Described as privileging the 'white Western notion of male honour' (Carline 2010: 80), the provocation defence has been heavily critiqued for 'excusing' the lethal actions of men who kill in unmeritorious circumstances (for more on the gendered operation of the provocation defence, see Fitz-Gibbon 2014; Horder 1992). This privileging may be linked back to the inherently masculine foundations of the defence in criminal law, as explained by Carline (2010: 82):

> While the law recognised that a man may feel anger and retaliation may result, there was also a societal expectation that a man

of honour would retaliate in anger, in order to restore the honour he had lost.

There are a number of common themes emerging here across these studies demonstrating the ways in which gendered assumptions and stereotypes permeate the operational practices of the criminal court system. When one takes a step back it is evident that the criminal justice system, perhaps unsurprisingly, is not immune from the stereotypes, myths and misconceptions that abound in wider society. While this may be unsurprising for some, it is striking in that the criminal justice system presents itself as a site of neutrality and a body of expert knowledge. Yet these studies, among many others, demonstrate the ways in which the criminal courts and those operating within them have differentially come to process, understand and respond to male and female defendants. This brings to the fore a key problem for feminists, as Kendall (1991: 80) points out in a different context:

> The question feminists face is whether justice for women is best achieved through legal recognition of sexual difference (special treatment) or by regarding sexual difference as largely irrelevant (equal treatment).

This poses a key theoretical dilemma. Should the law and its processes be changed to ensure equality for all and whose interests would this serve? Is this individual women who come before the law as perpetrators or victims, or women as a collective? Before moving to an examination of the ways in which reform has sought to improve legal processes for women victims of prolonged intimate partner violence, we first consider the gendered way in which victims of sexual violence are processed in the criminal courts.

Court responses to victims of sexual violence

Following on from the previous section, it is noted that research has consistently found that responses to victims – both male and female – in the criminal courts (and, beyond that, in the media and community) are heavily influenced by gendered stereotypes and expectations in ways that influence allocations of responsibility, and notions of guilt and innocence. Nowhere has this been more clearly documented than in criminal trials involving victims of sexual violence. It is here that we take the starting point for the following section, which considers what gains have been made in feminist and socio-legal attempts to improve justice outcomes for female victims of sexual violence.

Women's victim experiences of rape trials are governed by what Adler (1987) has called 'the importance of being perfect'. Her research examining rape trials before the Old Bailey in London revealed the number of strategies employed by defence barristers to discredit a woman's character and consequently her testimony against the defendant. Defence questioning of the victims in Adler's study focused on the woman's behaviour before, during and after the incident with the intention of establishing the woman's respectability (or lack thereof) and casting in doubt her credibility as a witness. Similar defence tactics continue to abound in the courts, as evidenced in a more recent Australian study by Powell and colleagues (2013). This work observed the continued salience of problematic courtroom narratives that supported the construction of a narrative of 'real rape' (read stranger rape) versus consensual sex (read cases where the 'men's active sexual desire was set against the women's passive receptivity') (Powell *et al.* 2013: 459).

The work of Powell and others demonstrates that in interpreting the notion of consent two things are apparent: first, that women's experiences of sexual violence are often disqualified; and second, that this is achieved through a process which privileges a male-centred view of both female and male sexuality. Adopting this stereotypical lens of responsibility for the act of rape is allocated to the female victim who should have acted differently so as not to *provoke* or *tempt* the male defendant. Thus men cannot be blamed for acting upon what are understood to be deep-seated and uncontrollable sexual desires. In attempting to counter such gendered narratives, feminist legal scholars have long challenged the practice of the law and, in some cases, have effectuated reform to challenge the ways in which consent is defined, interpreted and challenged within the setting of a criminal court trial. One of the aims of such reform has been to encourage broader attitudinal changes in the community towards victims of sexual violence and to counter long-held myths supporting a gendered understanding of a victim's behaviour and responsibility (see for example, Victorian Law Reform Commission 2004).

Beyond the specific interpretation of the notion of consent, attention has also been paid to the process of interpreting and corroborating evidence. This is a process which may involve heavy interrogation by the defence barrister which leads to the perception that it is the witness as opposed to the defendant who is put on trial. There have been attempts through legislation reform to address this, including through the introduction of what has been termed 'rape shield laws'. These laws, introduced in all Australian jurisdictions, for example, have sought to place clear limits on what evidence may be admitted about the victim, including to exclude evidence of prior sexual history, and to limit evidence which may function to discredit the victim's sexual reputation (Australian Law Reform Commission 2006).

The verdict on the extent to which these attempts at improving the laws targeted at sexual violence have improved victims' experiences of justice remains a heavily contested space (see, *inter alia*, Carline and Easteal 2014; Corrigan 2013; Spohn and Horney 2013), and reform in this area is certainly an ongoing project in many jurisdictions. The failure of criminal law reform to effect immediately positive change has led some advocates to question whether criminal law, as a response site, is appropriate for crimes of sexual violence (see for example, Graycar and Morgan 2005). As such the conversation is ongoing, as are the documented low reporting, prosecution and conviction rates for those cases of sexual violence that do come to the attention of the system. Beyond sexual assault law reform, a similar level of reform activity and feminist advocacy is evident in the changing nature of homicide laws to better meet the needs of women who kill in response to prolonged family violence. It is to this area of the law that we now turn.

The changing nature of legal responses to battered women

Feminist, socio-legal and criminological scholars have long acknowledged the difficulties 'battered women' face when brought within the confines of the traditionally masculine nature of the criminal justice system. While the law of homicide has been critiqued for privileging and 'excusing' the contexts within which men use lethal violence – namely via the partial defence of provocation – women who kill in the context of prolonged family violence have met the full brunt of the law via a system that is inadequately structured and lacks the nuanced understanding of family violence required to respond justly to such defendants. Take, for example, the high-profile case of Kiranjit Ahluwalia who, following ten years of intimate partner violence, killed her abusive husband. In December 1989 in the English courts Ahluwalia was convicted of murder and sentenced to life imprisonment, having been unsuccessful in raising a partial or complete defence to murder (see case overview in Fitz-Gibbon 2014: 79). In her 1992 Appeal, the court ruled that the traditional interpretation of criminal law failed to allow for women's experiences of intimate partner violence to be heard and that requirements in the law of self-defence – namely that of a 'sudden and temporary loss of control' – excluded women from the remit of such defences (Martin and Storey 2013). Heralded as 'an attempt to bring battered women within sight of the law's justice', in the nearly three decades since the original trial decision and sentencing in Ahluwalia a flurry of homicide law reform activity has sought to improve the ability of criminal law to respond to this circumstance of lethal violence.

The Ahluwalia case is not a unique example of the injustice of the law of homicide when responding to battered women who kill. Similar injustices have been documented in Australia, New Zealand, Canada and France (see Fitz-Gibbon and Vannier 2017; Sheehy 2014; Sheehy et al. 2012). While it is conceded that in each case other factors may be at play, the masculinist nature of defence to murder has been signalled as a contributing factor in such cases. As Yeo (1993: 104–105) explains:

> [T]here is a major problem confronting women who seek to rely on these criminal defences. It is that the defences have been developed through a long history of judicial precedents on the basis of male experiences and definitions of situations. Consequently, female defendants whose experiences and definitions fall outside

these male-inspired defences are confronted with the prospect of either failing to plead them successfully or having to distort their experiences in an effort to fit them into the defence.

To this end, and in response to clear injustices in the law's operation, reform of the law of self-defence across multiple jurisdictions provides one of the clearest examples of feminist-inspired criminal law reform activity. Such reform – introduced differentially in England and Wales, Canada, Australian states and territories among other jurisdictions – have sought to reform the timing and proportionality requirements in self-defence law as well as the evidential barriers that women face in explaining their lethal actions to a jury (Crofts and Tyson 2013; Fitz-Gibbon and Stubbs 2012).

Most recently, policy makers have sought to move beyond the specifics of legislation and to embark upon 'cultural change' reform, including but not limited to changes to the directions provided to the jury in cases involving family violence and the introduction of social framework evidence (see collection of contributions in Fitz-Gibbon and Freiberg (2015) for an analysis of the impact of such reform in the Victorian context). While the impact of reforms in practice are slow to emerge from case law, efforts to effect broader change in the way that the criminal law and justice system responds to women who have experienced family violence are encouraging.

The creation of new laws for gendered harms

Beyond the reform of existing laws, recognition of a wider range of gendered harms has led to the creation of new offences to transform criminal law to better accommodate the varying contexts within which gendered harms are perpetrated. A recent example is the emergence of what has been colloquially termed 'revenge pornography' laws. Revenge pornography refers to the distribution of nude and/ or sexually explicit images without the depicted person's consent (Powell and Henry 2017). Research has found that 'revenge porn' is a 'highly gendered' crime (Salter and Crofts 2015) that should be understood as one example of image-based abuse occurring along a continuum of sexual violence (McGlynn *et al.* 2017; for more on the continuum of sexual violence see Kelly 1988).

In 2015 the United Kingdom introduced a new offence to criminalise the sharing of an explicit sexual image without the depicted person's consent, punishable by two years' imprisonment or a fine (McGlynn and Rackley 2015). Similar moves towards criminalisation have occurred elsewhere. In Australia, for example, while there is no national law against revenge pornography (perhaps unsurprising given that criminal law is a state responsibility), at the state and territory level some jurisdictions have introduced new offences to criminalise 'image-based abuse', including the distribution of an intimate image without the person's consent (Powell *et al.* 2017). Other countries that have made efforts towards criminalising image-based abuse include the United States and Canada (McGlynn *et al.* 2017). While moves towards criminalisation have been welcomed, similar concerns to that already explored in this chapter have already begun to emerge – notably the question of the degree to which the law is an effective site through which to respond to gendered harm and, ultimately, through which to achieve cultural change (see, among others, McGlynn and Rackley 2015). As McGlynn and Rackley (2015: 1) note, 'the law can only play a limited role in bringing about that [cultural] change'.

Another example of the criminalisation of newly recognised gendered sexual harms is the proliferation of 'sexting' laws in countries such as the United States and Australia (for a discussion of the latter, see Crofts and Lee 2013). However, like the examples already provided of revenge pornography and sex defence law reform, there are emerging concerns that the criminalisation of new harms may serve to inadvertently capture a wider net of persons than that intended at the outset of the legislation. In this case, the concerns relate to the risk that children and young persons will become criminalised under child pornography laws for 'sexting' related behaviour (Crofts and Lee 2013). Given the infancy of sexting laws, as well as those pertaining to revenge pornography, their impact in practice is still emerging; however, over three decades of feminist critical inquiry provides reason to be cautious of assuming that the answer lies in law reform and to ensure ongoing monitoring of the law in practice.

In the intimate partner violence space, the past five years have evidenced a push towards criminalising coercive and controlling behaviour, in recognition of the inability of criminal justice practitioners (police, prosecutors and courts included) to date to effectively identify and respond to non-physical abuse between intimate partners. In England and Wales, for example, a stand-alone offence of controlling or coercive behaviour was introduced in 2015 with the expressed aim of improving legal responses to intimate partner violence (Home Office 2015). This piece of reform is unique in that it represents the translation of a concept derived in a clinical setting – that of coercive and controlling abuse (as theorised by Stark 2007) – into the legal realm through the enactment of legislation. While the first prosecutions and convictions are just emerging from the English courts, a body of scholarship has already begun to questions the merits of the new offence and the effectiveness of reforming legal categories per see to address long-held problems in legal system responses to gender-based harms (see, *inter alia*, Walklate *et al.* 2018).

Is there a case for a feminist jurisprudence?

In addition to the creation of new offences and reforms to transform existing laws, a body of research has emerged over the past two decades exploring the merits of feminist jurisprudence (see, *inter alia*, Hunter 2008a, 2012; Naffine 1990; Carlen 1990; Smart 1989). Returning to the earlier discussion of the male-centric nature of the criminal justice system, debates surrounding the need for a feminist jurisprudence call into question the ways in which the notion of the 'legal man' structures and influences legal responses to male and female victims and defendants, community perceptions of justice and broader experiences of the criminal justice system.

In her earlier work on the topic, Naffine (1990) identified three phases of the feminist response to understanding the law, through which a critical consideration of 'the man of law' could be achieved.

The first phase, which reflects the liberal feminist position, accepts that the law should be, and can be, fair and impartial to all. To this end, any sexist and gendered practices in law reflect an inability to apply its own professional standards to women – be it women victims, defendants, witnesses or practitioners. From this viewpoint the rationality of the law is assumed and, as such, a failure to recognise women's rights and an inability to respond in equal measures to men and women before the law should be addressed through substantive reform.

The second phase of feminist response to the law, according to Naffine (1990), labels the 'male culture of the law'. This position, which equates most readily with a radical feminist viewpoint, makes a strong statement about the central values of the law, arguing that it necessary to examine much more than who makes the law, who interprets the law and who gets to practise law – all of whom are predominately male. From this viewpoint the importance of critically examining the values within the law, those that underlie the patriarchal institution of law, is emphasised, including, but not limited to, the adversarial form, commitment to rationality and detachment. This response to law is not without its critics. Naffine (1990) and Smart (1989), for example, argue that this view assumes a consistency among law that does not exist and fails to account for the complexity in law and the interaction between legal vales and the wider society within which the justice system operates.

The third phase of feminist response to the law posed by Naffine (1990) seeks to understand the interconnections between legal rhetoric and the patriarchal social order. Writing from this vantage point, Smart (1989) argues that the law articulates a 'phallocentric discourse'. It is phallocentric because its character is centrally masculine, heterosexual and influenced by patriarchal social conditions. To demonstrate the influence of this discourse, Smart (1989) considers a rape trial whereby the construction of the law serves to disqualify the woman's experience while celebrating phallocentrism. From this perspective it is argued that the law is unable to address the structured relationships of power within which sexual violence occurs. Smart's approach, while not neglecting the importance of understanding the power and influence of the law's gendering strategies, calls for a greater critical awareness of how, and under what circumstances, strategies are played out.

While Naffine's analysis of the feminist response is centrally focused on understanding the practical impacts of the 'man of law', she also explores the ways in which some men are marginalised by the law's construction. She argues that while a middle-class, rational male entrepreneur may align with notions of the 'ideal man' (see Chapter 2 on hegemonic masculinity), men who do not neatly fit this stereotype experience hurdles in their interactions with the justice system – both as defendant, victim or practitioner.

Beyond the specifics of each viewpoint, Naffine's (1990) analysis is important in that it highlights the need to look beyond legislation when challenging gender stereotypes in law, a viewpoint shared by Smart. This does not mean to suggest that gains have not been made for women through changing the law. Rather, it reflects a view that placing too much emphasis on the law in isolation of other changes overlooks both its underlying presumptions and the complex way in which these influence practice. The degree to which this argument works in favour or against the case for a feminist jurisprudence depends on how that notion is itself understood.

One of the most prolific interpretations of what a 'feminist jurisprudence' would look like has emerged from the Feminist Judgments Project (FJP). First originating in Canada through the Women's Court of Canada initiative (Majury 2006), the FJP emerged from among a group of feminist legal scholars who decided to rewrite a series of legal judgments of relevance to the equality clause of the Canadian Charter of Rights and Freedoms. The motivation for the project is explained as follows:

> 'So why don't we show them how it could have been done, what substantive equality would look like in those cases? Why don't we rewrite these decisions that are so wrong?' The spark was ignited, and the Women's Court of Canada was created.
>
> (Majury, 2006: 2)

The process of rewriting sought to bring a feminist perspective to the decision and to attend to aspects of the case that may have otherwise been silenced in traditionally legal responses. Each judgment is written alongside a case commentary, which provides a summary of why the judgment was chosen for rewriting and what were the feminist concerns with the original legal judgment.

Since the 2008 publication of those first FJP judgments, the methodology of feminist judgment writing has travelled extensively. Iterations of the Feminist Judgment Project have now been carried out around the world, including the English Feminist Judgment Project (Hunter *et al.* 2010), the Australian Feminist Judgment Project (Douglas *et al.* 2014) and the United States Feminist Judgement (Stanchi *et al.* 2016). While several of these projects have provided an opportunity for scholars to rewrite the judgments of cases involving gender-based violence (see for example, Fitz-Gibbon and Maher (2015) for a critical reflection on rewriting an intimate partner homicide judgment), FJPs have also provided an opportunity for the feminist lens to be cast over decisions made about international law, environmental law and children's rights (see, *inter alia*, Stalford *et al.* 2017; Rogers and Maloney 2017).

Beyond the FJP there are other emerging instances of gender-informed policy and practice development. In 2017, for example, the Crown Prosecution Service (CPS) in England and Wales announced their intention to develop a guidance document specific to dealing with male victims of domestic and sexual abuse (CPS 2017; see also Rudgard 2017). Focused specifically on LGBT and ethnic minority males, the document seeks to improve responses to male victims by challenging problematic stereotypes surrounding male victimisation and increasing awareness of support services available for male victims. Discussing the new guidelines, Director of Public Prosecutions Alison Saunders explained:

> The way society views masculinity can make it very difficult for men and boys who are the victims of sexual and domestic offences to come forward. This 'public statement' formalises the CPS commitment to male victims and recognises that stereotypes

of masculinity and femininity can, and do, feed sexist and homo-
phobic assumptions. These can deter male victims from reporting
abuse and pursuing a prosecution.

(Cited in Rudgard 2017)

The guidelines were introduced as part of a wider strategy to better
acknowledge the barriers faced by and responded to male victimisation (for further details see CPS 2017).

Conclusion

This chapter has sought to focus on the ways in which criminal law
and criminal justice policy can impact differentially upon the men
and women who come before the law, and the ways in which criminal law reform has been enacted to address perceived shortcomings
in legal responses to victims of gendered violence. It has attempted
to identify the historical inadequacies of criminal law in this area as
well as the ongoing influence of gender in criminal law responses to
sexual and intimate partner violence. In doing so, the limits of law
have been highlighted and, while it is not to suggest that all reforms
have been without merit, the need to look beyond legislative reform
is emphasised in moving forward. For the disciplines of criminology and victimology, this chapter has sought to demonstrate why an
examination of the operation of the law from a gendered perspective
is an important exercise.

Of course, it is not only in relation to the law per se that the influence of gender may be found. Gendered assumptions are discernible
in a wide range of policy responses, from community safety (Davies
2008) to the prevention of terrorism (de Jonge Oudraat and Brown
2016), through to restorative justice (Daly and Stubbs 2006). In all
of these domains it is pertinent to ask: For whom have these policies been written with whom in mind? Critical criminological and
feminist-informed work has documented, for example, the paucity
of options and understandings of gender in all of the domains that
have taken women as their subject and/or the object of their concerns.
Of course, in many ways similar dilemmas are found here to those

raised in the questions posed by the gender-responsive policy initiatives informed by risk, as discussed in Chapter 3. Our focus here on the law, and its responsiveness or otherwise to gendered violence(s), is intended to afford the reader some continuity between the questions raised here and those discussed in Chapter 4. Moreover, while much of the discussion here has focused attention on adversarial legal systems, some of the issues and concerns it draws attention to are equally pertinent in other differently informed criminal justice systems (see for example, Fitz-Gibbon and Vannier (2017) in relation to France; United Nations (2017) on Thailand and Viet Nam, and Hetu (2017) on India). The ways in which these issues manifest themselves are not uniform and will be characterised by the specificity of the particular contexts in which they occur. Nonetheless, the questions raised in this chapter also direct attention to some fundamental issues concerning the domain assumptions of criminal justice processes across the world.

Recommendations for further reading

For readers interested in reading in more detail about the nature of the law from a gendered perspective, see Ngaire Naffine's (1990) *Law and the Sexes*. Building on this, Helena Kennedy's (1992) *Eve was Framed* explores in detail the gendered ways in which the law and legal training can influence those working as part of the legal profession. For a detailed analysis of the impact of law reform targeted at improving legal responses to gendered domestic and sexual violence, see Carline and Easteal's (2014) *Shades of Grey – Domestic and Sexual Violence against Women: Law Reform and Society*. For an analysis of the impact of law reform in the space of civil proceedings see Rosemary Hunter's (2008b) *Domestic Violence Law Reform and Women's Experience in Court: The Implementation of Feminist Reforms in Civil Proceedings*.

References

Adler, Z. (1987) *Rape on Trial*. London: Routledge and Kegan Paul.
Allen, J. (1987) *Justice Unbalanced: Gender, Psychiatry and Judicial Decision Making*. Milton Keynes: Open University Press.

Australian Law Reform Commission. (2006) *Uniform Evidence Law.* ALRC Report 102. Canberra: Australian Government.

Behrens, J. (1996) Ending the silence, but [.] family violence under the *Family Law Reform Act 1995. Australian Journal of Family Law* 10(1): 35–47.

Bond, C.E. and Jeffries, S. (2014) Similar punishment? Comparing sentencing outcomes in domestic and non-domestic violence cases. *British Journal of Criminology* 54: 849–872.

Cammiss, S. (2006) The management of domestic violence cases in the mode of trial hearing. *British Journal of Criminology* 46: 704–718.

Carlen, P. (1990) *Alternatives to Women's Imprisonment.* Buckingham: Open University Press.

Carline, A. (2010) Honour and shame in domestic homicide: a critical analysis of the provocation defence. In M.M. Idriss and T. Abbs (eds) *Honour, Violence, Women and Islam.* Hoboken: Taylor & Francis.

Carline, A. and Easteal, P. (2014) *Shades of Grey – Domestic and Sexual Violence against Women: Law Reform and Society.* London: Routledge.

Chesney-Lind, M (2006), Patriarchy, crime and justice: feminist criminology in an era of backlash. *Feminist Criminology* 1: 6–26.

Corrigan, R. (2013) *Up against a Wall.* New York: New York University Press.

Crofts, T. and Tyson, D. (2013) Homicide law reform in Australia: improving access to defences for women who kill their abusers. *Monash University Law Review* 39(3): 864–893.

CPS (Crown Prosecution Service). (2017) Public statement on male victims for crimes covered by the CPS Violence against Women and Girls (VAWG) Strategy.

Currie, S. (1995) Validating women in the legal system: an analysis of the invisibility of women's perspectives in the law. *Social Alternatives* 14(1): 14–17.

Daly, K. and Stubbs, J. (2006) Feminist engagement with restorative justice. *Theoretical Criminology* 10(1): 9–28.

Davies, P. (2008) Looking out a broken old window: community safety, gendered crimes and victimizations. *Crime Prevention and Community Safety* 10(4): 207–225.

Dawson, M. (2015) Punishing femicide: criminal justice responses to the killing of women over four decades. *Current Sociology* 64(7): 996–1016.

Douglas, H. and Fitzgerald, R. (2013) Legal processes and gendered violence: cross-applications for domestic violence protection orders. *UNSW Law Journal* 36(1): 56–87.

Douglas, H., Bartlett, F., Luker, T. and Hunter, R. (eds). (2014) *Australian Feminist Judgments: Righting and Rewriting Law.* Oxford: Bloomsbury Publishing.

Duggan, M. (2012) Using victims' voices to prevent violence against women: a critique. *British Journal of Community Justice* 10(2): 25–37.

Eaton, M. (1986) *Justice for Women? Family, Court and Social Control.* Milton Keynes: Open University Press.

Fehlberg, B., Kaspiew, R., Millbank, J., Kelly, F. and Behrens, J. (2015) *Australian Family Law.* Australia: Oxford University Press.

Fisher, S. (2012) From violence to coercive control: renaming men's abuse of women. *Australasian Policing* 4(1): 35–37.

Fitz-Gibbon, K. (2014) *Homicide Law Reform, Gender and the Provocation Defence: A Comparative Perspective.* London: Palgrave Macmillan.

Fitz-Gibbon, K. and Freiberg, A. (eds). (2015) *Homicide Law Reform in Victoria: Retrospect and Prospects.* Sydney: The Federation Press.

Fitz-Gibbon, K. and Maher, J, (2015) Feminist challenges to the constraints of law: donning uncomfortable robes? *Feminist Legal Studies* 23(3): 253–271.

Fitz-Gibbon, K. and Stubbs, J. (2012) Current directions in reforming legal responses to lethal violence. *Australian and New Zealand Journal of Criminology* 45(3): 318–336.

Fitz-Gibbon, K. and Vannier, M. (2017) Domestic violence and the gendered law of self-defence in France: the case of Jacqueline Sauvage. *Feminist Legal Studies.* Published First Online. doi: 10.1007/s10691-017-9358-8.

Fitz-Gibbon, K. and Walklate, S. (2016) The efficacy of Clare's Law in domestic violence law reform in England and Wales. *Criminology and Criminal Justice.* Published Online First. doi: 10.1177/1748895816671383.

Graycar, R. and Morgan, J. (2005) Law reform: what's in it for women? *Windsor Yearbook of Access to Justice* 23(2): 393–419.

Hedderman, C. and Gelsthorpe, L. (1997) *The Sentencing of Women.* Home Office Research Study 170. London: HMSO.

Hetu, V (2017) *Victims of Rape: Rights, Expectations and Restoration.* Gurgaon: ThomsonReuters.

Home Office. (2015) *Controlling or Coercive Behaviour in an Intimate or Family Relationship: Statutory Guidance Framework.* London: Home Office.

Horder, J. (1992) *Provocation and Responsibility.* Oxford: Clarendon Press.

Hudson, B. (2006) Beyond white man's justice: race, gender and justice in late modernity. *Theoretical Criminology* 10: 29–47.

Hunter, R. (2008a) Can feminist judges make a difference? *International Journal of the Legal Profession* 15: 7–36.

Hunter, R. (2008b) *Domestic Violence Law Reform and Women's Experience in Court: The Implementation of Feminist Reforms in Civil Proceedings.* Cambria.

Hunter, R. (2012) The power of feminist judgements? *Feminist Legal Studies* 20: 135–148.

Hunter, R., McGlynn, C. and Rackley, E. (eds) (2010) *Feminist Judgments: From Theory to Practice.* Oxford: Hart Publishing.

de Jonge Oudraat, C. and Brown, M.E. (2017) Women, gender, and terrorism: the missing link women in international security policy brief, August. Available at www.wiisglobal.org.

Kelly, L. (1988) *Surviving Sexual Violence.* Cambridge: Polity Press.

Kendall, K. (1991) The politics of premenstrual syndrome: implications for feminist justice. *Journal of Human Rights* 2(2): 77.

Kennedy, H. (1992) *Eve was Framed.* London: Chatto and Windus.

Laster, K. and O'Malley, P. (1996) Sensitive new age laws? The rediscovery of emotionality in law. *International Journal of the Sociology of Law* 24: 21–40.

MacDonald, H. (1998) *What's in a Name? Definitions and Domestic Violence.* Brunswick: Domestic Violence and Incest Resource Centre.

McGlynn, C. and Rackley, E. (2015) New law against 'revenge porn' is welcome, but no guarantee of success. *The Conversation,* 16 February.

McGlynn, C., Rackley, E. and Houghton, R. (2017) Beyond 'revenge porn': the continuum of image-based sexual abuse. *Feminist Legal Studies* 25(1): 25–46.

Majury, D. (2006) Introducing the Women's Court of Canada. *Canadian Journal of Women and the Law* 18(1): 1–12.

Martin, J. and Storey, T. (2013) *Unlocking Criminal Law,* 4th edition. London: Routledge.

Morris, A. and Gelsthorpe, L. (2000) Re-visioning men's violence against female partners. *Howard Journal of Criminal Justice* 39: 412–428.

Naffine, N. (1990) *Law and the Sexes*. London: Allen and Unwin.

National Domestic and Female Violence Bench Book. (2017) Available at http://dfvbenchbook.aija.org.au/contents.

Powell, A. and Henry, N. (2017) *Sexual Violence in a Digital Age*. London: Palgrave Macmillan.

Powell, A., Henry, N., Flynn, A. and Henderson, E. (2013) Meanings of 'sex' and 'consent': the persistence of rape myths in Victorian rape law. *Griffith Law Review* 22(2): 456–480.

Rogers, N. and Maloney, M. (2017) *Law as if Earth Really Mattered: The Wild Law Judgment Project*. London: Routledge.

Rudgard, O. (2017) CPS to issue first-ever guidance for prosecutors on handling male victims of sexual and domestic abuse. *The Telegraph*, 6 September.

Salter, M. and Crofts, T. (2015) Responding to revenge porn: challenges to online legal impunity. In L. Comella and S. Tarrant (eds) *New Views on Pornography: Sexuality, Politics, and the Law*. New York: Praeger, pp. 233–256.

Sheehy, E. (2014) *Defending Battered Women on Trial: Lessons from the Transcripts*. Toronto, Ont: University of Toronto Press.

Sheehy, E., Stubbs, J. and Tolmie, J. (2012) Battered women charged with homicide in Australia, Canada and New Zealand: how do they fare? *Australian and New Zealand Journal of Criminology* 45(3): 383–399.

Smart, C. (1989) *Feminism and the Power of Law*. London: Routledge.

Spohn, C. and Horney, J. (2013) *Rape Law Reform: A Grassroots Revolution and its Impact*. New York: Springer.

Stalford, H., Hollingsworth, K. and Gilmore, S. (2017) *Rewriting Children's Rights Judgments: From Academic Vision to New Practice*. London: Hart Publishing, Bloomsbury.

Stanchi, K.M., Berger, L.L. and Crawford, B.J. (2016) *Feminist Judgments: Rewritten Opinions of the United States Supreme Court*. Cambridge: Cambridge University Press.

Stark, E. (2007) *Coercive Control: How Men Entrap Women in Personal Life*. Oxford: Oxford University Press.

United Nations. (2017) The trial of rape: understanding criminal justice system response to sexual violence in Thailand and Viet Nam, United Nations, November. Downloaded 8 December 2017.

Victorian Law Reform Commission. (2004) *Sexual Offences: Final Report*. Victoria: Government of Victoria.

Walklate, S. (2008) What is to be done about violence against women? *British Journal of Criminology* 48: 39–54.

Walklate, S., Fitz-Gibbon, K. and McCulloch, J. (2018) Is more law the answer? Seeking justice for victims of intimate partner violence through the reform of legal categories. *Criminology and Criminal Justice* 18(1): 115–131.

Worrall, A. (1990) *Offending Women*. London: Routledge.

Yeo, S. (1993) Resolving gender bias in criminal defences. *Monash University Law Review* 19(1): 104–116.

CONCLUSION
REFLECTIONS ON GENDER, CRIME AND CRIMINAL JUSTICE

Introduction

This book has charted the variable influence gendered thinking has had on how criminologists and victimologists go about their work and the extent to which such thinking has penetrated the world of criminal justice policy, practice and reform. This is not an easy map to draw, since the politics present in all of these domains also serve to shape the nature and form that gendered thinking may take and the space in which it may have to operate. Moreover, even if such a space existed, gendered thinking still faces a number of dilemmas. Put simply, as Kruttschnitt (2016) has observed, it is still the case that not enough is known about how and under what conditions gender operates as the salient variable and when it does not. This observation returns us to several key questions running throughout the chapters of this book: should we be talking about women and crime or gender and crime (the Introduction); should we be talking about sameness or difference (Chapter 1); should we be talking about masculinity or masculinities (Chapter 2); what is the relationship between gender, race, ethnicity and class (all chapters); and what might be the role of the state in different global contexts in enhancing or denying gender as a variable (particularly Chapters 5 and 6)? All of these questions continue to raise difficult issues for criminology and victimology. Thus, as Naffine (1987: 133) commented some time ago, the threat that feminist theory 'poses to masculine criminology is [therefore] considerable'. This Conclusion reiterates the nature of that threat in five interconnected ways.

Criminology, victimology and gender: epistemic dilemmas?

Questions of epistemology ask us to consider how we know things. Chapter 1 mapped the origins of both criminology and victimology within nineteenth-century Northern theorising. This particularly marked both areas of investigation as being preoccupied with differentiation, determinism and pathology driven by the nomothetic impulse of positivism (Young 2011). In pointing to the powerful influence such epistemic thinking associated with positivism has had on criminology (and victimology), Young (2011) invites us to consider the dangers of abstracted empiricism as outlined in the seminal work of C. Wright Mills. In ignoring these dangers, Young (2011) argues that criminology in particular has become characterised by 'fetishism with number' (for a similar argument in relation to victimology see Walklate 2014). Importantly this fetishism rests on the assumption that numbers can capture social reality. However, lying behind the construction of such numbers within both criminology and victimology are deeper questions concerning how to count, who to count, when to count and what there is to be done once counting has been completed (ibid.). All of these questions are gendered, since they each in their different ways reflect who can know things and what it is that can be known (Chapter 1).

Of course, not all of criminological and/or victimological work is tainted by positivism. There is a wide range of work both cited in this book and evident elsewhere, starting from a different epistemological position. This goes without saying. However, the point of drawing this thread to the fore lies in recognising its dominance within both areas of investigation, particularly as the preferred source of knowledge on which to inform policy and practice. Positivist work still sets the policy agenda for the most part with other ways of knowing and thinking lying in its shadow. For Young (2011) and others, positivism also constitutes one of the key characteristics of the most dominant form of criminology (and victimology) across the globe: American criminology. This version of criminology and its associated intellectual imperialism, cemented during the Cold War (Morrison 2015), has had the capacity to 'other'/erase different ways of 'doing' criminology/victimology and is deeply entrenched in Northern theorising (Connell 2007). The gendered assumptions embedded in this agenda have, of course, been differently exposed and discussed in the preceding chapters. However, that exposure has not been uniform.

Arguably the kinds of gendered assumptions referred to above have been most thoroughly exposed in relation to sexual violence(s) (Chapter 6) but they nonetheless make their presence felt in a wide range of criminal justice policy and practice arenas. For example, notions of risk and the practices of risk assessment (discussed in

Chapter 3) and the potential of alternative ways of making legal judgments (discussed in Chapter 6), each in their different way, encourage us to critically reflect upon the questions of who can know things and what it is that can be known. The challenge posed by feminist work on these questions persists for both criminology and victimology. Such challenges also raise questions about the kinds of concepts used by both areas of investigation and how such concepts are interpreted.

Criminology, victimology and gender: conceptual dilemmas?

The epistemic dilemmas alluded to above are intimately connected to the kinds of concepts each of these areas of investigation deploy in making sense of the relationship between gender, crime and criminal justice. How an area of investigation assumes it can 'know' social reality is reflected in the kinds of questions asked and the concepts underpinning those questions used to make sense of social reality. The feminist challenge for criminology and victimology not only lies within whether or not *she* can answer *his* questions and the appropriateness of the methods used to ask those questions but historically whether or not feminism and criminology/victimology can speak to each other at all. Considering this very question, Smart (1990) concluded that criminology needs feminism more than feminism needs criminology, and the tensions between feminism and victimology have been well documented by Rock (1990) and Walklate (2003), among others (it should be noted that Davies (2018) offers a somewhat more optimistic analysis in relation to victimology). However, whichever position is adopted in relation to these debates, for criminology/victimology the challenge lies in gendered concepts to be both understood and deployed in such a way that makes this possible.

In this book, for example, Chapter 3 explored the key concepts of fear, security, risk, responsibility and vulnerability. All of these concepts fuel the concerns of both criminology and victimology historically and contemporarily, yet each of them can be deployed more or less sensitively to questions of gender. Some concepts (like fear and risk) have been subjected to a much more thorough gendered critique in each of these areas of investigation than perhaps have responsibility and/or vulnerability (though see the edited collection by Fitz-Gibbon and Walklate (2016) on the former). Gendered approaches to fear (of crime), as Chapters 3 and 4 have particularly illustrated, start from the position in which fear is situated in people's (women's) real lives and as something that cuts across public–private and wartime/peacetime boundaries. Viewing fear in this way offers a much more nuanced and contextualised understanding of its manifestation in different geographical locations than that proffered, for example, by analyses routed in criminal victimisation survey data. At the same time gendered approaches to security engage in similar transgressive conceptual challenges for criminological concerns on this issue (see Walklate *et al.* 2017). Gendered approaches to the law, and the conceptual framework in which it operates, also afford a differently nuanced appreciation of the law and the differential impact it has upon both victims and offenders, particularly for those whose shared characteristics ensure that they fall outside of the white, heterosexual maleness of the law (Naffine 1990; see also Chapter 6). These kinds of conceptual dilemmas in relation to gender raise the further issue of when and under what conditions gender is or is not the salient variable through which to make sense of the realities of crime and criminal victimisation.

Criminology, victimology and gender: salient variable dilemmas?

Some time ago, Messerschmidt (1997: 113) made the following point:

> Gender, race and class are not absolutes and are not equally significant in every social setting, where crime is realised. That is, depending on the social setting accountability to certain categories is more salient than accountability to other categories.

Moreover, Daly (1997) has also outlined the different ways in which it is possible to conceptualise the interrelationship between sex and gender, and if other structural variables are added to the mix the puzzle generated is a complex one. The corollary of recognising this complexity means embracing not only the possibility of masculinities and femininities (see Chapters 1 and 2), but also different sexualities (Collier 1998), whiteness, blackness, classness, faith, age and so on. From the outset this book took as its starting point the appreciation of just one of these variables: gender. However, this does not mean that by implication other variables do not count. The emergence and refinement of studies in criminology and victimology concerned with intersectionality provide an insight into the variable interaction of a wide range of structural conditions in which any individual has the capacity for choosing different courses of action.

The term 'intersectionality' is attributed to Crenshaw (1991) emanating from her work in critical race theory that focused attention not on the either/or of gender or race but how each interacted with the other to effect a different level of experience. While Gunnarsson (2017) has subjected intersectionality to critique and pointed to the inherent epistemological problem of either/orism and separable/inseparable, not dissimilar to those found within criminology/victimology (as discussed above), it is nonetheless evident that different variables do interact differently with each. This was an observation made some time ago by Carlen (1994) in discussing issues surrounding women's imprisonment and has been afforded added recognition for criminology more generally in the work of Potter (2015). She argues that intersectionality studies both disrupt and revolutionise how criminology and criminal justice practice is done.

More recent interventions, like that of Duhaney (2018) on intersectionality and intimate partner violence, Chakraborti (2018) in relation to hate crime, and Steffensmeier *et al.* (2017) on sentencing, all point to the ways in which different structural variables and experiences can compound to produce different outcomes. Indeed, age is still as important an ingredient in this cocktail as it was when criminologists were particularly preoccupied with 'juvenile delinquency' in the 1950s. However, contemporarily such concerns have shifted to equally address young people as victims (see for example, Stanley 2018), how young people may be better responded to as offenders (see for example, Fitz-Gibbon and O'Brien 2017) as well as shining a light at the other end of the spectrum on elder persons as victims (see for example, Bows 2017). Appreciation of the compounding effects of intersectionality is an ongoing, unfolding agenda for both criminology and victimology, all of which, setting aside the ontological questions posed by Gunnarsson (2017), raise questions for criminal justice policy and reform of criminal law.

Criminology, victimology and gender: policy dilemmas?

As the opening section of this book demonstrated, criminology and victimology have both been historically and contemporaneously intimately connected to the policy domain. The origins of both disciplines lie in the modernist assumptions that knowing the world enabled better informed interventions in the world. While the relationship between both of these areas of investigation within the world of policy has varied over time and does vary by geographical location, this fundamental connection remains. For example, the World Society of Victimology has an important influence on setting standards for victim service responses across the globe. Setting aside the debate that such interconnectionsmay raise concerns surrounding the nature of the role of a public social scientist (Buroway 2005), it remains the case that much of the work conducted under the auspices of criminology/victimology carries policy implications.

Sometimes, of course, such policy connections have unintended consequences. One example of this is the shift towards the term 'gender' – now commonly used by policy makers and practitioners (and indeed some academics) as a substitute for sex, as though this has dealt with the contested nature of the relationship between the two terms (see the Introduction of this volume for the problems associated in doing this). Nevertheless, as Part III has illustrated, focal attention on the impact that a male-dominated criminal justice system (which most are) may and does have in responding to gendered crimes like domestic violence and rape remains important. Simultaneously understanding the impact of experiences with a male-dominated criminal justice system leads to an appreciation of whether or not it is possible to do justice differently in order to take account of such experiences (for example, women-only police stations discussed in Chapter 5) and/or the development of the Feminist Judgment Project (discussed in Chapter 6). Whether it is in relation to the emergence of gender-responsive justice (discussed in Chapter 3) or improved training for police officers in relation to responding to intimate partner violence (discussed in Chapter 5), how to be heard and what to do on the basis of being heard remain dilemmas for both criminologists and victimologists.

At this juncture it is also important to note that criminal justice policies travel frequently from the global north to the global south and just as frequently within and across what may be termed the Anglo-speaking world. In this latter respect this often refers to criminal justice policies generated in the United States travelling to other countries (see e.g. Jones and Newburn 2013; Madlingozi 2014; Waklate 2016; Walklate and Fitz-Gibbon 2018). In the context of policies relating to violence against women, Goodmark (2015) labels this 'exporting without a licence'. This label itself conveys much that is problematic in the policy transfer process which, on the one hand, may serve to problematise behaviour previously considered unproblematic; on the other hand, it can also erase and silence the issues of location, specificity and cultural difference. Walklate and Fitz-Gibbon (2018) have subjected Clare's Law (the Domestic Violence Disclosure Scheme introduced in England and Wales in 2014) and the pro-arrest stance for domestic violence incidents (introduced in the United States in the late 1980s) to critical scrutiny. Both policies have travelled the globe in spite of (or in the absence of) evidence, and serve as examples of the problems that arise when particular voices in particular settings are erased by such policies. Cunneen and Rowe (2015: 15) provide some insight into how and why this erasure and silencing occurs. They point the finger at the epistemic violence found in entrenched beliefs about the superiority of what they call 'Eurocentric thinking'. This, they observe, has crucial consequences insofar as:

> Eurocentric domestic violence, law and policy imposed in Indigenous contexts is often predicated on an incongruent ontological

and epistemological reality – a reality based on the potential for autonomous and individualised decision making.

This observation invites consideration of the relationship between criminology, victimology and gender in a global context and what this implies for the presumptions with which each of these areas of investigation operates. Here the global consequences of the interconnections between epistemology, concepts, saliency and policy come to the fore.

Criminology, victimology and gender: global dilemmas?

Connell (2007), Young (2011) and Aas (2012) have offered some reflections on the nature of social scientific knowledge that pose fundamental questions for criminology and victimology. Connell (2007), for example, offers a detailed analysis of the way in which theoretical assumptions about globalisation has led commentators to conclude that the processes of globalisation take their toll on all of us, in the same way, and to the same extent. This, she suggests, has resulted in the Westo-centric bias of Northern theorising becoming reified with the consequent 'systematic violence of the metropole' (Connell 2007: 378) on the periphery being overlooked. These kinds of theoretical blinkers assume a linear progression from a pre-modern, to an industrial, to a world risk society, and have three consequences: other voices and visions of social processes are excluded, non-metropolitan experiences are erased and the gathering of data from the 'periphery' becomes framed and informed by Northern concepts and methods (ibid.: 380). In a critique more focused on criminology, Aas (2012: 14) asks the discipline to think about the importance of geography, stating:

The global does therefore not present itself as a smooth, unified surface, a plane of immanence accessible through a zoom function, but rather as a dynamic multiplicity of surfaces and tectonic boundaries. It is in these meeting points and frictions between the global north and south, between licit and illicit worlds, that criminology has an opportunity to gain (and provide other social sciences with) invaluable insight into the nature of the contemporary world order.

The questions posed by Connell, Young, Aas and others have crystallised into voices calling for a 'southern criminology' (though in many ways an equal case for a southern victimology may also be made). The arguments made by Carrington *et al.* (2016) and Carrington and Hogg (2017) resonate with Cain's (2000) discussion of criminology's Occidentalism, and are further developed by Walklate (2008) in relation to victimology.

The possibilities raised by a southern criminology are not intended to add another version of criminology or victimology to an ever-growing fragmentary disciplinary list of labels: radical, critical, cultural, narrative and so on. They do however demand that both areas of investigation recognise their Northern origins and the epistemological, conceptual and policy consequences that flow from this. Southern criminology builds on Connell's (2007) use of the term 'Southern' as a metaphor designed to capture all those knowledges and practices rendered peripheral by the metropolitan preoccupations of Northern social science (see also de Sousa Santos 2014). This is a demand for an intellectual space that:

> seek[s] to adjust the theoretical lens of interpretation and to recover histories rooted in colonialism to enable it to more usefully account for the divergent patterns of crime, violence and justice that occur outside the metropole and their power effects on everyday life in the global South. (Carrington *et al.* 2016: 15).

Victimology is not immune to this agenda. Indeed, it is intimately connected with and exposed to the very same issues also exemplified in what Cunneen and Tauri (2016) call an 'indigenous criminology'. Their concern is to challenge the imperialism of Western social science and to situate indigenous people's experiences within their own colonial histories in which they have become readily framed as offenders. For the purposes of this discussion, the point is that the domain disciplinary assumptions of both criminology and victimology, adhering as they have been to Northern theorising, have each contributed to silencing, erasure, blurring and masking, the harms done through the vehicles of settler colonialism and the presumptions of globalisation. Concrete examples of the ways in which this has occurred and the toll it has taken are scattered through the pages of this book but are particularly pertinent to the discussion of gendering sexual violence in Chapter 4. Arguably it is also within the gendered thinking generated from within the feminist movement that the origins of these Southern voices may be found (see in particular Carrington 2015), thus endorsing Naffine's (1987) prescient observation with which this Conclusion began: the threat of feminist theory to masculine criminology has been, and still is, considerable indeed.

Conclusion: gender, politics and the state

The ongoing dilemmas summarised above, addressed both implicitly and explicitly in the pages of this book, do not of course persist in the vacuum of other academic and/or policy debates. The extent to which the implications derivable from them may be acted on and/or resisted is highly contingent upon the spaces afforded for different ways of doing criminal justice that may demand starting in a different place. Understanding the nature of the gendered state and its associated politics is crucial to appreciating how far such changes may and do occur. As Connell (1987: 130) commented some time ago, the state comprises a 'reverberating set of power relations and political processes in which patriarchy is both constructed and contested'. The presence of those contested power relations seeps through the pages of this book in full recognition that politics and policy processes can work both progressively and regressively, as previously observed by Smart (1989) and discussed in Chapter 6. Nonetheless, recognition of this is not a justification for ignoring the questions that gender raises for criminology/victimology broadly and for criminal justice policy more specifically. The question remains as to whether or not criminology/victimology is man enough to take gender seriously (Jefferson 1992).

Recommendations for further reading

The implications of the themes identified in this Conclusion raise fundamental questions about the concerns of this book that go beyond issues of gender. In order to appreciate these questions further we suggest that Cunneen and Tauri's (2016) *Indigenous Criminology*, Potter's (2015) *Intersectionality and Criminology*, and Carrington's (2015) *Feminism and Global Justice* would be good places to start.

References

Aas, K. (2012). 'The Earth is but one but the world is not': criminological theory and its geopolitical divisions. *Theoretical Criminology* 16(1): 5–20.

Bows, H. (2017) Sexual violence against older people: a review of the empirical literature. *Trauma, Violence & Abuse*. Published online first. doi: 10.1177/1524838016683455.

Buroway, M. (2005) For public sociology. *American Sociological Review* 70: 4–28.

Cain, M. (2000) Orientalism, Occidentalism and the sociology of crime. *British Journal of Criminology* 40(2): 239–260.

Carlen, P. (1994) Why study women's imprisonment? Or anyone else's. *British Journal of Criminology* 34 (Special Issue): 131–140.

Carrington, K. (2015) *Feminism and Global Justice*. London: Routledge.

Carrington, K. and Hogg, R. (2017) Deconstructing criminology's origin stories. *Asian Journal of Criminology* 12(3): 181–197.

Carrington, K., Hogg, R. and Sozzo, M. (2016) Southern criminology. *British Journal of Criminology* 56 (1): 1–20.

Chakraborti, N. (2018) Victims of hate crime. In S. Walklate (ed.) *Handbook of Victims and Victimology* (2nd edition). London: Routledge, pp. 141–155.

Collier, R. (1998) *Masculinities, Crime and Criminology*. London: Sage.

Connell, R.W. (1987) *Gender and Power*. Oxford: Polity Press.

Connell, R. (2007) The Northern theory of globalization. *Sociological Theory* 25(4): 368–385.

Crenshaw, K. (1991) Mapping the margins: intersectionality, identity politics, and violence against women of color. *Stanford Law Review* 43: 1241–1279.

Cunneen, C. and Tauri, J. (2016) *Indigenous Criminology*. Bristol: Policy Press.

Cunneen, C. and Rowe, S. (2015) Decolonising indigenous victimisation. In D. Wilson and S. Ross (eds) *Crime, Victims and Policy: International Contexts, Local Experiences*. London: Palgrave-Macmillan, pp. 10–32.

Daly, K. (1997) Different ways of conceptualising sex/gender in feminist theory and their implications for criminology. *Theoretical Criminology* 1(1): 23–52.

Davies, P. (2018) Feminist voices, gender and victimisation. In S. Walklate (ed.) *Handbook of Victims and Victimology* (2nd edition). London: Routledge, pp. 107–123.

de Sousa Santos, B. (2014) *Epistemologies of the South: Justice against Epistemicide*. Boulder, CO: Paradigm Publishers.

Duhaney, P. (2018) A critical race feminist perspective on racialized women's experiences of intimate partner abuse. In S. Walklate (ed.) *Handbook of Victims and Victimology* (2nd edition). London: Routledge, pp. 174–188.

Fitz-Gibbon, K. and O'Brien, W. (2017) The naming of child homicide offenders in England and Wales: the need for a change in law and practice. *British Journal of Criminology* 57(5): 1061–1079.

Fitz-Gibbon, K. and Walklate, S. (eds) (2016) *Homicide, Gender and Responsibility: An International Perspective*. London: Routledge.

Goodmark, L. (2015) Exporting without license: the American attempt to end intimate partner abuse worldwide. In R. Goel and L. Goodmark (eds) *Comparative Perspectives on Gender Violence: Lessons from Efforts Worldwide*. Oxford: Oxford University Press, pp. 3–14.

Gunnarsson, L. (2017) Why we keep separating the 'inseparable': dialecticizing intersectionality. *European Journal of Women's Studies* 24(2): 114–127.

Jefferson, T. (1992) Wheelin and stealin. *Achilles Heel* 13(summer).

Jones, T. and Newburn, T. (2013) Policy convergence, politics and comparative penal reform: sex offender notification schemes in the USA and UK. *Punishment and Society* 15(5): 439–467. doi: 10.1177/1462474513504801.

Kruttschnitt, C. (2016) The politics, and place, of gender in research on crime. *Criminology* 54(1): 8–29.

Madlingozi, T. (2014) On transitional justice entrepreneurs and the production of victims. In D. Buss, J. Lebert, B. Rutherford, D. Sharkey and O. Aginam (eds) *Sexual Violence in Conflict and Post-conflict Societies: International Agendas and African Contexts*. London: Routledge, pp. 169–192.

Messerschmidt, J. (1997) *Crime as Structured Action*. London: Sage.

Morrison, W. (2015) War and normative visibility: interactions in the Nomos. In P. Francis, T. Wyatt and P. Davies (eds) *Invisible Crimes and Social Harms*. London: Palgrave-Macmillan, pp. 178–198.

Naffine, N. (1987) *Female Crime*. Sydney: Allen and Unwin.

Naffine, N. (1990) *Law and the Sexes*. London: Allen and Unwin.

Potter, H. (2015) *Intersectionality and Criminology*. London: Routledge.

Rock, P. (1990) *Helping Victims of Crime*. Oxford: Clarendon Press.

Smart, C. (1989) *Feminism and the Power of Law*. London: Routledge.

Smart, C. (1990) Feminist approaches to criminology; or post-modern woman meets atavistic man. In L. Gelsthorpe and A. Morris (eds) *Feminist Perspectives in Criminology*. Buckingham: Open University Press, pp. 40–84.

Stanley, L. (2018) Child victims of human rights violations. In S. Walklate (ed.) *Handbook of Victims and Victimology* (2nd edition). London: Routledge, pp. 124–140.

Steffensmeier, D., Painter-Davis, N. and Ulmer, J. (2017) Intersectionality of race, ethnicity, gender, and age on criminal punishment. *Sociological Perspectives* 60(4): 810–833.

Walklate, S. (2003) Can there be a feminist victimology? In P. Davies and P. Francis (eds) *Understanding Victimisation*. pp. 28–45. London: Macmillan, pp. 28–45.

Walklate, S. (2008) Local contexts and globalised knowledge: what can international criminal victimisation surveys tell us about women's diverse lives? In M. Cain and A. Howe (eds) *Women, Crime and Social Harm*. Oxford: Hart Publishing, pp. 201–214.

Walklate, S. (2014) Sexual violence against women? Still a controversial issue for victimology? *International Review of Victimology* 20(1): 71–84.

Walklate, S. (2016) The metamorphosis of the victim of crime: from crime to culture and the implications for justice. *International*

Journal for Crime, Justice and Social Democracy 5(4): 4–16. doi: 10.5204/ijcjsd.v5i4.280.

Walklate, S. and Fitz-Gibbon, K. (2018) The violence of 'Northern' theorising for policy responses to intimate partner violence. In K. Carrington, M. Sozzo, R. Hogg and J. Scott (eds) *Palgrave Handbook on Criminology and the Global South*. London: Palgrave.

Walklate, S., McCulloch, J., Fitz-Gibbon, K. and Maher, J.M. (2017) Criminology, gender and security in the Australian context: making women's lives matter. *Theoretical Criminology*. doi: 10.1177/1362480617719449.

Young, J. (2011). *The Criminological Imagination*. Cambridge: Polity Press.

Index